Home Landscaping

Other titles available in the *Home Landscaping* series:

Home Landscaping: California Region

Home Landscaping: Mid-Atlantic Region

Home Landscaping: Midwest Region, including Southern Canada

Home Landscaping: Northeast Region, including Southeast Canada

Home Landscaping: Southeast Region

CRE▲TIVE
HOMEOWNER®

Home Landscaping

Northwest Region, including Western British Columbia

Roger Holmes
&
Don Marshall

CREATIVE HOMEOWNER®, Upper Saddle River, New Jersey

Produced by WordWorks.

Editors: Roger Holmes and Don Marshall
Editorial consultant: Rita Buchanan
Creative Homeowner editor: Neil Soderstrom
Copyeditor: Nancy J. Stabile
Design and layout: Deborah Fillion
Illustrators: Portfolio of Designs by Steve Buchanan;
    Guide to Installation by Michelle Angle Farrar, Lee Hov,
    Robert La Pointe, Rick Daskam, and Teresa Nicole Green
Indexer: Brigid A. O. Wilson
Cover design: Michelle Halko

Printed in the United States of America

Current Printing (last digit)
10 9 8 7 6 5 4 3 2 1

Library of Congress Catalog Card Number: 2001094076
ISBN: 1-58011-088-6

CREATIVE HOMEOWNER®
A Division of Federal Marketing Corp.
24 Park Way
Upper Saddle River, NJ 07458
Web site: **www.creativehomeowner.com**

Safety First

Though all concepts and methods in this book have been re-
viewed for safety, it is not possible to overstate the importance
of using the safest working methods possible. What follows
are reminders—do's and don'ts for yard work and landscaping. They are not substitutes for your own common sense.

▲ *Always* use caution, care, and good judgment when following the procedures described in this book.

▲ *Always* determine locations of underground utility lines
before you dig, and then avoid them by a safe distance.
Buried lines may be for gas, electricity, communications,
or water. Start research by contacting your local building
officials. Also contact local utility companies; they will
often send a representative free of charge to help you map
their lines. In addition, there are private utility locator
firms that may be listed in your Yellow Pages. *Note:* Previous owners may have installed underground drainage,
sprinkler, and lighting lines without mapping them.

▲ *Always* read and heed the manufacturer's instructions for
using a tool, especially the warnings.

▲ *Always* ensure that the electrical setup is safe; be sure that
no circuit is overloaded and that all power tools and electrical outlets are properly grounded and protected by a
ground-fault circuit interrupter (GFCI). Do not use power
tools in wet locations.

▲ *Always* wear eye protection when using chemicals, sawing
wood, pruning trees and shrubs, using power tools, and
striking metal onto metal or concrete.

▲ *Always* read labels on chemicals, solvents, and other products; provide ventilation; heed warnings.

▲ *Always* wear heavy rubber gloves rated for chemicals, not
mere household rubber gloves, when handling toxins.

▲ *Always* wear appropriate gloves in situations in which your
hands could be injured by rough surfaces, sharp edges,
thorns, or poisonous plants.

▲ *Always* wear a disposable face mask or a special filtering
respirator when creating sawdust or working with toxic
gardening substances.

▲ *Always* keep your hands and other body parts away from
the business ends of blades, cutters, and bits.

▲ *Always* obtain approval from local building officials before
undertaking construction of permanent structures.

▲ *Never* work with power tools when you are tired or under
the influence of alcohol or drugs.

▲ *Never* carry sharp or pointed tools, such as knives or saws,
in your pockets. If you carry such tools, use special-pur-
pose tool scabbards.

The Landscape Designers

Lee Buffington and her husband, Gordon Iwata, operate a design-build landscape company, Arcadia Design, in Mercer Island, Washington. They specialize in residential landscapes. Lee's designs appear on pp. 40–43, 88–91, and 92–95.

Laura Crockett, owner and principal of Sylvan Designs of Hillsboro, Oregon, has been designing gardens for clients in the Northwest since 1988. An avid plantswoman, she designs and consults for residential and public-space projects. She is also an instructor at hands-on gardening workshops. Her designs appear on pp. 24–27, 36–39, and 52–55.

Kate Day is a landscape architect and certified arborist. She designs for The Portico Group of Seattle and is a private consulting arborist-horticulturist for several municipalities and developments in the Seattle area. She has received several design awards as a member of project teams honored by the American Society of Landscape Architects and by the Native Plant Society at the Northwest Flower and Garden Show. Her designs appear on pp. 16–19, 48–51, and 80–83.

Lucy Hardiman is the principal of Perennial Partners, a garden-design collective in Portland. A plant enthusiast, she writes for *Garden Design* and *Horticulture* magazines, as well as regional publications, and lectures on garden design throughout the United States and Canada. Her own garden has been featured in many magazines and books and has appeared on HGTV's *Gardener's Diary* and PBS's *Victory Garden*. Her designs appear on pp. 56–59 and 60–63.

Daniel Lowery is owner of the design-build firm Queen Anne Gardens, where he seeks to improve the health and happiness of his clients through garden design. His work has been featured in national magazines and has won a variety of awards. At a recent Northwest Flower and Garden Show, he was joint winner of the Founder's Cup (Best of Show) and the *Horticulture* Magazine Award for the most interesting use of plants. His designs appear on pp. 20–23, 32–35, and 64–67.

Ruth Olde is a principal with Blasig Landscape Design and Construction Ltd. in Vancouver, British Columbia. Her designs have won many awards, and she has presented landscaping seminars in Canada and the United States. She is author of *Landscaping Made Easy by Design*. Her designs appear on pp. 44–47, 68–71, and 84–87.

Phil Wood owns Phil Wood Garden Design in Seattle. His designs have won numerous awards, including gold medals at the Northwest Flower and Garden Show. He is also a board member of the Seattle Chinese Garden Society. His designs appear on pp. 28–31, 72–75, and 76–79.

Contents

PORTFOLIO OF DESIGNS

GUIDE TO INSTALLATION

PLANT PROFILES

About This Book

Of all the home improvement projects homeowners tackle, few offer greater rewards than landscaping. Paths, patios, fences, arbors, and, most of all, plantings can enhance home life in countless ways, large and small, functional and pleasurable, every day of the year. At the main entrance, an attractive brick walkway flanked by eye-catching shrubs and perennials provides a cheerful send-off in the morning and welcomes you home from work in the evening. A carefully placed grouping of small trees, shrubs, and fence panels creates privacy on the patio or screens a nearby eyesore from view. An island bed showcases your favorite plants, while dividing the backyard into areas for several different activities.

Unlike with some home improvements, the rewards of landscaping can be as much in the activity as in the result. Planting and caring for lovely shrubs, perennials, and other plants can afford years of enjoyment. And for those who like to build things, outdoor construction projects can be especially satisfying.

While the installation and maintenance of plants and outdoor structures are within the means and abilities of most people, few of us are as comfortable determining exactly which plants or structures to use and how best to combine them. It's one thing to decide to dress up the front entrance or patio, another to come up with a design for doing so.

That's where this book comes in. Here, in the Portfolio of Designs, you'll find designs for 20 common home-landscaping situations, created by landscape professionals who live and work in the Northwest. Drawing on years of experience, these designers balance functional requirements and aesthetic possibilities, choosing the right plant or structure for the task,

confident of its proven performance in similar situations.

Complementing the Portfolio of Designs is the Guide to Installation, the book's second section, which will help you install and maintain the plants and structures called for in the designs. The third section, Plant Profiles, gives information on all the plants used in the book. The discussions that follow take a closer look at each section; we've also printed representative pages of the sections on pp. 9 and 10 and pointed out their features.

Portfolio of Designs

This section is the heart of the book, providing examples of landscaping situations and solutions that are at once inspiring and accessible. Some are simple, others more complex, but each one can be installed in a few weekends by homeowners with no special training or experience.

For each situation, we present two designs, the second a variation of the first. As the sample pages on the facing page show, the first design is displayed on a two-page spread. A perspective illustration (called a "rendering") depicts what the design will look like several years after installation, when the perennials and many of the shrubs have reached mature size. (For more on how plantings change as they age, see "As Your Landscape Grows," pp. 12–13.) The rendering also shows the planting as it will appear at a particular time of year. A site plan indicates the positions of the plants and structures on a scaled grid. Text introduces the situation and the design and describes the plants and projects used.

The second design, presented on the second two-page spread, addresses the same situation as the first but differs in one or more important aspects. It might show a

planting suited for a shady rather than a sunny site, or it might incorporate different structures or kinds of plants to create a different look. As for the first design, we present a rendering, site plan, and written information, but in briefer form. The second spread also includes photographs of a selection of the plants featured in the two designs. The photos showcase noteworthy qualities — lovely flowers, handsome foliage, or striking form — that these plants contribute to the designs.

Installed exactly as shown here, the designs will provide years of enjoyment. But individual needs and properties will differ, and we encourage you to alter the designs to suit your site and desires. Many types of alterations are easy to make. You can add or remove plants and adjust the sizes of paths, patios, and arbors to accommodate larger or smaller sites. You can rearrange groupings and substitute favorite plants to suit your taste. Or you can integrate the design with your existing landscaping. If you are uncertain about how to solve specific problems or about the effects of changes you'd like to make, consult with staff at a local nursery or with a landscape designer in your area.

Guide to Installation

In this section you'll find detailed instructions and illustrations covering all the techniques you'll need to install any design from start to finish. Here we explain how to think your way through a landscaping project and anticipate the various steps. Then you'll learn how to do each part of the job: readying the site; laying out the design; choosing materials; addressing basic irrigation needs; building paths, trellises, or other structures; preparing the soil for planting; buying the recommended plants and putting them in place; and car-

Portfolio of Designs

First Design Option
An overview of the situation and the design.

Concept Box
Summarizes an important aspect of the design; tells whether the site is sunny or shady and what season is depicted in the rendering.

Plants & Projects
Noteworthy qualities of the plants and structures and their contributions to the design.

Plant Portraits
Photos of a selection of the plants used in both designs.

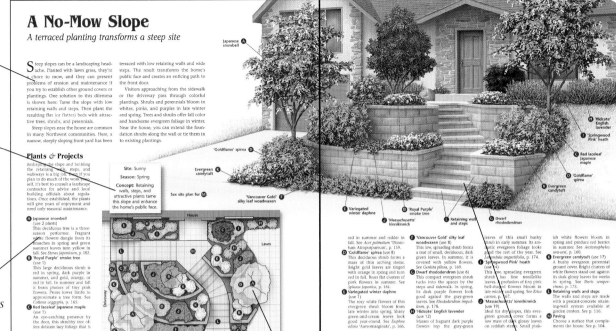

Second Design Option
Addressing the same situation as the first design, this variation may differ in design concept, site conditions, or plant selection.

Site Plan
Positions all plants and structures on a scaled grid.

Rendering
Shows how the design will look when plants are well established.

Concept Box
Site, season, and design summary.

Rendering
Depicts the design when plants are well established.

Site Plan
Plants and structures on a scaled grid.

Guide to Installation

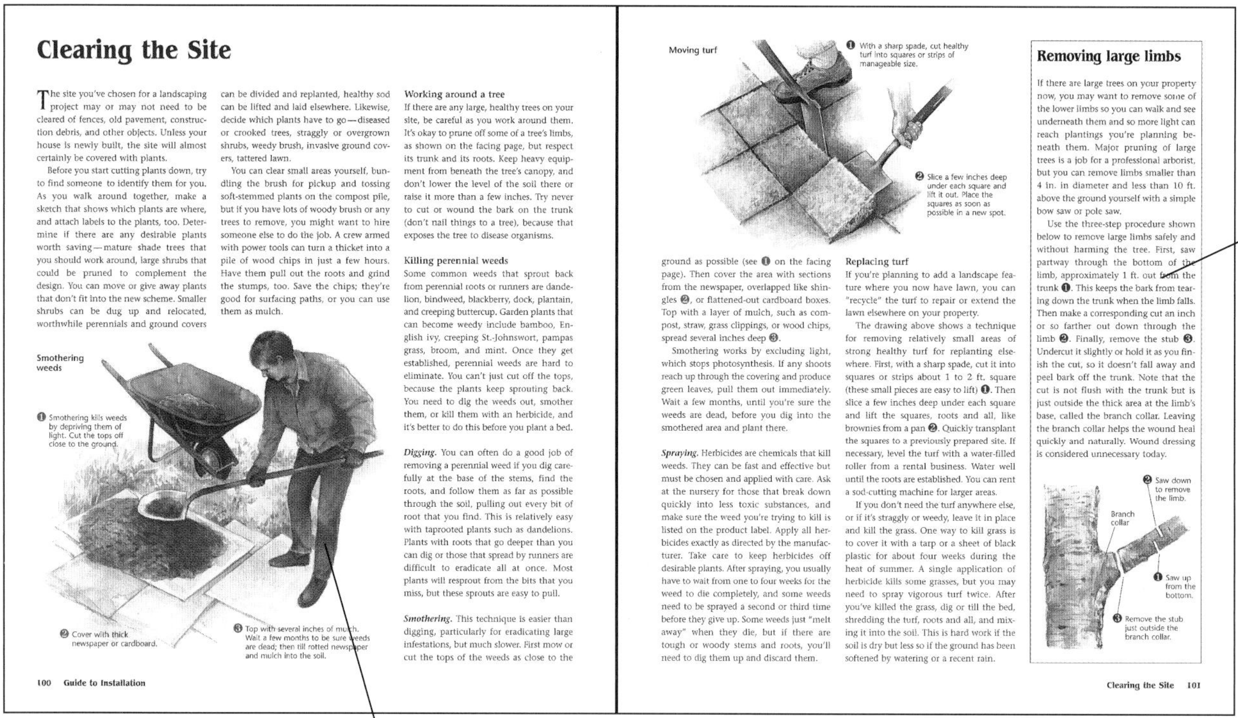

Clearing the Site

The site you've chosen for a landscaping project may or may not need to be cleared of fences, old pavement, construction debris, and other objects. Unless your house is newly built, the site will almost certainly be covered with plants.

Before you start cutting plants down, try to find someone to identify them for you. As you walk around together, make a sketch that shows which plants are where, and attach labels to the plants, too. Determine if there are any desirable plants worth saving—mature shade trees that you should work around, large shrubs that could be pruned to complement the design. You can move or give away plants that don't fit into the new scheme. Smaller shrubs can be dug up and relocated, worthwhile perennials and ground covers can be divided and replanted, healthy sod can be lifted and laid elsewhere. Likewise, decide which plants have to go—diseased or crooked trees, straggly or overgrown shrubs, weedy brush, invasive ground covers, tattered lawn.

You can clear small areas yourself, bundling the brush for pickup and tossing soft-stemmed plants on the compost pile, but if you have lots of woody brush or any trees to remove, you might want to hire someone else to do the job. A crew armed with power tools can turn a thicket into a pile of wood chips in just a few hours. Have them pull out the roots and grind the stumps, too. Save the chips; they're good for surfacing paths, or you can use them as mulch.

Working around a tree

If there are any large, healthy trees on your site, be careful as you work around them. It's okay to prune off some of a tree's limbs, as shown on the facing page, but respect its trunk and its roots. Keep heavy equipment from beneath the tree's canopy, and don't lower the level of the soil there or raise it more than a few inches. Try never to cut or wound the bark on the trunk (don't nail things to a tree), because that exposes the tree to disease organisms.

Killing perennial weeds

Some common weeds that sprout back from perennial roots or runners are dandelion, bindweed, blackberry, dock, plantain, and creeping buttercup. Garden plants that can become weedy include bamboo, English ivy, creeping St.-Johnswort, pampas grass, broom, and mint. Once they get established, perennial weeds are hard to eliminate. You can't just cut off the tops, because the plants keep sprouting back. You need to dig the weeds out, smother them, or kill them with an herbicide, and it's better to do this before you plant a bed.

Digging. You can often do a good job of removing a perennial weed if you dig carefully at the base of the stems, find the roots, and follow them as far as possible through the soil, pulling out every bit of root that you find. This is relatively easy with taprooted plants such as dandelions. Plants with roots that go deeper than you can dig or those that spread by runners are difficult to eradicate all at once. Most plants will resprout from the bits that you miss, but these sprouts are easy to pull.

Smothering. This technique is easier than digging, particularly for eradicating large infestations, but much slower. First mow or cut the tops of the weeds as close to the ground as possible (see ❶ on the facing page). Then cover the area with sections from the newspaper, overlapped like shingles ❷, or flattened-out cardboard boxes. Top with a layer of mulch, such as compost, straw, grass clippings, or wood chips, spread several inches deep ❸.

Smothering works by excluding light, which stops photosynthesis. If any shoots reach up through the covering and produce green leaves, pull them out immediately. Wait a few months, until you're sure the weeds are dead, before you dig into the smothered area and plant there.

Spraying. Herbicides are chemicals that kill weeds. They can be fast and effective but must be chosen and applied with care. Ask at the nursery for those that break down quickly into less toxic substances, and make sure the weed you're trying to kill is listed on the product label. Apply all herbicides exactly as directed by the manufacturer. Take care to keep herbicides off desirable plants. After spraying, you usually have to wait from one to four weeks for the weed to die completely, and some weeds need to be sprayed a second or third time before they give up. Some weeds just "melt away" when they die, but if there are tough or woody stems and roots, you'll need to dig them up and discard them.

Smothering weeds
❶ Smothering kills weeds by depriving them of light. Cut the tops off close to the ground.
❷ Cover with thick newspaper or cardboard.
❸ Top with several inches of mulch. Wait a few months to be sure weeds are dead; then till rotted newspaper and mulch into the soil.
Moving turf
❶ With a sharp spade, cut healthy turf into squares or strips of manageable size.
❷ Slice a few inches deep under each square and lift it out. Place the squares as soon as possible in a new spot.

Replacing turf

If you're planning to add a landscape feature where you now have lawn, you can "recycle" the turf to repair or extend the lawn elsewhere on your property.

The drawing above shows a technique for removing relatively small areas of strong healthy turf for replanting elsewhere. First, with a sharp spade, cut it into squares or strips about 1 to 2 ft. square (these small pieces are easy to lift) ❶. Then slice a few inches deep under each square and lift the squares, roots and all, like brownies from a pan ❷. Quickly transplant the squares to a previously prepared site. If necessary, level the turf with a water-filled roller from a rental business. Water well until the roots are established. You can rent a sod-cutting machine for larger areas.

If you don't need the turf anywhere else, or if it's straggly or weedy, leave it in place and kill the grass. One way to kill grass is to cover it with a tarp or a sheet of black plastic for about four weeks during the heat of summer. A single application of herbicide kills some grasses, but you may need to spray vigorous turf twice. After you've killed the grass, dig or till the bed, shredding the turf, roots and all, and mixing it into the soil. This is hard work if the soil is dry but less so if the ground has been softened by watering or a recent rain.

Removing large limbs

If there are large trees on your property now, you may want to remove some of the lower limbs so you can walk and see underneath them and so more light can reach plantings you're planning beneath them. Major pruning of large trees is a job for a professional arborist, but you can remove limbs smaller than 4 in. in diameter and less than 10 ft. above the ground yourself with a simple bow saw or pole saw.

Use the three-step procedure shown below to remove large limbs safely and without harming the tree. First, saw partway through the bottom of the limb, approximately 1 ft. out from the trunk ❶. This keeps the bark from tearing down the trunk when the limb falls. Then make a corresponding cut an inch or so farther out down through the limb ❷. Finally, remove the stub ❸. Undercut it slightly or hold it as you finish the cut, so it doesn't fall away and peel bark off the trunk. Note that the cut is not flush with the trunk but is just outside the thick area at the limb's base, called the branch collar. Leaving the branch collar helps the wound heal quickly and naturally. Wound dressing is considered unnecessary today.

❷ Saw down to remove the limb.
Branch collar
❶ Saw up from the bottom.
❸ Remove the stub just outside the branch collar.

100 Guide to Installation

Clearing the Site 101

"Sidebar"
Detailed information on special topics, set within a ruled box.

Step-by-Step
Illustrations show process; steps are keyed by number to discussion in the main text.

Detailed Plant Information
Descriptions of each plant's noteworthy qualities and requirements for planting and care.

Plant Portraits
Photos of selected plants.

Plant Profiles

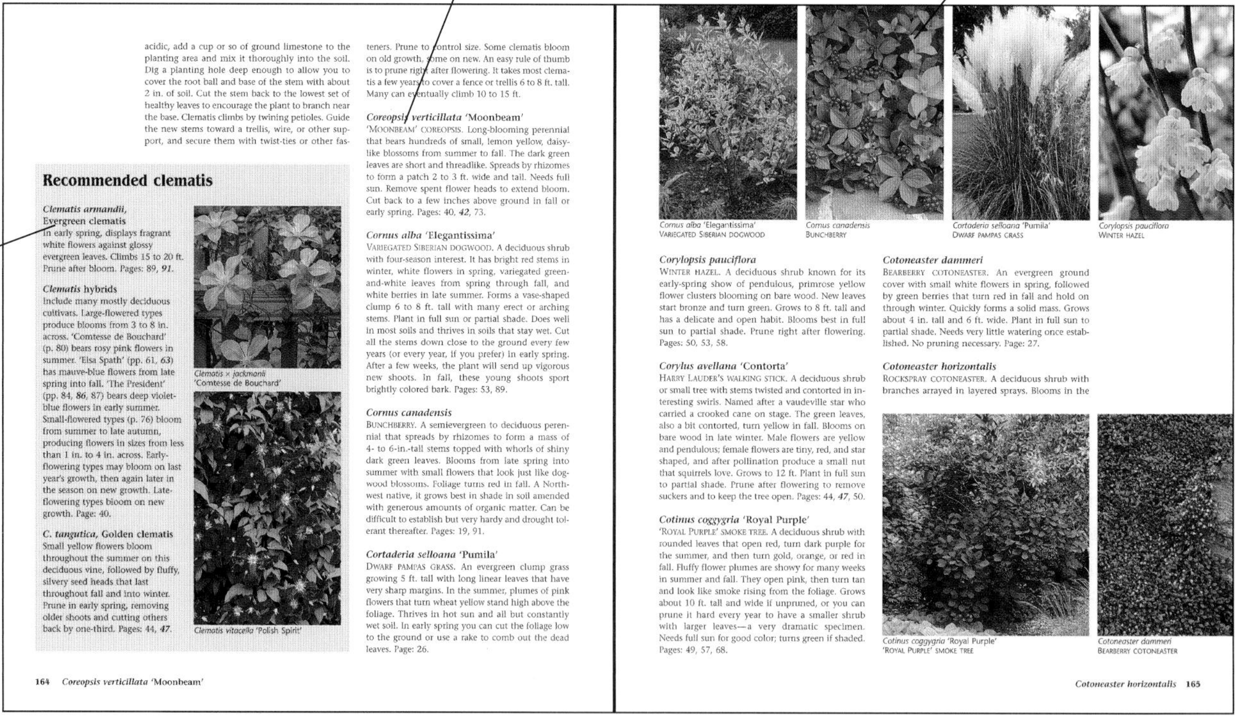

acidic, add a cup or so of ground limestone to the planting area and mix it thoroughly into the soil. Dig a planting hole deep enough to allow you to cover the root ball and base of the stem with about 2 in. of soil. Cut the stem back to the lowest set of healthy leaves to encourage the plant to branch near the base. Clematis climbs by twining petioles. Guide the new stems toward a trellis, wire, or other support, and secure them with twist-ties or other fasteners. Prune to control size. Some clematis bloom on old growth, some on new. An easy rule of thumb is to prune right after flowering. It takes most clematis a few years to cover a fence or trellis 6 to 8 ft. tall. Many can eventually climb 10 to 15 ft.

Recommended clematis

Clematis armandii, Evergreen clematis
In early spring, displays fragrant white flowers against glossy evergreen leaves. Climbs 15 to 20 ft. Prune after bloom. Pages: 89, *91*.

Clematis hybrids
Include many mostly deciduous cultivars. Large-flowered types produce blooms from 3 to 8 in. across. 'Comtesse de Bouchard' (p. 80) bears rosy pink flowers in summer. 'Elsa Spath' (pp. 61, *63*) has mauve-blue flowers from late spring into fall. 'The President' (pp. 84, *86*, 87) bears deep violet-blue flowers in early summer. Small-flowered types (p. 76) bloom from summer to late autumn, producing flowers in sizes from less than 1 in. to 4 in. across. Early-flowering types may bloom on last year's growth, then again later in the season on new growth. Late-flowering types bloom on new growth. Page: 40.

C. tangutica, Golden clematis
Small yellow flowers bloom throughout the summer on this deciduous vine, followed by fluffy, silvery seed heads that last throughout fall and into winter. Prune in early spring, removing older shoots and cutting others back by one-third. Pages: 44, *47*.

Clematis × jackmanii 'Comtesse de Bouchard'

Clematis viticella 'Polish Spirit'

Coreopsis verticillata 'Moonbeam'
'MOONBEAM' COREOPSIS. Long-blooming perennial that bears hundreds of small, lemon yellow, daisy-like blossoms from summer to fall. The dark green leaves are short and threadlike. Spreads by rhizomes to form a patch 2 to 3 ft. wide. Needs full sun. Remove spent flower heads to extend bloom. Cut back to a few inches above ground in fall or early spring. Pages: 40, *42*, 73.

Cornus alba 'Elegantissima'
VARIEGATED SIBERIAN DOGWOOD. A deciduous shrub with four-season interest. It has bright red stems in winter, white flowers in spring, variegated green-and-white leaves from spring through fall, and white berries in late summer. Forms a vase-shaped clump 6 to 8 ft. tall with many erect or arching stems. Plant in full sun or partial shade. Does well in most soils and thrives in soils that stay wet. Cut all the stems down close to the ground every few years (or every year, if you prefer) in early spring. After a few weeks, the plant will send up vigorous new shoots. In fall, these young shoots sport brightly colored bark. Pages: 53, 89.

Cornus canadensis
BUNCHBERRY. A semievergreen to deciduous perennial that spreads by rhizomes to form a mass of 4- to 6-in.-tall stems topped with whorls of shiny dark green leaves. Blooms from late spring into summer with small flowers that look just like dogwood blossoms. Foliage turns red in fall. A Northwest native, it grows best in shade in soil amended with generous amounts of organic matter. Can be difficult to establish but very hardy and drought tolerant thereafter. Pages: 19, 91.

Cortaderia selloana 'Pumila'
DWARF PAMPAS GRASS. An evergreen clump grass growing 5 ft. tall with long linear leaves that have very sharp margins. In the summer, plumes of pink flowers that turn wheat yellow stand high above the foliage. Thrives in hot sun and all but constantly wet soil. In early spring you can cut the foliage low to the ground or use a rake to comb out the dead leaves. Page: 26.

164 *Coreopsis verticillata* 'Moonbeam'

Cornus alba 'Elegantissima'
VARIEGATED SIBERIAN DOGWOOD

Cornus canadensis
BUNCHBERRY

Cortaderia selloana 'Pumila'
DWARF PAMPAS GRASS

Corylopsis pauciflora
WINTER HAZEL

Corylopsis pauciflora
WINTER HAZEL. A deciduous shrub known for its early-spring show of pendulous, primrose yellow flower clusters blooming on bare wood. New leaves start bronze and turn green. Grows to 8 ft. tall and has a delicate and open habit. Blooms best in full sun to partial shade. Prune right after flowering. Pages: 50, 53, 58.

Corylus avellana 'Contorta'
HARRY LAUDER'S WALKING STICK. A deciduous shrub or small tree with stems twisted and contorted in interesting swirls. Named after a vaudeville star who carried a crooked cane on stage. The green leaves, also a bit contorted, turn yellow in fall. Blooms on bare wood in late winter. Male flowers are yellow and pendulous; female flowers are tiny, red, and star shaped, and after pollination produce a small nut that squirrels love. Grows to 12 ft. Plant in full sun to partial shade. Prune after flowering to remove suckers and to keep the tree open. Pages: 44, *47*, 50.

Cotinus coggygria 'Royal Purple'
'ROYAL PURPLE' SMOKE TREE. A deciduous shrub with rounded leaves that open red, turn dark purple for the summer, and then turn gold, orange, or red in fall. Fluffy flower plumes are showy for many weeks in summer and fall. They open pink, then turn tan and look like smoke rising from the foliage. Grows about 10 ft. tall and wide if unpruned, or you can prune it hard every year to have a smaller shrub with larger leaves—a very dramatic specimen. Needs full sun for good color; turns green if shaded. Pages: 49, 57, 68.

Cotoneaster dammeri
BEARBERRY COTONEASTER. An evergreen ground cover with small white flowers in spring, followed by green berries that turn red in fall and hold on through winter. Quickly forms a solid mass. Grows about 4 in. tall and 6 ft. wide. Plant in full sun to partial shade. Needs very little watering once established. No pruning necessary. Page: 27.

Cotoneaster horizontalis
ROCKSPRAY COTONEASTER. A deciduous shrub with branches arrayed in layered sprays. Blooms in the

Cotinus coggygria 'Royal Purple'
'ROYAL PURPLE' SMOKE TREE

Cotoneaster dammeri
BEARBERRY COTONEASTER

Cotoneaster horizontalis 165

Choices
Selections here help you choose from the many varieties of certain popular plants.

ing for the plants to keep them healthy and attractive year after year.

We've taken care to make installation of built elements simple and straightforward. The paths, trellises, and arbors all use basic, readily available materials, and they can be assembled by people who have no special skills or tools beyond those commonly used for home maintenance. The designs can easily be adapted to meet specific needs or to fit in with the style of your house or other landscaping features.

Installing different designs requires different techniques. You can find the techniques that you need by following the cross-references in the Portfolio to pages in the Guide to Installation, or by skimming the Guide. You'll find that many basic techniques are reused from one project to the next. You might want to start with one of the smaller, simpler designs. Gradually you'll develop the skills and confidence to do any project you choose.

Most of the designs in this book can be installed in several weekends; some will take a little longer. Digging planting beds and erecting fences and arbors can be strenuous work. If you lack energy for such tasks, consider hiring a neighborhood teenager to help out; local landscaping services can provide more comprehensive help.

Plant Profiles

The final section of the book includes a description of each of the plants featured in the Portfolio. These profiles outline the plants' basic preferences for environmental conditions—such as soil, moisture, and sun or shade—and provide advice about planting and ongoing care.

Working with plant experts in the Northwest, we selected plants carefully, following a few simple guidelines: Every plant should be a proven performer in the region; once established, it should thrive without pampering. All plants should be available from a major local nursery or garden center. If they're not in stock, they could be

ordered, or you could ask the nursery staff to recommend suitable substitutes.

In the Portfolio section, you'll note that plants are referred to by their common name but are cross-referenced to the Plant Profiles section by their latinized scientific name. While common names are familiar to many people, they can be confusing. Distinctly different plants can share the same common name, or one plant can have several different common names. Scientific names, therefore, ensure greatest accuracy and are more appropriate for a reference section such as this. Although you can confidently purchase most of the plants in this book from local nurseries using the common name, knowing the scientific name allows you to ensure that the plant you're ordering is the same one shown in our design.

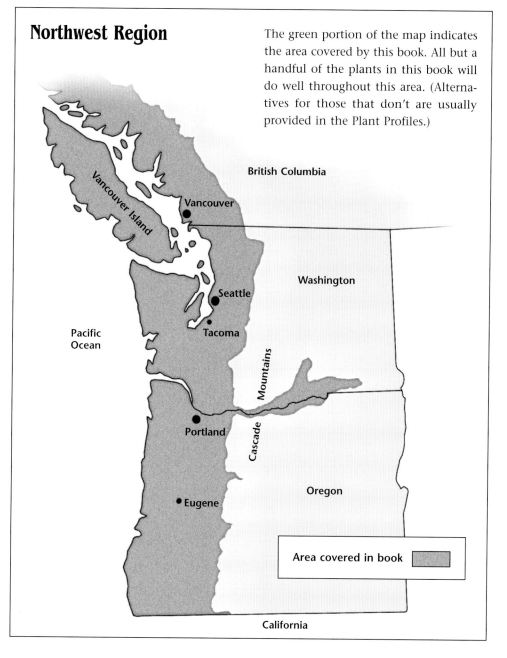

Northwest Region

The green portion of the map indicates the area covered by this book. All but a handful of the plants in this book will do well throughout this area. (Alternatives for those that don't are usually provided in the Plant Profiles.)

British Columbia

Vancouver Island

Vancouver

Washington

Pacific Ocean

Seattle

Tacoma

Cascade Mountains

Portland

Oregon

Eugene

Area covered in book

California

As Your Landscape Grows

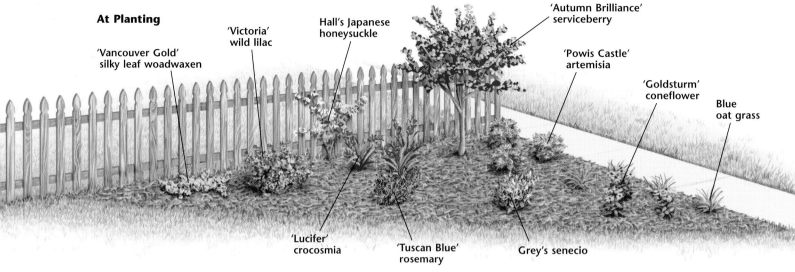

At Planting

'Vancouver Gold' silky leaf woadwaxen

'Victoria' wild lilac

Hall's Japanese honeysuckle

'Autumn Brilliance' serviceberry

'Powis Castle' artemisia

'Goldsturm' coneflower

Blue oat grass

'Lucifer' crocosmia

'Tuscan Blue' rosemary

Grey's senecio

Landscapes change over the years. As plants grow, the overall look evolves from sparse to lush. Trees cast cool shade where the sun used to shine. Shrubs and hedges grow tall and dense enough to provide privacy. Perennials and ground covers spread to form colorful patches of foliage and flowers. Meanwhile, paths, arbors, fences, and other structures gain the comfortable patina of age.

Continuing change over the years—sometimes rapid and dramatic, sometimes slow and subtle—is one of the joys of landscaping. It is also one of the challenges. Anticipating how fast plants will grow and how big they will eventually become is difficult, even for professional designers, and was a major concern in formulating the designs for this book.

To illustrate the kinds of changes to expect in a planting, these pages show one of the designs at three different "ages." Even though a new planting may look sparse at first, it will soon fill in. And because of careful spacing, the planting will look as good in 10 to 15 years as it does after 3 to 5. It will, of course, look different, but that's part of the fun.

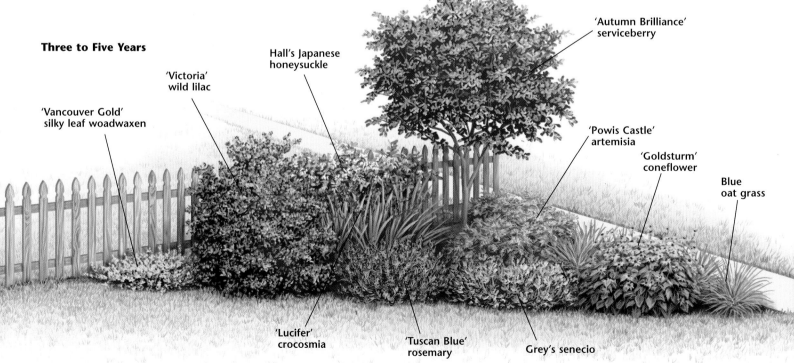

Three to Five Years

'Vancouver Gold' silky leaf woadwaxen

'Victoria' wild lilac

Hall's Japanese honeysuckle

'Autumn Brilliance' serviceberry

'Powis Castle' artemisia

'Goldsturm' coneflower

Blue oat grass

'Lucifer' crocosmia

'Tuscan Blue' rosemary

Grey's senecio

At Planting—Here's how the corner planting (pp. 28–31) might appear in spring immediately after planting. The branches of the Hall's honeysuckle, 2 to 3 ft. long, have been tied to the fence, where they can begin to twine. The serviceberry is 4 to 5 ft. tall, and the shrubby wild lilac is about 18 in. tall. Bought in 1-gal. containers, the rosemary, Grey's senecio, coneflower, artemisia, and blue oat grass are about a foot in height; the crocosmia, a little taller. Silky leaf woadwaxen hugs the ground near the fence. In addition to mulch, you can fill the spaces between the small plants with short annuals.

Three to Five Years—As shown here in early summer, the planting has filled out nicely. The serviceberry rises to a height of about 8 ft. Below, the honeysuckle twines along much of the fence. The wild lilac has filled in significantly. Its blue flowers pair attractively with the carpet of yellow woadwaxen flowers. The rosemary, senecio, coneflower, and artemisia have become bushy plants with handsome foliage and flowers. The blue oat grass has grown into bristly clumps 12 to 18 in. tall; the taller crocosmia now forms a small patch.

Ten to Fifteen Years—Shown again in early summer, the serviceberry, now 10 to 12 ft. tall, has a graceful habit and casts dappled shade over the planting. Its lower limbs have been removed as the tree has grown, making room for the wild lilac, which has overgrown the woadwaxen. Annual pruning has kept the honeysuckle vigorous but confined to the fence. The crocosmia has been divided over the years to keep it in scale (and provide starts for other clumps around the yard). The rosemary, senecio, coneflower, artemisia, and blue oat grass commingle, with just enough pruning each year to keep the planting tidy and the clumps defined.

Ten to Fifteen Years

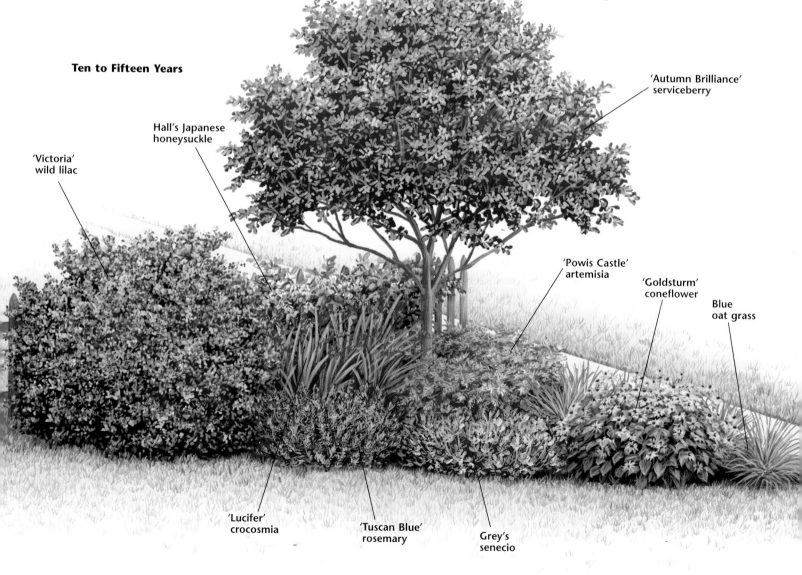

'Victoria' wild lilac

Hall's Japanese honeysuckle

'Autumn Brilliance' serviceberry

'Powis Castle' artemisia

'Goldsturm' coneflower

Blue oat grass

'Lucifer' crocosmia

'Tuscan Blue' rosemary

Grey's senecio

Portfolio of Designs

This section presents designs for 20 situations common in home landscapes. You'll find designs to enhance entrances, decks, and patios. There are gardens of colorful perennials and shrubs, as well as structures and plantings that create shady hideaways, dress up nondescript walls, and even make a centerpiece of a lowly recycling area. Large color illustrations show what the designs will look like, and site plans delineate the layout and planting scheme. Texts explain the designs and describe the plants and projects appearing in them. Installed as shown or adapted to suit your site and personal preferences, these designs can make your property more attractive, more useful, and—most important—more enjoyable for you, your family, and your friends.

First Impressions

Make a pleasant passage to your front door

Site: Sunny

Season: Midsummer

Concept: Easy-care plantings and distinctive walkway enhance a home's main entrance.

Why wait until a visitor reaches the front door to extend a cordial greeting? An entryway landscape of well-chosen plants and a revamped walkway make the short journey a pleasant one. They also enrich your home's most public face and help settle it comfortably in its surroundings.

The flagstone paving here creates a walkway with the feel of a cozy courtyard, an atmosphere enhanced by the small trees, shrubs, and bench.

Extending along the driveway, the paving makes it easier for passengers to get in and out of a car. Attractive plants lead the way to the door and make the stroll inviting, while providing interest to viewers inside the house and on the street.

Flowering trees and shrubs bloom from spring through fall in whites and pinks. Perennial flowers add blues, reds, and purples. A mix of evergreen leaves and eye-catching fruit and bark make winter visitors welcome, too.

Sourwood **A**

Plants & Projects

Preparing the planting beds and laying the flagstone walkway are the main tasks in this design. Once plants are established, they require only seasonal cleanup and pruning to keep them looking their best.

A **Sourwood** (use 7 plants)
This small deciduous tree provides light shade and helps create a casual privacy for the entryway. Leaves change from bronze to green to orangy red from spring to summer to fall. Clusters of bell-shaped white flowers dangle from the ends of branches in mid- to late summer. See *Oxydendrum arboreum*, p. 176.

B **Peegee hydrangea** (use 1)
Pruned as a standard (a mass of foliage above a single bare trunk), this deciduous shrub greets visitors by the drive. Elongated clusters of creamy white flowers stand out against the dull green foliage from midsummer into fall. See *Hydrangea paniculata* 'Grandiflora', p. 172.

C **Bigleaf hydrangea** (use 3)
Large hemispherical clusters of white, pink, red, or blue flowers grace this vase-shaped shrub from midsummer into fall. Deciduous leaves are shiny green. See *Hydrangea macrophylla*, p. 172.

D **Compact strawberry tree** (use 3)
Framing the window and door, this upright shrub offers glossy evergreen leaves with red margins and stems and colorful peeling bark. Bears clusters of white flowers and red fruit simultaneously in fall. See *Arbutus unedo* 'Compacta', p. 160.

E **'Wood's Dwarf' heavenly bamboo** (use 21)
This multistemmed shrub produces feathery evergreen foliage that is bright orange when new, green in summer, and scarlet-orange in fall and winter. See *Nandina domestica*, p. 175.

F **'Goldflame' spirea** (use 10)
This deciduous shrub has striking leaves—red in spring and fall and golden yellow in summer. In addition, flattened clusters of carmine-pink flowers bloom in summer and again in early fall. See *Spiraea japonica*, p. 181.

G **'Harmony' reticulata iris** (use 9)
Sky blue flowers with yellow throats bloom in spring before the grassy foliage of this perennial appears. See *Iris reticulata*, p. 173.

H **Perennial salvia** (use 7)
This popular plant bears numerous upright spikes of violet-blue flowers on a mass of dull green foliage. Blooms off and on from spring through fall. See *Salvia × superba*, p. 180.

I **'Autumn Joy' sedum** (use 9)
The fleshy gray-green leaves of this perennial are topped by flat clusters of tiny flowers in late summer. Clusters turn from pale greenish pink to russet over a long period. See *Sedum*, p. 181.

J **Columbine** (use 3)
From spring into summer, exquisite flowers of blue, pink, or purple float on wiry stems over this perennial's airy blue-green foliage. See *Aquilegia*, p. 160.

K **Wintergreen** (use 16)
This low, creeping evergreen shrub displays small, glossy green leaves at the ends of short stems. In summer, bell-shaped, white-to-pink flowers dangle among the foliage. Red berries follow. Leaves and berries have wintergreen scent when crushed. See *Gaultheria procumbens*, p. 169.

L **Paving**
Laid on a sand-and-gravel base, rectangular flagstones in a variety of sizes provide an attractive, level surface. See p. 104.

'Wood's Dwarf' **E** heavenly bamboo

House

Stoop

Bench

Lawn

1 square = 1 ft.

B Peegee hydrangea

C Bigleaf hydrangea

I 'Autumn Joy' sedum

H Perennial salvia

J Columbine

L Paving

F 'Goldflame' spirea

I 'Autumn Joy' sedum

K Wintergreen

Compact **D** strawberry tree

E 'Wood's Dwarf' heavenly bamboo

See site plan for **G**.

Native plants offer a shady welcome

Site: Shady

Season: Spring

Concept: A selection of plants native and adapted to the region creates an enticing entryway on a shaded site.

House

Stoop

Lawn

1 square = 1 ft.

If your entry is shady, perhaps with morning sun and afternoon shade, you can try this planting scheme. The configuration remains the same as that of the previous design, but here we've used Northwest native plants and others well adapted to shadier conditions in the region. Overall, the emphasis is still on year-round good looks.

Following nature's woodland models, the planting is layered. The vine maples' leafy canopy casts dappled summer shade on flowering evergreen shrubs and richly textured ground covers below. Spring (shown here) bursts with bloom, and a profusion of evergreen foliage guarantees interest throughout the rest of the year.

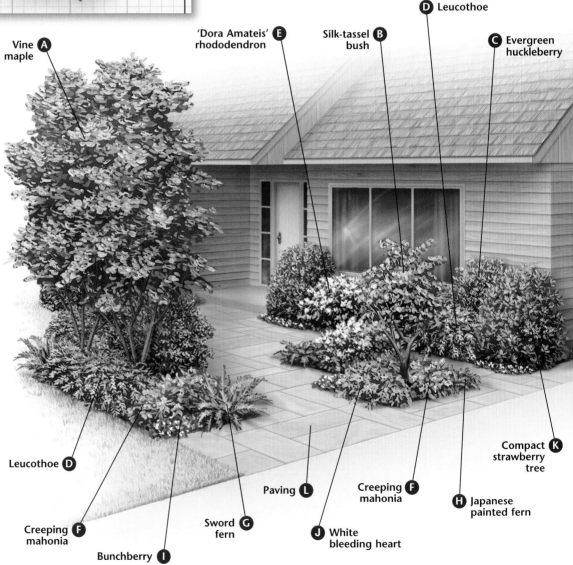

Vine maple **A**

'Dora Amateis' rhododendron **E**

Silk-tassel bush **B**

D Leucothoe

C Evergreen huckleberry

Leucothoe **D**

Creeping mahonia **F**

Bunchberry **I**

Sword fern **G**

Paving **L**

White bleeding heart **J**

Creeping mahonia **F**

H Japanese painted fern

Compact strawberry tree **K**

Plants & Projects

A Vine maple (use 7 plants)
Choose multitrunked specimens of this deciduous tree to make the most of its striking form. Broad, lobed leaves are colorful in the spring and fall. See *Acer circinatum*, p. 158.

B Silk-tassel bush (use 1)
An evergreen tree or shrub, pruned here as a shrub with room for underplantings. Elliptical, wavy-edged leaves are dark green above and gray below. Male plants produce long pendulous catkins in winter. See *Garrya elliptica*, p. 169.

C Evergreen huckleberry (use 11)
A low-branching evergreen shrub. Its small, glossy green leaves are tinged with red, and new stems are burgundy. Bears pinkish white flowers in spring. Berries are edible. See *Vaccinium ovatum*, p. 182.

D **Leucothoe** (use 16)
A low-growing evergreen shrub with arching branches. Small clusters of white flowers nestle on stems at the base of the lance-shaped leaves in spring. Foliage turns bronze with cold weather in fall. See *Leucothoe axillaris*, p. 174.

E **'Dora Amateis' rhododendron** (use 8)
A compact form of the popular evergreen shrub. In spring, it lights up the space beneath the window with a blizzard of green-throated white flowers. Glossy green foliage is attractive year-round. See *Rhododendron*, p. 178.

F **Creeping mahonia** (use 7)
An evergreen shrub with holly-like blue-green leaflets, it spreads by underground stems to form a patch. Bears clusters of dusty yellow flowers in spring. Leaves turn bronze-green in winter. See *Mahonia repens*, p. 174.

G **Sword fern** (use 9)
The shiny evergreen fronds of this Northwest native fern contrast handsomely with nearby foliage. See Ferns: *Polystichum munitum*, p. 168.

H **Japanese painted fern** (use 15)
A smaller, lacier fern with delicately colored fronds showing shades of purple, green, and silver. See Ferns: *Athyrium nipponicum* 'Pictum', p. 168.

I **Bunchberry** (use 12)
The small oval leaves of this semievergreen ground cover appear near the ends of short stems. A perennial, bunchberry bears small flowers with showy white bracts in spring, followed by eye-catching shiny red fruit in autumn. See *Cornus canadensis*, p. 164.

J **White bleeding heart** (use 3)
A perennial with lacy, fernlike, blue-green foliage. In late spring, rows of small white heart-shaped flowers dangle from arching stems. See *Dicentra spectabilis* 'Alba', p. 166.

See p. 16 for the following:

K **Compact strawberry tree** (use 3)

L **Paving**

Plant portraits

In sun or shade, these plants will provide a warm welcome at the front entry of your home.

● = First design, pp. 16–17
▲ = Second design, pp. 18–19

Wintergreen
(*Gaultheria procumbens*, p. 169) ●

'Wood's Dwarf' heavenly bamboo
(*Nandina domestica*, p. 175) ●

'Dora Amateis' rhododendron
(*Rhododendron*, p. 178) ▲

Evergreen huckleberry (*Vaccinium ovatum*, p. 182) ▲

White bleeding heart
(*Dicentra spectabilis* 'Alba', p. 166) ▲

Columbine (*Aquilegia*, p. 160) ●

Creeping mahonia (*Mahonia repens*, p. 174) ▲

A Foundation with Flair

Create a front garden of striking foliage

Rare is the home without foundation plantings. These simple skirtings of greenery hide unattractive underpinnings and help integrate a house with its surroundings. Useful as these plantings are, they are too frequently no more than monochromatic expanses of clipped evergreens, dull as dishwater. But, as this design shows, a low-maintenance foundation planting can be varied, colorful, and fun.

The planting enhances the house as seen from the street, frames the walkway to the front door for visitors, and can be enjoyed when viewed from inside the house as well. Extending the planting beyond the ends of the house helps "set-tle" an upright, boxy house more comfortably on its site.

The design combines trees and shrubs in a deep, gently curving bed. Small maples and a plume cedar lend height and presence, while providing some screening and privacy from the street. Lower evergreen shrubs and ferns add a variety of leaf textures and colors that make an eye-catching display for much of the year, peaking in fall, the season shown here. In addition to woody plants, carefully chosen perennials accent the entry and, in spring, swaths of tulips brighten the scene.

B Plume cedar

Amur A maple

David viburnum D

Plants & Projects

This is a low-care planting. Once established, the plants will thrive without much more attention than seasonal cleanup and renewing the mulch in the summer to conserve water. Shear the candytuft after bloom and divide and refurbish the tulips every fall.

A Amur maple (use 3 plants)
This small multitrunked deciduous tree offers months of interest. In spring, fragrant yellow flowers are followed by bright red, winged seeds. Summer's glossy green leaves cast a dappled shade and turn striking colors in fall. See *Acer ginnala*, p. 158.

B Plume cedar (use 1)
Making a neat cone, this evergreen tree contrasts nicely with the nearby maples. Needlelike blue-green foliage turns bronze in winter. Peeling, cinnamon-colored bark is also attractive. See *Cryptomeria japonica* 'Elegans', p. 166.

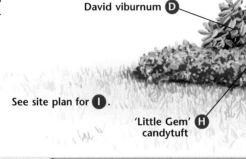

See site plan for I.

'Little Gem' H candytuft

David D viburnum

'Lucifer' G crocosmia

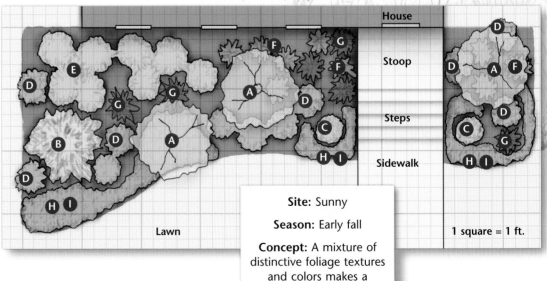

House

Stoop

Steps

Sidewalk

Lawn

Site: Sunny

Season: Early fall

Concept: A mixture of distinctive foliage textures and colors makes a foundation planting with four-season interest.

1 square = 1 ft.

A Amur maple

E 'Moyers Red' heavenly bamboo

C Dwarf Hinoki cypress

F Barnes' narrow male fern

D David viburnum

C Dwarf Hinoki cypress

H 'Little Gem' candytuft

F Barnes' narrow male fern

G 'Lucifer' crocosmia

C **Dwarf Hinoki cypress** (use 2)
Flanking the steps, a pair of these small evergreen trees form mounds of layered emerald green, scalelike foliage. Plant has a sculpted look. See *Chamaecyparis obtusa* 'Nana Gracilis', p. 163.

D **David viburnum** (use 11)
A compact evergreen shrub with handsome, leathery, dark green leaves. In spring, pink buds produce flat clusters of small white flowers. It bears metallic blue fruits in fall. See *Viburnum davidii*, p. 182.

E **'Moyers Red' heavenly bamboo** (use 8)
This evergreen shrub forms a clump of erect stems bearing soft lacy foliage that is bronze in spring, green in summer, and an intense red throughout fall and winter. Bears fluffy white flowers in summer, sometimes off and on throughout the year, and orange-red berries. See *Nandina domestica*, p. 175.

F **Barnes' narrow male fern** (use 9)
This semievergreen fern forms a narrow clump of upright fronds with slightly ruffled leaflets. See Ferns: *Dryopteris filix-mas* 'Barnesii', p. 168.

G **'Lucifer' crocosmia** (use 6)
Clusters of bright red-orange flowers hover on graceful arching stems among this perennial's swordlike leaves from summer into fall. See *Crocosmia*, p. 166.

H **'Little Gem' candytuft** (as needed)
This perennial ground cover forms mounds of glossy evergreen leaves. Flat clusters of white flowers cover the foliage in spring. See *Iberis sempervirens*, p. 173.

I **Tulips** (as needed)
Plant a generous number (100 or more) of these colorful bulbs in the candytuft for a striking spring display. See Bulbs: *Tulipa*, p. 161.

A Foundation with Flair 21

Plant portraits

These plants will dress up the most nondescript foundation or front porch, while requiring little care.

● = First design, pp. 20–21
▲ = Second design, pp. 22–23

Weeping hemlock
(*Tsuga canadensis* 'Pendula', p. 182) ▲

Tulips (*Tulipa*, p. 161) ●

'Setsugekka' sasanqua camellia
(*Camellia sasanqua*, p. 162) ▲

Amur maple (*Acer ginnala*, p. 158) ●

Bird's-nest Norway spruce
(*Picea abies* 'Nidiformis', p. 177) ▲

Setting for a shady porch

This foundation planting graces a front porch on a site shaded from the afternoon sun. Like the previous design, this one mixes the year-round attractions of evergreens with deciduous trees and perennials. From spring through fall, many-stemmed vine maples screen porch sitters from activity on the street. In late winter, fragrant flowers entice visitors to linger on the porch.

Here again, foliage is the key. Conifers, broad-leaved evergreens, ferns, and leafy hostas combine a pleasing variety of forms, leaf textures, and colors. Unlike many plantings, this one reaches its flowering peak in late winter (shown here). Seasonally planted hanging baskets and containers accent the foliage during the rest of the year.

Plants & Projects

A **Vine maple** (use 6 plants)
This deciduous Northwest native tree forms an open thicket of stems that is interesting year-round. Green leaves turn red, yellow, and purple in fall. See *Acer circinatum*, p. 158.

B **Weeping hemlock** (use 1)
A slow-growing evergreen tree, its arching branches forming a wide mound of soft blue-green foliage. A striking contrast to the vine maples. See *Tsuga canadensis* 'Pendula', p. 182.

C **Bird's-nest Norway spruce** (use 3)
Another slow-growing evergreen tree. It makes a hassock-like mound of dark green needles. Commonly has a slight depression on top, which gives rise to its name. See *Picea abies* 'Nidiformis', p. 177.

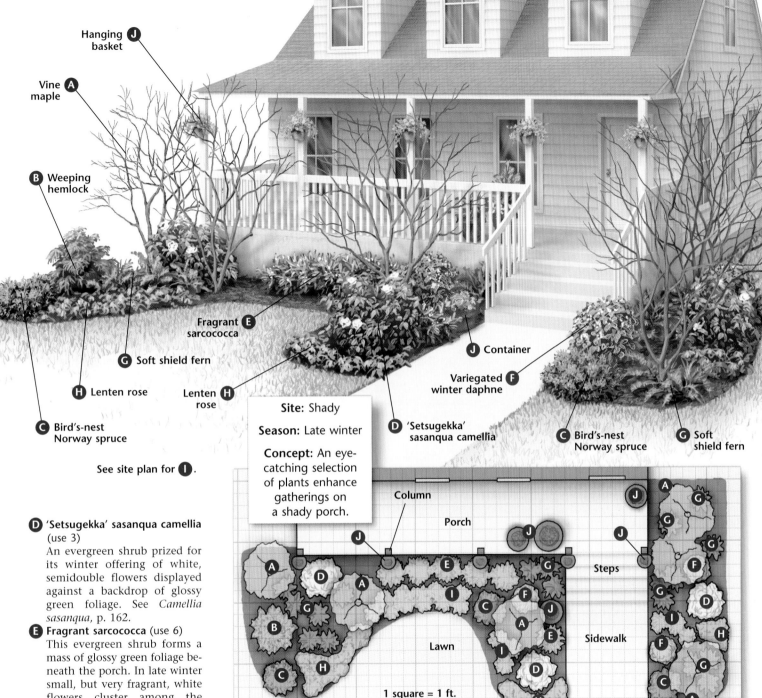

Hanging basket J

Vine maple A

Weeping hemlock B

Fragrant sarcococca E

Soft shield fern G

Lenten rose H

Lenten rose H

Bird's-nest Norway spruce C

See site plan for I.

J **Container**

F **Variegated winter daphne**

D **'Setsugekka' sasanqua camellia**

C **Bird's-nest Norway spruce**

G **Soft shield fern**

Site: Shady

Season: Late winter

Concept: An eye-catching selection of plants enhance gatherings on a shady porch.

Column

Porch

Steps

Lawn

Sidewalk

1 square = 1 ft.

D **'Setsugekka' sasanqua camellia** (use 3)
An evergreen shrub prized for its winter offering of white, semidouble flowers displayed against a backdrop of glossy green foliage. See *Camellia sasanqua*, p. 162.

E **Fragrant sarcococca** (use 6)
This evergreen shrub forms a mass of glossy green foliage beneath the porch. In late winter small, but very fragrant, white flowers cluster among the leaves. See *Sarcococca ruscifolia*, p. 180.

F **Variegated winter daphne** (use 3)
The glossy green leaves of this evergreen shrub are edged in gold. Fragrant, rose-tinged white flowers bloom from late winter into spring. See *Daphne odora* 'Aureomarginata', p. 166.

G **Soft shield fern** (use 18)
Clumps of lacy bright green fronds accent the planting in several spots. The foliage is evergreen and soft to the touch. See Ferns: *Polystichum setiferum*, p. 168.

H **Lenten rose** (use 12)
A popular late-winter-blooming perennial with distinctive fleshy flowers and shiny evergreen leaves. See *Helleborus orientalis*, p. 170.

I **Hosta** (use 20)
A popular perennial that is prized for its foliage. To complement this planting, choose a medium-size cultivar with variegated white-and-green leaves. See *Hosta*, p. 171.

J **Containers and hanging baskets** (as needed)
For winter we've shown trailing glacier ivy and primroses in the baskets hanging on the porch columns. For the large pots on the porch and by the steps, use a tall plant (such as a dwarf conifer, evergreen fern, or spike plant) underplanted with seasonal annuals. Here we've shown winter pansies and kale.

Up Front and Formal
Garden geometry transforms a small front yard

Formal gardens have a special appeal. Their simple geometry can be soothing in a hectic world, and the look is timeless, never going out of style. Homes with balanced or symmetrical facades are especially suited to formal makeovers, which complement and accent the architecture.

This design enhances both approaches to a front door—from the sidewalk and the driveway—while echoing the house facade when viewed from the street. The result is formal, but comfortably so.

Visitors approaching from sidewalk or drive are drawn to a small "courtyard" at the intersection of the two walkways where they can pause to enjoy the plantings before proceeding to the door. A nearby bench encourages lingerings under the shade of a small tree. Low wooden screens provide privacy from the street.

Overcrowded, intricate plantings can make a small space seem smaller. So here, a limited palette of plants is arrayed in bold masses to impart a comfortably spacious feel to a small garden. Flowers can be enjoyed from spring through fall, and a balance of deciduous and evergreen foliage ensures a year-round presence.

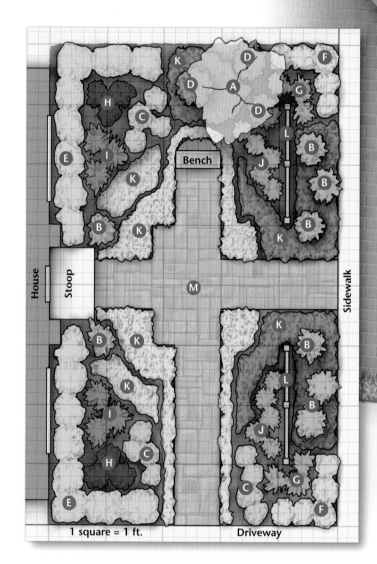

1 square = 1 ft.

'Green Island' **E**
Japanese holly

Plants & Projects

Installing new paving and wooden privacy screens is a big job, but not complicated. Contact a landscape contractor if you prefer to expend your energy on the planting. Once established, these plants are not particularly demanding. Clip the hedges regularly to keep them tidy. Prune trees and shrubs as needed to maintain size and shape.

A Japanese stewartia
(use 1 plant)
This deciduous tree provides white flowers in midsummer, dappled shade in summer, colorful fall foliage, and flaking bark for winter interest. See *Stewartia pseudocamellia*, p. 181.

B 'Flower Carpet Pink' rose
(use 8)
A deciduous shrub, its shiny green foliage is covered from spring to fall with clusters of pink flowers. See *Rosa*, p. 178.

C 'Ramapo' rhododendron
(use 12)
This compact evergreen shrub forms a mound of silvery blue foliage. Bright violet flowers bloom in spring. See *Rhododendron*, p. 178.

D 'Preziosa' hydrangea (use 3)
Prized for its long-lasting, showy midsummer flowers, this deciduous shrub also has attractive foliage. Flowers start out white, then turn red, mauve, or blue. See *Hydrangea macrophylla*, p. 172.

E 'Green Island' Japanese holly
(use 16)
This evergreen shrub's small shiny green leaves are borne on compact, twiggy branches ideal for shearing. Trim as a tidy, but loose, hedge. See *Ilex crenata*, p. 173.

F 'Helleri' Japanese holly
(use 10)
Similar to 'Green Island', this evergreen shrub makes a smaller, tighter mass of dark green leaves. Trim formally to neat geometric lines. See *Ilex crenata*, p. 173.

G 'Sarabande' Japanese silver grass (use 6)
A perennial grass, this forms a large clump of slender leaves

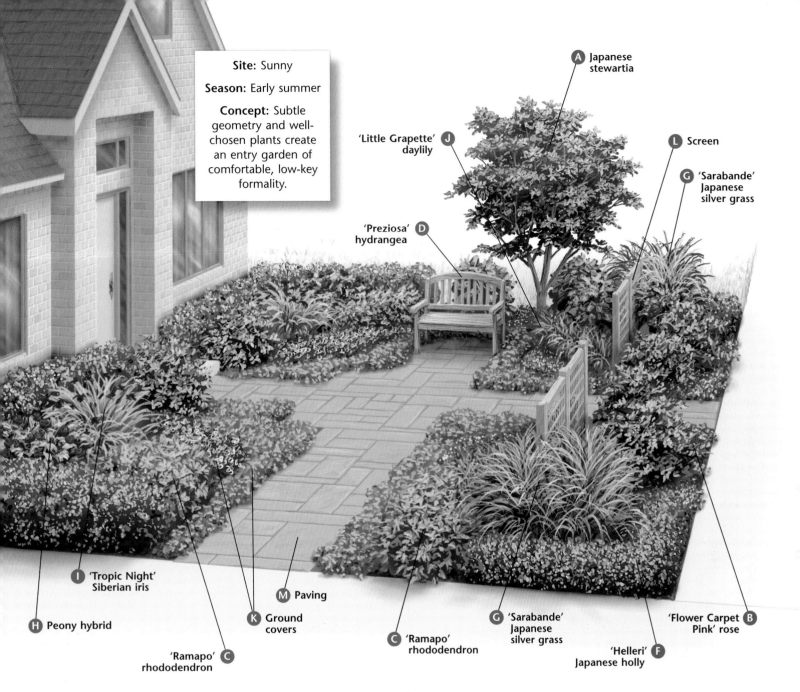

Site: Sunny

Season: Early summer

Concept: Subtle geometry and well-chosen plants create an entry garden of comfortable, low-key formality.

A Japanese stewartia

J 'Little Grapette' daylily

L Screen

G 'Sarabande' Japanese silver grass

D 'Preziosa' hydrangea

I 'Tropic Night' Siberian iris

M Paving

K Ground covers

H Peony hybrid

C 'Ramapo' rhododendron

C 'Ramapo' rhododendron

G 'Sarabande' Japanese silver grass

F 'Helleri' Japanese holly

B 'Flower Carpet Pink' rose

that arch at their tips. White-striped green leaves appear to be silver from a distance. See *Miscanthus sinensis*, p. 175.

H Peony hybrids (use 6)
These perennials bear large fragrant flowers in late spring or early summer on bushy clumps of compound foliage. A cultivar with burgundy-red flowers suits this design well. See *Paeonia*, p. 176.

I 'Tropic Night' Siberian iris (use 6)
In late spring and early sum-mer, elegant deep purple flow-ers rise on long stalks above this perennial's slender upright leaves. Foliage continues to look good after bloom has faded. See *Iris sibirica*, p. 173.

J 'Little Grapette' daylily (use 10)
Echoing the irises closer to the house, this perennial also forms a clump of long slender leaves and bears deep rosy pur-ple flowers on long stalks. Blooms in early summer. See *Hemerocallis*, p. 170.

K Ground covers (as needed)
Of the three ground covers used in this design, two are shrubs. Nearest the house, 'Sil-ver Queen' euonymus (see *Eu-onymus fortunei*, p. 167) forms a low mass of small green leaves edged in white. Space plants 2 ft. on center. Around the low screens, 'Massachusetts' kin-nikinnick (see *Arctostaphylos uva-ursi*, p. 160) forms a dark green carpet. Its white spring flowers produce red berries. Plant 18 in. on center. Edging

the walkways is moss phlox (see *Phlox subulata*, p. 176), a perennial with grayish ever-green leaves and pink spring flowers. Plant 18 in. on center.

L Screen
Low wooden screens adjacent to the walkway help separate the public and private spaces in the front yard. See p. 126.

M Paving
Rectangular, random-sized flag-stones are durable and rein-force the formality of the design. See p. 104.

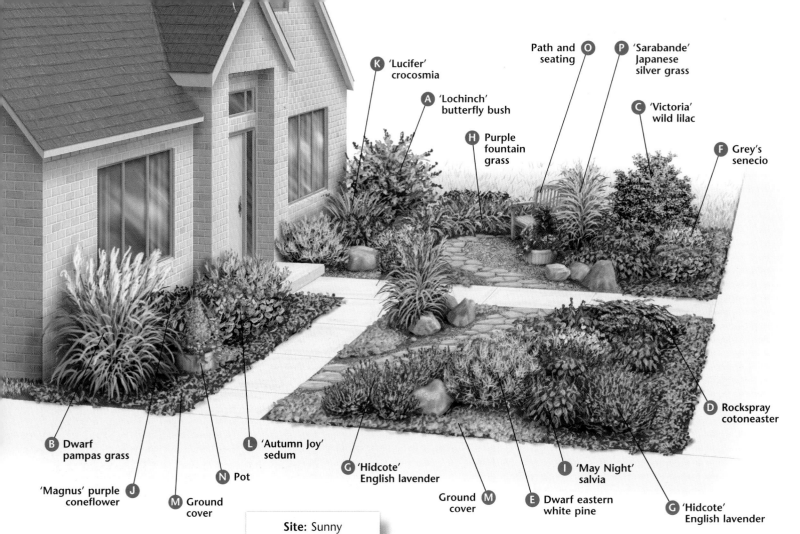

K 'Lucifer' crocosmia

A 'Lochinch' butterfly bush

H Purple fountain grass

Path and seating **O**

P 'Sarabande' Japanese silver grass

C 'Victoria' wild lilac

F Grey's senecio

D Rockspray cotoneaster

B Dwarf pampas grass

L 'Autumn Joy' sedum

'Magnus' purple coneflower **J**

N Pot

M Ground cover

G 'Hidcote' English lavender

Ground cover **M**

E Dwarf eastern white pine

I 'May Night' salvia

G 'Hidcote' English lavender

Free-spirited front yard

If formality isn't your style and you prefer gardens to lawns, consider this design. Here, sweeping masses of shrubs and perennials create a colorful undulating landscape. The foliage is varied in form, color, and texture, and there are flowers and striking seed heads from spring through fall.

Though informal, the composition is subtly purposeful. Eye-catching plants define the planting at the corners. Distinctive pines frame the doorway, while walkways from drive and sidewalk invite entry.

Site: Sunny

Season: Late summer

Concept: An imaginative informal planting transforms a front yard into a pleasant stroll garden.

But for the visitor or resident inclined to dally, a meandering flagstone path leads not to the front door but to a comfortable bench where the plants can be enjoyed at leisure. You might consider removing any concrete walkway from the drive to emphasize the garden stroll.

You need undertake no major construction for this design, and you can install the planting in stages, retaining lawn in areas yet to be planted.

Plants & Projects

A **'Lochinch' butterfly bush** (use 1 plant)
Long clusters of fragrant violet-blue flowers bloom from midsummer through fall on this deciduous shrub. See *Buddleia davidii*, p. 161.

B **Dwarf pampas grass** (use 1)
An evergreen perennial with arching leaves. In summer and fall it bears pink flowers and pale yellow seed heads. See *Cortaderia selloana* 'Pumila', p. 164.

C **'Victoria' wild lilac** (use 1)
This upright shrub offers attractive evergreen foliage and clusters of deep blue flowers in spring. See *Ceanothus*, p. 163.

D **Rockspray cotoneaster** (use 1)
A low deciduous shrub with pinkish white spring flowers and long-lasting red berries. Leaves turn red in fall. See *Cotoneaster horizontalis*, p. 165.

E **Dwarf eastern white pine** (use 3)
This evergreen tree or shrub grows slowly and has soft blue-green needles. See *Pinus strobus* 'Nana', p. 177.

F **Grey's senecio** (use 3)
An evergreen shrub with small gray leaves and yellow daisy-like flowers in summer. See *Senecio greyi*, p. 181.

G **'Hidcote' English lavender** (use 23)
The gray foliage of this compact evergreen shrub bristles with spikes of dark purple flowers in early summer. See *Lavandula angustifolia*, p. 174.

H **Purple fountain grass** (use 9)
This perennial forms a clump of very thin reddish leaves topped during the summer with striking plumes of tiny purple flowers. See *Pennisetum setaceum* 'Rubrum', p. 176.

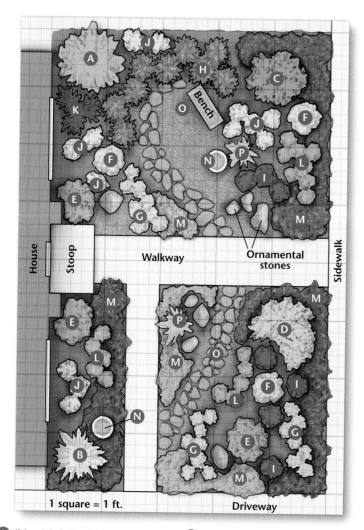

Bench

House

Stoop

Walkway

Ornamental stones

Sidewalk

1 square = 1 ft.

Driveway

Plant portraits

These plants add character to front yards that are geometric or free-ranging, formal or informal.

● = First design, pp. 24–25
▲ = Second design, pp. 26–27

Moss phlox (*Phlox subulata*, p. 176) ●

'Ramapo' rhododendron (*Rhododendron*, p. 178) ●

I 'May Night' salvia (use 7)
For months in summer this perennial bears numerous spikes of deep purple flowers above dark green leaves. See *Salvia × superba*, p. 180.

J 'Magnus' purple coneflower (use 13)
Large daisylike purple flowers with orange centers rise on stiff stems above this perennial's dark green leaves. See *Echinacea purpurea*, p. 166.

K 'Lucifer' crocosmia (use 3)
This perennial makes a clump of long narrow leaves. In summer, arching stalks bear sprays of red-orange flowers. See *Crocosmia*, p. 166.

L 'Autumn Joy' sedum (use 18)
A perennial with fleshy gray-green foliage and flat clusters of tiny flowers that turn from pink to russet from summer through fall. See *Sedum*, p. 181.

M Ground covers (as needed)
Woolly thyme (see *Thymus pseudolanuginosus*, p. 182) runs through the center of the planting. Plant 1 ft. apart. Bearberry cotoneaster (see *Cotoneaster dammeri*, p. 165) carpets areas at the front of the planting and to the left of the stoop. Plant 2 ft. on center.

N Pots
Large, colorfully planted pots accent the planting. Try combinations of boxwood, amaranth, zinnias, verbena, coleus, scaevola, and helichrysum.

O Path and seating
A path of irregular flagstones leads to a seating area of crushed rock (for both, see p. 104) and a comfortable bench.

See p. 24 for the following:

P 'Sarabande' Japanese silver grass (use 2)

'Lochinch' butterfly bush (*Buddleia davidii*, p. 161) ▲

'Preziosa' hydrangea (*Hydrangea macrophylla*, p. 172) ●

An Eye-Catching Corner

Beautify a boundary with easy-care plants

The corner where two properties and the sidewalk meet is often a kind of grassy no-man's-land. Neighbors hesitate to garden there for fear of offending one another. This design defines that boundary with a planting that can be enjoyed by both property owners, as well as by passersby. Good gardens make good neighbors, so we've used well-behaved, low-maintenance plants that won't make extra work for the person next door—or for you.

Because of its exposed location, remote from the house and close to the street, a corner planting is often less personal than those in more private and frequently used parts of a property. This design is meant to be appreciated from a distance. Anchored by a small tree, the planting combines shrubs and perennials in an attractive scheme of colorful foliage and flowers. An existing fence provides scaffolding for a vigorous vine. While not intended as a barrier, the planting also provides a modest psychological, if not physical, screen from activity on the sidewalk and street.

Here, something is in bloom from spring through fall, with flowers in shades of yellow, blue, orange-red, and white. The foliage is also colorful, mixing gray, silver, and blue with green. The small tree provides a blaze of color in fall, while evergreen plants ensure a year-round presence.

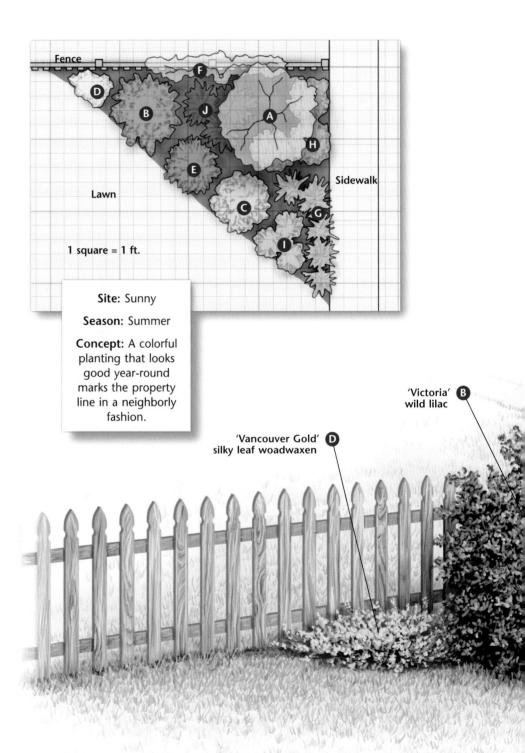

Site: Sunny

Season: Summer

Concept: A colorful planting that looks good year-round marks the property line in a neighborly fashion.

'Victoria' **B** wild lilac

'Vancouver Gold' **D** silky leaf woadwaxen

Plants & Projects

As befits a planting some distance from the house, these durable, reliable plants require little care beyond some seasonal pruning and cleanup. As they reach maturity, the shrubs and vine may need occasional pruning to control size.

A **'Autumn Brilliance' serviceberry** (use 1 plant)
This small deciduous tree is a three-season performer, with white flowers in spring, blue berries in summer, and colorful foliage in fall. See *Amelanchier × grandiflora*, p. 160.

B **'Victoria' wild lilac** (use 1)
In spring, this evergreen shrub displays small deep blue flowers at the ends of its branches. Small, glossy dark green leaves make an effective background. See *Ceanothus*, p. 163.

C **Grey's senecio** (use 1)
Grown primarily for its soft gray foliage, this evergreen shrub bears pretty yellow flowers in summer. Bloom is unreliable. Flowers are sometimes sheared off, as shown here, to emphasize the foliage. See *Senecio greyi*, p. 181.

D **'Vancouver Gold' silky leaf woadwaxen** (use 1)
A low deciduous ground cover whose twiggy matlike stems are covered with tiny green leaves. In late spring and early summer it bears a mass of bright yellow pealike flowers. See *Genista pilosa*, p. 169.

E **'Tuscan Blue' rosemary** (use 3)
This evergreen shrub has fragrant gray-green leaves. Periwinkle blue flowers bloom in late winter and sporadically the rest of the year. See *Rosmarinus officinalis*, p. 179.

F **Hall's Japanese honeysuckle** (use 1)
A vigorous semievergreen vine with dull green leaves. Late-spring flowers are trumpet-shaped and turn from yellow to white with age. See *Lonicera japonica* 'Halliana', p. 174.

G **Blue oat grass** (use 5)
This evergreen grass forms a clump bristling with thin pale blue leaves. Trim off the sparse flower spikes, as shown here, if you wish. See *Helictotrichon sempervirens*, p. 170.

H **'Powis Castle' artemisia** (use 3)
A perennial, this forms a spreading mound of deeply cut silvery leaves that adds a striking accent to the planting. See *Artemisia*, p. 160.

I **'Goldsturm' coneflower** (use 3)
From summer into fall this perennial's daisylike flowers rise on sturdy stems above clumps of green leaves. Flowers are yellow with dark centers. See *Rudbeckia*, p. 179.

J **'Lucifer' crocosmia** (use 3)
This perennial forms attractive clumps of sword-shaped leaves. In summer, bright red-orange flowers line the ends of tall branched stems. See *Crocosmia*, p. 166.

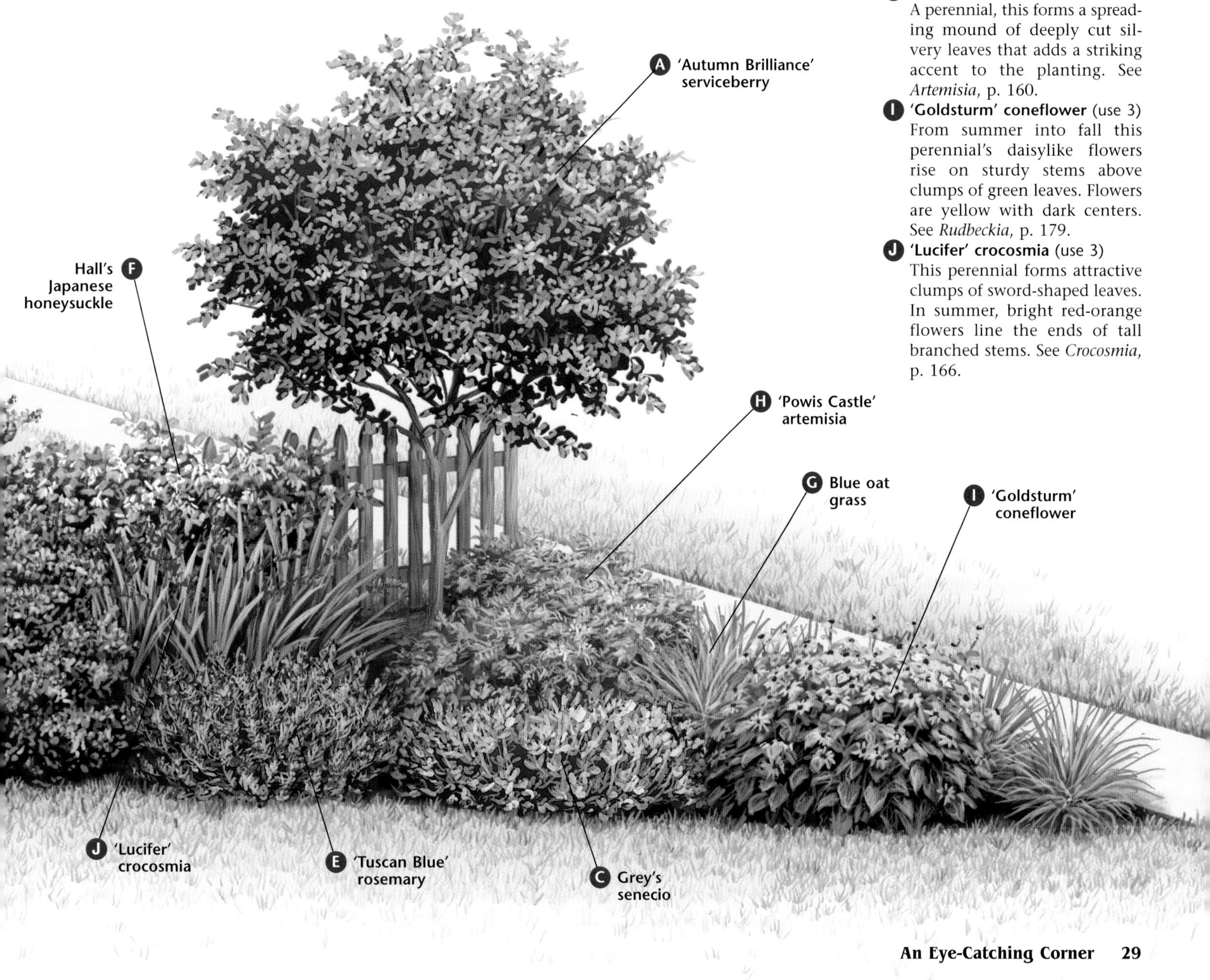

A 'Autumn Brilliance' serviceberry

F Hall's Japanese honeysuckle

H 'Powis Castle' artemisia

G Blue oat grass

I 'Goldsturm' coneflower

J 'Lucifer' crocosmia

E 'Tuscan Blue' rosemary

C Grey's senecio

A winter full of flowers

Like the previous design, this one provides a handsome mix of foliage and flowers, but for a shady site. Again, low maintenance and year-round interest are priorities. To relieve the dreary days of the rainy season, this planting offers a lovely, often fragrant, array of flowers from fall to spring.

A large deciduous viburnum anchors the design, while evergreen or nearly evergreen plants fill out the space. Foliage colors and textures take center stage from late spring through fall. Mounding and spreading shrubs are accented by lacy fern fronds and sword-leaved irises. The dominant flower colors are pink and white. Adding highlights are splashes of yellow barrenwort and magenta geranium blossoms, along with the bright orange-red seedpods of the Gladwin irises.

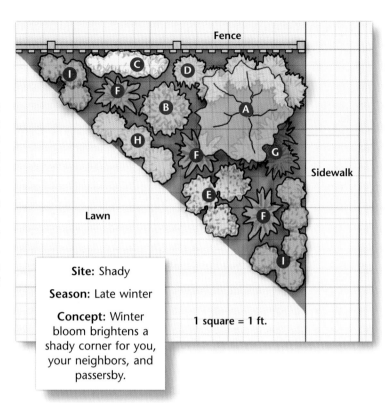

Site: Shady

Season: Late winter

Concept: Winter bloom brightens a shady corner for you, your neighbors, and passersby.

1 square = 1 ft.

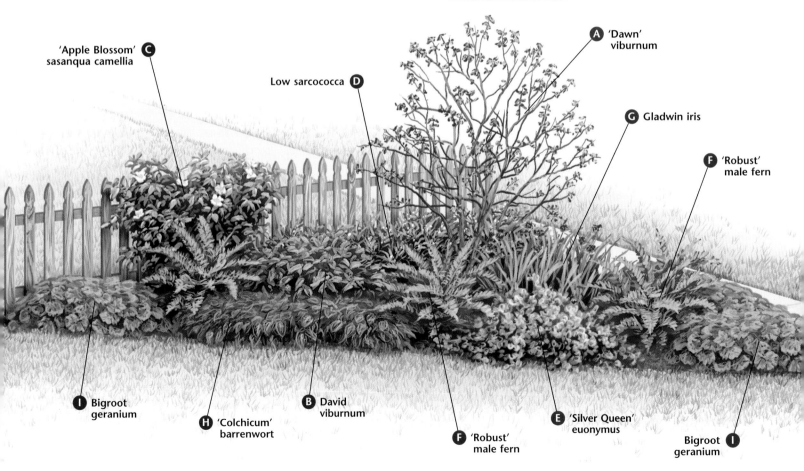

C 'Apple Blossom' sasanqua camellia

D Low sarcococca

A 'Dawn' viburnum

G Gladwin iris

F 'Robust' male fern

I Bigroot geranium

H 'Colchicum' barrenwort

B David viburnum

F 'Robust' male fern

E 'Silver Queen' euonymus

I Bigroot geranium

Plants & Projects

A 'Dawn' viburnum (use 1 plant)
A large deciduous shrub with very fragrant pink flowers from fall into spring, peaking in late winter. Its dark green leaves turn scarlet in fall. See *Viburnum × bodnantense*, p. 182.

B David viburnum (use 1)
This compact evergreen shrub has leathery dark green leaves. In spring, pink buds open into flat-topped clusters of white flowers. See *Viburnum davidii*, p. 182.

C 'Apple Blossom' sasanqua camellia (use 1)
Trained along the fence, this shrub displays pink-and-white flowers against a backdrop of glossy evergreen leaves from late fall into winter. See *Camellia sasanqua*, p. 162.

D Low sarcococca (use 5)
This low, spreading evergreen shrub bears tiny white flowers that nestle at the base of its green lancelike leaves. Blooms in late winter. See *Sarcococca humilis*, p. 180.

E 'Silver Queen' euonymus (use 3)
Another low-growing evergreen, this shrub has small, white-edged green leaves that take on a pink tinge in winter. See *Euonymus fortunei*, p. 167.

F 'Robust' male fern (use 3)
A graceful bright green fern. Its lacy evergreen fronds do well in winter conditions. See Ferns: *Dryopteris × complexa*, p. 168.

G Gladwin iris (use 3)
This perennial forms a clump of glossy upright leaves and bears clusters of purple flowers in summer. Long-lasting pods follow, splitting to reveal bright orange-red seeds. See *Iris foetidissima*, p. 173.

H 'Colchicum' barrenwort (use 3)
This perennial ground cover is prized for its heart-shaped evergreen foliage, which changes color with the seasons. Bears yellow flowers in spring. See *Epimedium pinnatum*, p. 167.

I Bigroot geranium (use 8)
Bushy clumps of colorful and fragrant semievergreen foliage distinguish this perennial. Late-spring flowers are magenta or purple. See *Geranium macrorrhizum*, p. 169.

Plant portraits

Viewed from house, sidewalk, or street, these easy-care plants provide good-looking foliage and flowers year-round.

● = First design, pp. 28–29
▲ = Second design, pp. 30–31

'Apple Blossom' sasanqua camellia
(*Camellia sasanqua*, p. 162) ▲

'Dawn' viburnum
(*Viburnum × bodnantense*, p. 182) ▲

Hall's Japanese honeysuckle
(*Lonicera japonica* 'Halliana', p. 174) ●

Blue oat grass
(*Helictotrichon sempervirens*, p. 170) ●

Gladwin iris (*Iris foetidissima*, p. 173) ▲

'Powis Castle' artemisia (*Artemisia*, p. 160) ●

Streetwise and Stylish

Give your curbside strip a new look

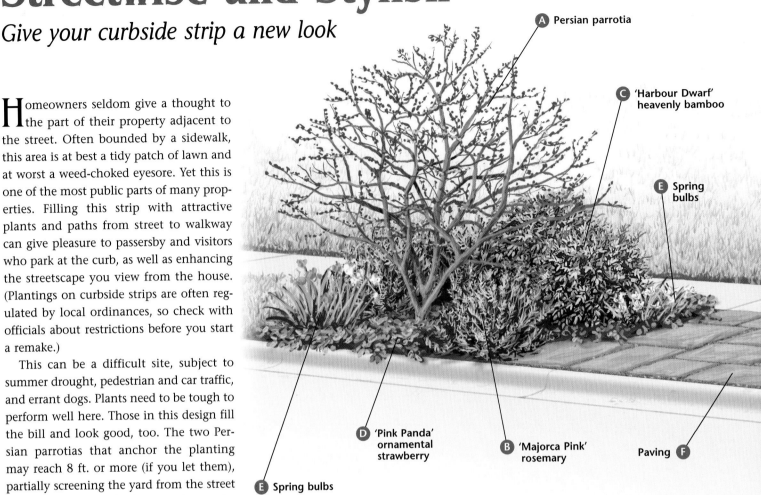

A Persian parrotia

C 'Harbour Dwarf' heavenly bamboo

E Spring bulbs

D 'Pink Panda' ornamental strawberry

B 'Majorca Pink' rosemary

Paving **F**

E Spring bulbs

Homeowners seldom give a thought to the part of their property adjacent to the street. Often bounded by a sidewalk, this area is at best a tidy patch of lawn and at worst a weed-choked eyesore. Yet this is one of the most public parts of many properties. Filling this strip with attractive plants and paths from street to walkway can give pleasure to passersby and visitors who park at the curb, as well as enhancing the streetscape you view from the house. (Plantings on curbside strips are often regulated by local ordinances, so check with officials about restrictions before you start a remake.)

This can be a difficult site, subject to summer drought, pedestrian and car traffic, and errant dogs. Plants need to be tough to perform well here. Those in this design fill the bill and look good, too. The two Persian parrotias that anchor the planting may reach 8 ft. or more (if you let them), partially screening the yard from the street in the summer. While the parrotias are deciduous, the other plants are evergreen, providing an all-season display. Bloom peaks in spring (shown here). Small red flowers sprout from the bare branches of the parrotias, while the ornamental strawberry, rosemary, and spring bulbs bloom beneath them.

Easily laid pavers afford access from the street to the sidewalk and front-entry walk. To unify the look of your front yard, incorporate the same plants in plantings on the other side of the sidewalk. If your curbside property doesn't include a sidewalk, you can extend the planting farther into the yard.

Plants & Projects

The flagstone paving is easy to lay on a sand-and-gravel base. Once established, the plants require very little care. You can let the parrotias grow into small trees, or prune them in spring to keep them whatever size you wish. Heavily planted bulbs will require dividing after several years.

A **Persian parrotia** (use 2 plants)
An all-season performer, this large deciduous shrub bears small clusters of red flowers before the leaves appear in spring. Dark green leaves turn yellow, red, and then purple in fall. Peeling bark looks good in winter. Use single-trunked, low-branching specimens here. See *Parrotia persica*, p. 176.

B **'Majorca Pink' rosemary** (use 6)
This evergreen shrub bears narrow, fragrant blue-green leaves on upright branches. Small lavender-pink flowers bloom from late winter into spring. See *Rosmarinus officinalis*, p. 179.

C **'Harbour Dwarf' heavenly bamboo** (use 5)
An evergreen shrub, it features soft lacy foliage. New leaves are light orange-red, then turn green in summer and bright crimson in fall and winter. This cultivar doesn't flower. See *Nandina domestica*, p. 175.

D **'Pink Panda' ornamental strawberry** (as needed)
This fast-growing evergreen ground cover resembles the

Site: Sunny

Season: Spring

Concept: Tall plants help separate your property from the street, while welcoming visitors parked at curbside.

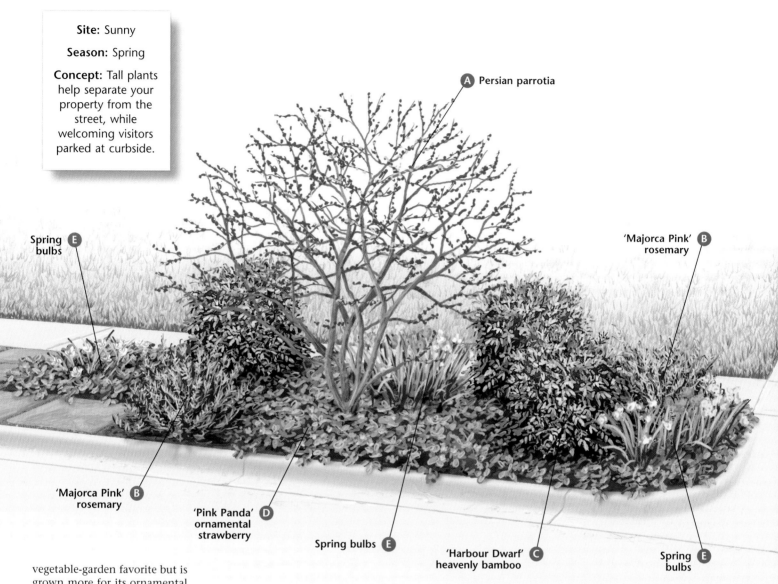

Ⓐ Persian parrotia

Ⓔ Spring bulbs

Ⓑ 'Majorca Pink' rosemary

Ⓑ 'Majorca Pink' rosemary

Ⓓ 'Pink Panda' ornamental strawberry

Ⓔ Spring bulbs

Ⓒ 'Harbour Dwarf' heavenly bamboo

Ⓔ Spring bulbs

vegetable-garden favorite but is grown more for its ornamental qualities than its fruit (which is edible). Bears pink flowers in spring. See *Fragaria,* p. 169.

Ⓔ **Spring bulbs** (as needed)
Underplant the strawberry ground cover with crocuses and daffodils for a long spring blooming season. Swaths of white and blue crocuses edge the pavers, while groups of white, yellow, and orange daffodils appear in several spots. Large numbers of bulbs make a bigger splash. See Bulbs: *Crocus* and *Narcissus,* p. 161.

Ⓕ **Paving**
Rectangular flagstones in random sizes provide easy access. See p. 104.

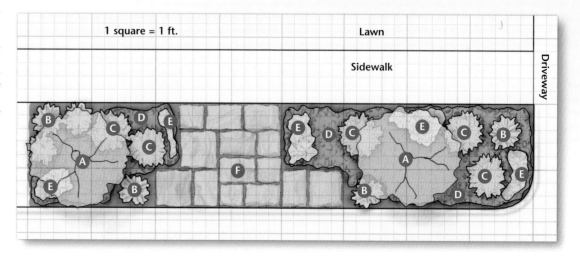

1 square = 1 ft.   Lawn

Sidewalk

Driveway

A low-profile planting

As in the previous design, this planting dresses up the often neglected curbside, while accommodating visitors who park on the street. Lacking tall shrubs, it offers less privacy but makes a smoother transition to the street than the other design.

Though there are flowers from spring into fall, foliage is the main event here. Planted in bold masses that echo the angled lines of the paving, the foliage makes a simple but effective composition of varied colors and textures. There are also seasonal accents, from cheerful daffodils in the spring to flat-topped russet seed heads of sedum in the fall. Most of the planting is evergreen and is attractive in winter as well.

Plants & Projects

A **'Newport Dwarf' escallonia** (use 6 plants)
This low, bushy evergreen shrub carpets the planting with glossy red-edged green leaves. It is sprinkled with small clusters of red flowers in summer. See *Escallonia rubra*, p. 167.

B **Mugo pine** (use 2)
This popular evergreen conifer forms a low shrubby mound of dark green needles. Its solid mass contrasts nicely with the airy Russian sage nearby. See *Pinus mugo*, p. 177.

C **'Silver Queen' euonymus** (use 20)
The white-and-green variegated foliage of this low, spreading shrub makes a distinctive edging for the pavers, sidewalk, and driveway. Evergreen leaves take on a pink tinge in winter. See *Euonymus fortunei*, p. 167.

D **'Longin' Russian sage** (use 2)
A multistemmed perennial with fine gray-green leaves. Delicate spikes of lavender-blue flowers hover among foliage and woody light gray stems from summer into fall. See *Perovskia atriplicifolia*, p. 176.

E **'Autumn Joy' sedum** (use 8)
This perennial forms a mound of fleshy light green leaves. Flat-topped clusters of tiny greenish pink flowers appear in late summer, turning deeper red with age, finally becoming long-lasting russet-colored seed heads. See *Sedum*, p. 181.

F **Daffodils** (as needed)
Plant your favorite daffodils among the euonymus for a spring spectacular. Use 100 or more of the same color for a strong showing. See Bulbs: *Narcissus*, p. 161.

G **Paving**
Use materials that go with your house. Here, roughly square flagstones are laid with fairly large gaps on a sand-and-gravel base. The stair-stepped outline is echoed in the adjacent plantings. See p. 104.

Site: Sunny

Season: Summer

Concept: Simple massings of handsome foliage transform an often neglected area and treat visitors and passersby to an eye-catching display.

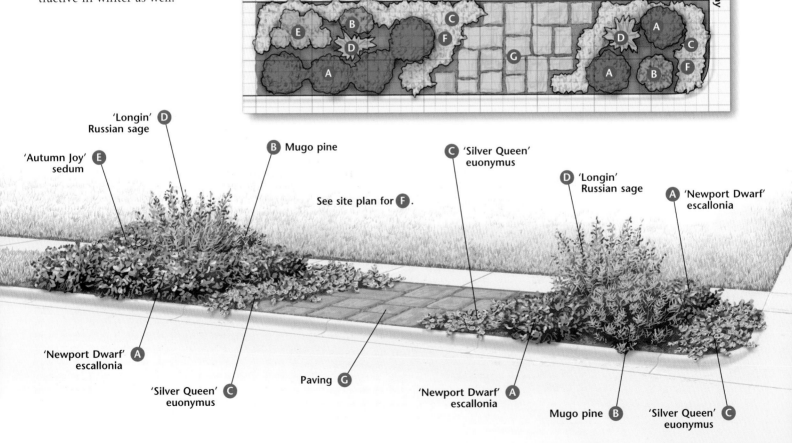

1 square = 1 ft.

Lawn

Sidewalk

Driveway

'Longin' **D** Russian sage

'Autumn Joy' **E** sedum

B Mugo pine

See site plan for **F**.

C 'Silver Queen' euonymus

D 'Longin' Russian sage

A 'Newport Dwarf' escallonia

'Newport Dwarf' **A** escallonia

'Silver Queen' **C** euonymus

Paving **G**

'Newport Dwarf' **A** escallonia

Mugo pine **B**

'Silver Queen' **C** euonymus

Plant portraits

These low-maintenance plants will improve any curbside area, while withstanding the rigors of life by the street.

● = First design, pp. 32–33
▲ = Second design, p. 34

Crocus (Bulbs: *Crocus*, p. 161) ●

'Harbour Dwarf' heavenly bamboo (*Nandina domestica*, p. 175) ●

Mugo pine (*Pinus mugo*, p. 177) ▲

'Pink Panda' ornamental strawberry
(*Fragaria*, p. 169) ●

'Majorca Pink' rosemary
(*Rosmarinus officinalis*, p. 179) ●

Persian parrotia
(*Parrotia persica*, p. 176) ●

Landscaping a Low Wall

A colorful two-tier garden replaces a bland slope

Site: Sunny

Season: Early summer

Concept: Low retaining wall creates easy-to-maintain beds for a distinctive two-level planting of shrubs and perennials.

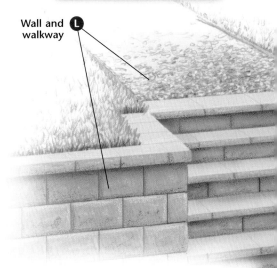

Wall and walkway **L**

Some things may not love a wall, but plants and gardeners do. For plants, walls offer warmth for an early start in spring. Gardeners appreciate the rich visual potential of composing a garden on two levels, as well as the practical advantage of working on two relatively flat surfaces instead of a single sloping one.

This design places two complementary perennial borders above and below a wall bounded at one end by a set of stairs. While each bed is relatively narrow, when viewed from the lower level they combine to form a border almost 10 ft. deep, with plants rising to eye level or more. The planting can be extended farther along the wall with the same or similar plants.

Anchored by its wall, steps, and path, this design can separate two areas on your property, serving as an entrance and boundary for both. Its mix of foliage textures and colors, including a number of evergreens, gives it a year-round presence. And flowers displayed from spring to fall make the planting a destination on its own.

Building the wall that makes this design possible doesn't require the time or skill it once did. Nor is it necessary to scour the countryside for tons of fieldstone or to hire an expensive contractor. Thanks to precast retaining-wall systems, anyone with a healthy back (or access to energetic teenagers) can install a knee-high do-it-yourself wall in as little as a weekend.

Plants & Projects

Installing the wall and steps is the major task in this design. Once the plants are established, they'll thrive with just some seasonal pruning, mulching, and cleanup. You'll need to renew the spade-cut edge between beds and lawn several times a year to keep it tidy.

A **'Victoria' wild lilac** (use 1 plant)
Anchoring the top bed, this evergreen shrub is a mass of small glossy crinkled leaves. In spring it bears blue to purple lilac-like flowers. See *Ceanothus*, p. 163.

B **Grey's senecio** (use 1)
Soft woolly gray foliage covers this evergreen shrub. Yellow daisylike flowers appear in summer; some gardeners remove them to emphasize the foliage. See *Senecio greyi*, p. 181.

C **New Zealand flax** (use 1)
Focal point of the lower bed, this perennial forms a clump of long, upright, swordlike leaves. Cultivars offer a range of eye-catching leaf colors. See *Phormium tenax*, p. 177.

D **'Blue Star' juniper** (use 5)
This evergreen shrub makes a low sculpted mass of silvery blue foliage. Plants will eventually grow together and form a single clump. See *Juniperus squamata*, p. 174.

E **'Hidcote' English lavender** (use 3)
Spikes of small purple flowers rise above this perennial's mounding blue-green foliage in early summer. Leaves are fragrant and evergreen. See *Lavandula angustifolia*, p. 174.

F **Fountain grass** (use 3)
This deciduous perennial forms a mound of thin leaves that turn light brown in fall. Fluffy flower and seed heads nod above foliage in summer. See *Pennisetum orientale*, p. 176.

G **Russian sage** (use 3)
This woody perennial makes an airy upright clump of stiff gray stems and small silver-gray, lance-shaped leaves. Tiny lavender-blue flowers appear to float above the leaves in summer. See *Perovskia*, p. 176.

H **Cushion spurge** (use 3)
A many-stemmed perennial, this forms a compact mound of neat green leaves. Long-lasting bright yellow flowers form at the ends of the stems in spring. Foliage turns red in fall. See *Euphorbia polychroma*, p. 168.

I **Corsican hellebore** (use 1)
This perennial produces distinctive pale green flowers in late winter. Leathery leaves are dark green and edged with small spines. See *Helleborus argutifolius*, p. 170.

J **Ground covers** (as needed)
The planting uses three ground covers. On the right side of the top bed, Carpathian bellflower (see *Campanula carpatica*, p. 162) makes a mass of green heart-shaped leaves and light blue flowers. At left in the top bed and covering much of the bottom bed is a carpet of creeping thyme (see *Thymus praecox* ssp. *articus*, p. 182), which bears tiny green leaves and violet flowers. On the left side of the bottom bed, 'Dragon's Blood' sedum (see *Sedum spurium*, p. 181) forms a mat of small fleshy evergreen leaves and rosy red flowers.

K **Planters**
Available at many garden centers, troughs formed of lightweight cement make excellent planters. You can plant them with fibrous begonias in a mix of colors, as we've shown here. They're also ideal for small sedums or alpine plants.

L **Wall and walkway**
The low, precast retaining wall shown here is typical of those available at home-and-garden centers and local landscaping suppliers. (See p. 116.) The walkway is made of durable crushed stone. (See p. 104.)

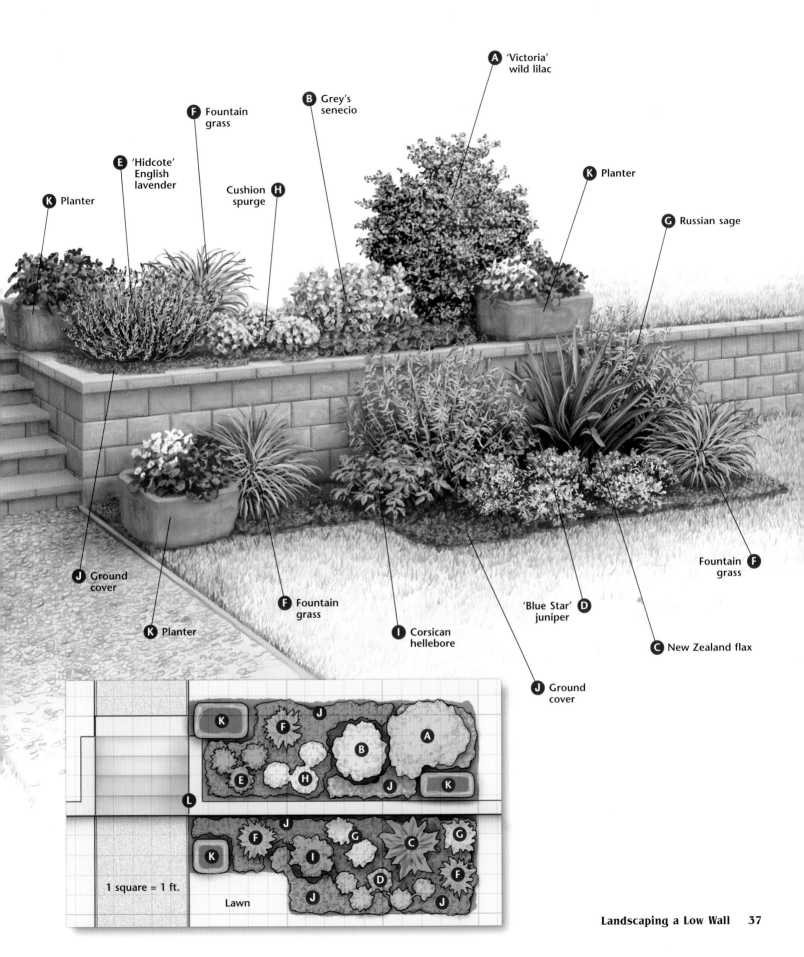

A 'Victoria' wild lilac

B Grey's senecio

F Fountain grass

E 'Hidcote' English lavender

H Cushion spurge

K Planter

K Planter

G Russian sage

J Ground cover

F Fountain grass

K Planter

I Corsican hellebore

J Ground cover

F Fountain grass

D 'Blue Star' juniper

C New Zealand flax

1 square = 1 ft.

Lawn

Two tiers in the shade

A retaining wall and plantings can be equally alluring in a shady backyard. This design echoes the one on the preceding pages, but with plants that thrive in morning sun and afternoon shade. The planting provides an enjoyable setting for relaxing or reading on the bench.

The top level has a striking and rather exotic look, combining the rustling warm yellow culms of bamboo, the dramatic leaves and flowers of bear's breeches, and the upright ruffled fronds of narrow ferns. The lower level is less flamboyant but offers a pleasant range of flowers and foliage.

Site: Shady

Season: Early summer

Concept: Bold plants create a shade-tolerant planting of interest from a distance or up close.

1 square = 1 ft.   Lawn

Plants & Projects

A **Golden bamboo** (use 7 plants) An evergreen bamboo, both its culms and foliage have a golden yellow cast. Makes a distinctive focal point and small screen. See *Phyllostachys aurea,* p. 177.

B **Bear's breeches** (use 1) A perennial grown for its dramatic boldly cut leaves and tall spikes of tubular white-and-purple flowers. Blooms rise several feet above the foliage in late spring. See *Acanthus mollis,* p. 158.

C **'Nana Gracilis' dwarf Hinoki cypress** (use 1) This small evergreen tree forms a narrow cone of glossy green, scalelike foliage. See *Chamaecyparis obtusa,* p. 163.

D **Sasanqua camellia** (use 1) From late fall into winter, this evergreen shrub displays lovely

E Barnes' narrow male fern

M Wall and walkway

J Ground cover

K River rock

A Golden bamboo

B Bear's breeches

G 'Tropic Night' Siberian iris

C 'Nana Gracilis' dwarf Hinoki cypress

D Sasanqua camellia

I 'Velvet Night' heuchera

H 'Cattleya' astilbe

L Seating area

F Large-leaved hosta

J Ground cover

flowers against a background of glossy foliage. Train on wires attached to the wall and prune to maintain size. See *Camellia sasanqua*, p. 162.

E **Barnes' narrow male fern** (use 5)
Small ruffled leaflets add character to the fronds of this narrow upright fern. It is evergreen in mild winters. See Ferns: *Dryopteris filix-mas* 'Barnesii', p. 168.

F **Large-leaved hosta** (use 1)
A large-leaved form of this popular perennial nestles next to the bench. A cultivar with large chartreuse leaves would look good in this planting. See *Hosta*, p. 171.

G **'Tropic Night' Siberian iris** (use 1)
A perennial with striking slender, upright leaves and even more striking deep purple flowers. Blooms in late spring. See *Iris sibirica*, p. 173.

H **'Cattleya' astilbe** (use 5)
This perennial's lacy greenbronze foliage is attractive for many months. In early summer, clusters of tiny crimsonpink flowers are borne on tall stalks above the foliage. See *Astilbe × arendsii*, p. 161.

I **'Velvet Night' heuchera** (use 7)
This perennial is prized for its deep purple foliage. From spring into summer, it bears airy plumes of small brownish green flowers. See *Heuchera americana*, p. 171.

J **Ground covers** (as needed)
Two perennial ground covers are used here. Blue star creeper (see *Pratia pedunculata*, p. 177) edges the lower bed with tiny bright green leaves and sky blue flowers. In the top bed, Irish moss (see *Sagina subulata*, p. 180) forms a mat of kelly green mosslike foliage.

K **River rock**
Round rocks in a range of sizes add interest to the beds.

L **Seating area**
Set a comfortable bench on a graveled surface (see p. 104) for enjoying the planting.

See p. 36 for the following:

M Wall and walkway

Plant portraits

These plants make the most of a two-tiered garden created by a low retaining wall.

● = First design, pp. 36–37
▲ = Second design, pp. 38–39

Fountain grass (*Pennisetum orientale*, p. 176) ●

Irish moss (*Sagina subulata*, p. 180) ▲

Golden bamboo (*Phyllostachys aurea*, p. 177) ▲

Corsican hellebore (*Helleborus argutifolius*, p. 170) ●

New Zealand flax (*Phormium tenax*, p. 177) ●

'Dragon's Blood' sedum (*Sedum spurium*, p. 181) ●

Large-leaved hosta (*Hosta*, p. 171) ▲

Beautify a Blank Wall

A vertical garden makes the most of a narrow site

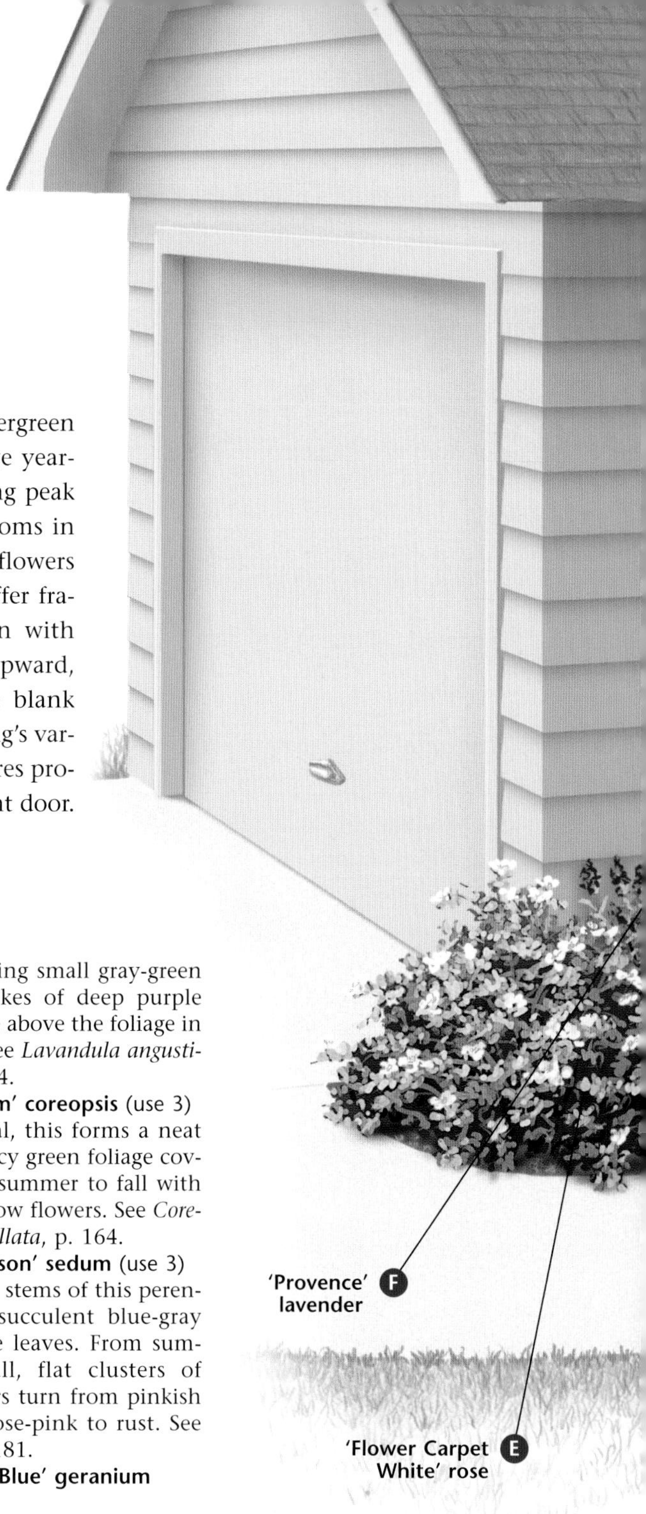

Just as you can enhance a wall in your home with a painting, you can decorate a blank wall outdoors with plants. The design shown here transforms a nondescript front entrance by showcasing perennials, shrubs, and vines against an adjacent garage wall. Such entrances are common in suburban homes, but a vertical garden like this is also ideal for other spots where yard space is limited.

Selected for a sunny site, these plants offer something in every season. There are flowers spring through fall, and evergreen shrubs provide fresh-looking foliage year-round. The garden is at its flowering peak in early and midsummer, with blooms in yellow, blue, purple, and red. The flowers and foliage of the two lavenders offer fragrance as well. Two trellises laden with clematis flowers draw the eye upward, making a canvas of an otherwise blank wall. When flowers fade, the planting's varied foliage colors, shapes, and textures provide interest on the walk to the front door.

Plants & Projects

Once established, these plants require little more than seasonal maintenance. As they mature, the shrubs will need to be pruned to limit their size. In late fall, cut down the perennials along the walk to keep the bed tidy. Or, instead, let the escallonia expand to displace the perennials and fill their space during the winter.

A Clematis hybrid (use 2 plants)
Trained up matching trellises, the generous foliage of these deciduous vines is covered with eye-catching flowers for months. Choose from numerous cultivars. For winter presence, try an evergreen type. See *Clematis*, p. 163.

B 'Sunshine' Grey's senecio (use 1)
An evergreen shrub, this makes a loose mound of soft paddle-shaped green leaves. Bears yellow flowers in summer. See *Senecio greyi*, p. 181.

C 'Newport Dwarf' escallonia (use 4)
Shading the roots of the clematis, this evergreen shrub has a tight, compact form. Shiny green leaves have red margins. Red flowers cluster at the ends of stems in summer. See *Escallonia rubra*, p. 167.

D 'Tuscan Blue' rosemary (use 1)
The upright stems of this evergreen shrub are lined with fragrant blue-green leaves. Bears deep blue flowers sporadically throughout the year. See *Rosmarinus officinalis*, p. 179.

E 'Flower Carpet White' rose (use 3)
This shrub forms a low, spreading ground cover of reddish green leaves. From spring through autumn it bears clusters of single white flowers. See *Rosa*, p. 178.

F 'Provence' lavender (use 1)
This evergreen shrub's spikes of fragrant deep purple flowers and fragrant gray-green foliage combine well with the nearby roses. It blooms in early summer. See *Lavandula × intermedia*, p. 174.

G 'Hidcote' English lavender (use 6)
An evergreen shrub, it forms a compact clump of upright stems bearing small gray-green leaves. Spikes of deep purple flowers rise above the foliage in summer. See *Lavandula angustifolia*, p. 174.

H 'Moonbeam' coreopsis (use 3)
A perennial, this forms a neat patch of lacy green foliage covered from summer to fall with sunny yellow flowers. See *Coreopsis verticillata*, p. 164.

I 'Vera Jameson' sedum (use 3)
The floppy stems of this perennial bear succulent blue-gray and purple leaves. From summer to fall, flat clusters of tiny flowers turn from pinkish green to rose-pink to rust. See *Sedum*, p. 181.

J 'Johnson's Blue' geranium (use 3)
This perennial makes a sprawling mass of pretty lobed green leaves. Bears periwinkle blue flowers in early summer. See *Geranium*, p. 169.

K Trellis
This pair of simple trellises provide support for the clematis and look good in winter, too. See p. 127.

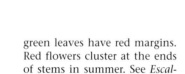

'Provence' **F** lavender

'Flower Carpet **E** White' rose

Site: Sunny

Season: Summer

Concept: Handsome plants arrayed against a blank wall make a picture that pleases year-round.

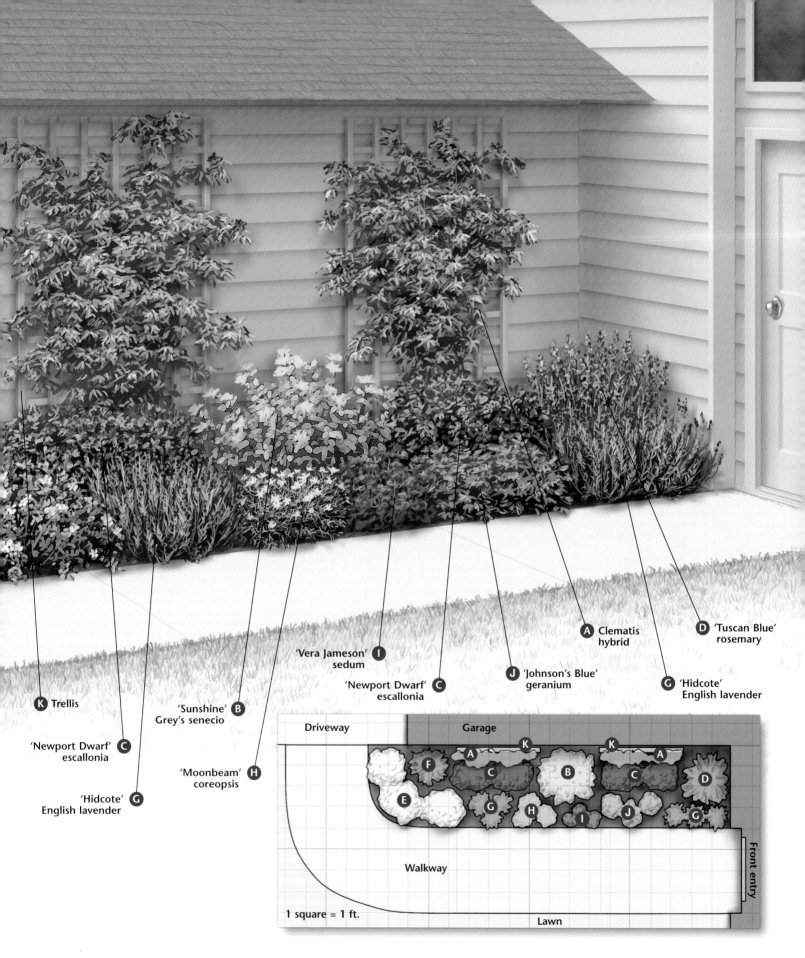

A Clematis hybrid

D 'Tuscan Blue' rosemary

I 'Vera Jameson' sedum

C 'Newport Dwarf' escallonia

J 'Johnson's Blue' geranium

G 'Hidcote' English lavender

K Trellis

C 'Newport Dwarf' escallonia

B 'Sunshine' Grey's senecio

H 'Moonbeam' coreopsis

G 'Hidcote' English lavender

Driveway

Garage

Walkway

Front entry

1 square = 1 ft.

Lawn

Plant portraits

These perennials and shrubs enhance a blank wall and narrow entry walk with handsome foliage and pretty flowers all year.

● = First design, pp. 40–41
▲ = Second design, pp. 42–43

'Moonbeam' coreopsis (*Coreopsis verticillata*, p. 164) ●

Barrenwort (*Epimedium*, p. 167) ▲

'Provence' lavender (*Lavandula × intermedia*, p. 174) ●

'Tuscan Blue' rosemary
(*Rosmarinus officinalis*, p. 179) ●

'Bressingham White' bergenia
(*Bergenia cordifolia*, p. 161) ▲

Dressing up a shady wall

A site with morning sun and afternoon shade calls for a different palette of plants. The basic idea of this design remains the same as before: incorporate wall space to make the best use of a narrow plot.

Arrayed on a wooden trellis, the star of this planting is a striking camellia. It graces the late-winter to early-spring floral display (shown here) with soft white flowers. At its feet, a supporting cast of plants adds flowers in pink, white, and blue. And the powerful scent of winter daphne welcomes visitors on the entry walk. After the spring show has faded, the foliage creates a pleasant scene through summer, fall, and winter.

Plants & Projects

A Sasanqua camellia
(use 1 plant)
Trained to the trellis, this shrub displays lovely flowers against glossy evergreen foliage from late fall through early spring. Choose a white-flowered cultivar suitable for trellis training. See *Camellia sasanqua*, p. 162.

B 'Cilpinense' evergreen rhododendron (use 1)
Branching low to the ground, this shrub forms a handsome mound of small evergreen leaves. In late winter and early spring, it bears pale pink flowers that fade to white. See *Rhododendron*, p. 178.

C Variegated winter daphne
(use 1)
An evergreen shrub with shiny green leaves edged in yellow. In spring, purple buds open into clusters of rose-tinged white flowers near the ends of the branches and perfume the entire area. See *Daphne odora* 'Aureomarginata', p. 166.

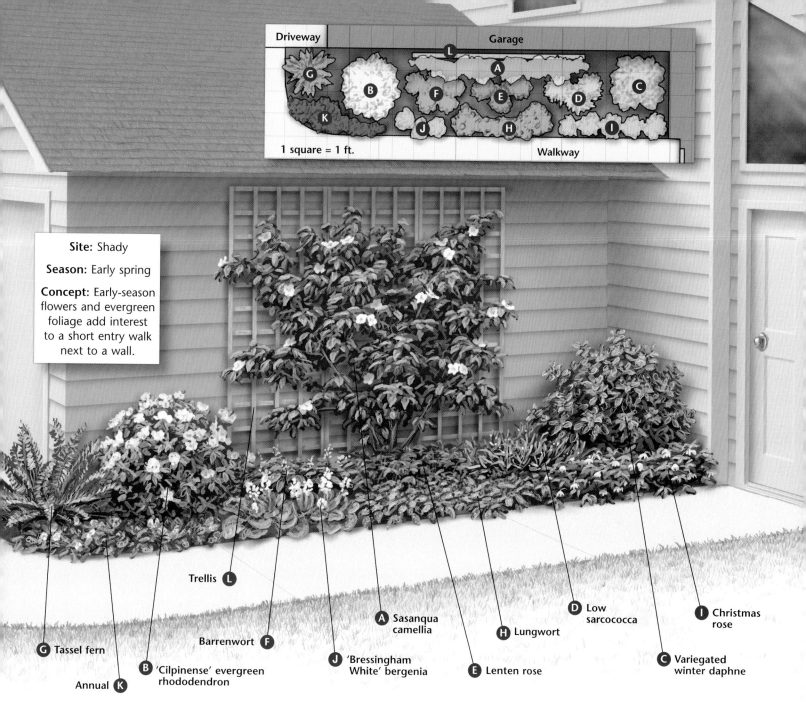

Site: Shady

Season: Early spring

Concept: Early-season flowers and evergreen foliage add interest to a short entry walk next to a wall.

Driveway

Garage

1 square = 1 ft.

Walkway

Trellis **L**

Barrenwort **F**

A Sasanqua camellia

H Lungwort

D Low sarcococca

I Christmas rose

G Tassel fern

B 'Cilpinense' evergreen rhododendron

J 'Bressingham White' bergenia

E Lenten rose

C Variegated winter daphne

Annual **K**

D Low sarcococca (use 3)
A spreading evergreen shrub with glossy green, leathery leaves. Bears clusters of very fragrant, tiny white flowers in late winter. See *Sarcococca humilis,* p. 180.

E Lenten rose (use 3)
Grown for its distinctive flowers and shiny evergreen leaves, this perennial blooms in late winter and early spring. See *Helleborus orientalis,* p. 170.

F Barrenwort (use 5)
This perennial's evergreen leaves change from bronze to green to maroon from spring to winter. Bears flowers in yellow, pink, red, or white in spring. See *Epimedium,* p. 167.

G Tassel fern (use 1)
This evergreen fern forms an attractive clump of stiff, finely divided, and glossy fronds. See Ferns: *Polystichum polyblepharum,* p. 168.

H Lungwort (use 6)
The fuzzy gray-green leaves of this perennial are sprinkled with white spots. Spikes of tiny blue, red, or pink flowers appear in early spring. See *Pulmonaria saccharata,* p. 178.

I Christmas rose (use 5)
This perennial closely resembles Lenten rose but bears showy white flowers in winter and early spring. See *Helleborus niger,* p. 170.

J 'Bressingham White' bergenia (use 3)
A perennial with large shiny green leaves and white flowers that bloom on stalks in spring. See *Bergenia cordifolia,* p. 161.

K Annuals (as needed)
Use seasonal annuals, such as the pansies shown here.

L Trellis
You can make this trellis using the same construction as in the previous design. See p. 127.

A Shady Hideaway

Build a cozy retreat in a corner of your yard

One of life's little pleasures is sitting in a shady, private spot reading a book or newspaper or just looking out onto your garden, relishing the fruits of your labors. If your property is long on lawn and short on shade or privacy, a bench under a leafy arbor can provide a welcome respite from the cares of the day. Tucked into a corner of the yard and set among attractive shrubs, vines, and perennials, the arbor shown here is a desirable destination in all four seasons.

Shrubs of medium height and a vine overhead help create a cozy sense of enclosure, affording privacy as well as shade. Plantings in front of the arbor and extending along the property lines integrate the hideaway with the lawn (or other plantings) and make a pleasing scene when viewed from the house. The design is equally effective in an open corner or backed by a property-line fence.

There are flowers from late winter through fall in yellow, pink, white, and purple. English lavender adds fragrance by the bench, while thyme releases aroma when underfoot. Attracted to the abelia, butterflies will put on a show. The contorted stems of the small tree, Harry Lauder's walking stick, are an extraordinary sight. Water trickling over the basalt column adds a soothing touch.

Plants & Projects

The arbor and plants can be installed in a few weekends. Once the plants are established, seasonal maintenance and cleanup should keep this durable planting looking good for years. As the abelia and rhododendron approach maturity, you'll need to prune them to maintain the desired size.

A **'Edward Goucher' abelia**
(use 3 plants)
This shrub forms a loose mound behind the arbor. Clusters of pink flowers bloom in summer. Semievergreen leaves have bronze tints in spring and are purple-bronze in fall. Copper sepals (leaflike structures below the flowers) add winter interest. See *Abelia × grandiflora*, p. 158.

B **Harry Lauder's walking stick**
(use 1)
A deciduous shrub or small tree with spectacularly twisted branches and stems. In late winter it bears tiny red female flowers or pendulous catkins of yellow male flowers. In fall, leaves turn yellow. See *Corylus avellana* 'Contorta', p. 165.

C **Fuchsia** (use 1)
This upright, open shrub bears dangling red-and-purple flowers all summer. Leaves are tinged with red. May be evergreen in mild winters. See *Fuchsia magellanica*, p. 169.

D **'Gomer Waterer' rhododendron** (use 3)
In late spring, this evergreen shrub bears lovely white flowers with pink margins. Deep green foliage looks good all year. See *Rhododendron*, p. 178.

E **'Hidcote' English lavender** (use 3)
An evergreen shrub, this forms a compact mound of thin, aromatic, gray-green leaves. In early summer, it bristles with spikes of tiny, fragrant, deep purple flowers. See *Lavandula angustifolia*, p. 174.

F **'Vancouver Gold' silky leaf woadwaxen** (use 7)
This deciduous shrub makes a low mat of green, twiggy stems covered with tiny green leaves. It bears a mass of bright yellow pealike flowers from late spring into summer. See *Genista pilosa*, p. 169.

G **Golden clematis** (use 2)
Numerous small, lantern-shaped yellow flowers bloom on this deciduous vine all summer. Fluffy seed heads appear in fall and last into winter. See *Clematis tangutica*, p. 163.

H **'Johnson's Blue' geranium** (use 3)
This perennial's pretty blue flowers and attractive foliage are a pleasing sight at the foot of the bench. It blooms from late spring into summer. See *Geranium*, p. 169.

I **'Autumn Joy' sedum** (use 3)
A popular perennial grown for its fleshy gray-green foliage and flat clusters of tiny flowers that start out pale pink and turn deep rusty red from summer into fall. See *Sedum*, p. 181.

J **'Goldsturm' coneflower** (use 5)
Sunny yellow daisylike flowers,

Property line

Lawn

1 square = 1 ft.

Site: Sunny

Season: Summer

Concept: Enjoy colorful, eye-catching plants while you relax under a shady arbor.

M Arbor

G Golden clematis

J 'Goldsturm' coneflower

H 'Johnson's Blue' geranium

K 'Birch Hybrid' bellflower

A 'Edward Goucher' abelia

B Harry Lauder's walking stick

Ornament **O**

Paving **N**

L Creeping thyme

D 'Gomer Waterer' rhododendron

E 'Hidcote' English lavender

'Vancouver Gold' **F** silky leaf woadwaxen

C Fuchsia

I 'Autumn Joy' sedum

each with a dark "eye," rise on stiff leafy stalks above this perennial's basal mound of coarse green foliage. Blooms summer into fall. See *Rudbeckia,* p. 179.

K 'Birch Hybrid' bellflower (use 12)
This perennial forms a low, spreading mass of green heart-shaped leaves with crinkled margins. Bears bell-shaped blue

flowers in summer. See *Campanula,* p. 162.

L Creeping thyme (as needed)
Planted among the flagstones, this evergreen perennial has gray-green leaves that release a scent when stepped on. Bears tiny purplish white flowers in summer. See *Thymus praecox* ssp. *arcticus,* p. 182.

M Arbor
This simple structure can be

built in a weekend. See p. 128.

N Paving
Flagstones in random sizes and shapes complement the casual feel of the planting. See p. 104.

O Ornament
A specially bored basalt rock makes a pleasing water feature. Can be bought bored with reservoir, pump, and installation instructions at garden centers and rock suppliers.

Grow your hideaway

In this design, instead of building your shade, you plant it. Here, the open canopy of a Japanese maple provides dappled shade for the bench and its comfortable occupants. A leafy screen of shrubs and ornamental grasses creates a sense of privacy but not confinement.

As in the previous design, there are flowers almost year-round. Eye-catching flower buds on the viburnum add winter interest. In early spring, fragrant white blossoms entice strollers to the bench. A rhododendron and evergreen candytuft round out the spring bloom. Although flowering picks up again in midsummer, the garden is at its most colorful in fall, with oranges, reds, yellows, and russets supplied by perennial flowers and the foliage of the Japanese maple and ornamental grasses.

See site plan for **D**.

Site: Sunny

Season: Early fall

Concept: Anchored by a shade tree, this hideaway, from ground cover to canopy, is homegrown.

Property line

Bench

Lawn

1 square = 1 ft.

A Japanese maple

B 'Spring Bouquet' viburnum

E 'Magnus' purple coneflower

C 'Purpurascens' Japanese silver grass

K Ornament

H 'Goldsturm' coneflower

I Creeping thyme

F 'Little Gem' candytuft

J Paving

G 'Autumn Joy' sedum

Plants & Projects

Ⓐ Japanese maple (use 1 plant)
This deciduous tree provides dappled shade in summer. Here we've shown a seed-grown plant (not a cultivar) with green summer foliage that turns red-purple in fall. See *Acer palmatum,* p. 159.

Ⓑ 'Spring Bouquet' viburnum (use 3)
An upright evergreen shrub with dark green leaves on reddish stems. Pretty pink buds appear in fall and open in early spring as fragrant white flowers. Metallic blue berries follow and last for months. See *Viburnum tinus,* p. 182.

Ⓒ 'Purpurascens' Japanese silver grass (use 5)
This perennial makes a graceful upright fountain of thin green leaves, each with a pink midrib. Turns orange-red in fall. In late summer and fall, it is topped by fluffy flowers and seed heads. See *Miscanthus sinensis,* p. 175.

Ⓓ Dwarf rhododendron (use 3)
This low, spreading evergreen shrub bears dark purple flowers in spring. Small blue-gray leaves look good the rest of the year. See *Rhododendron impeditum,* p. 178.

Ⓔ 'Magnus' purple coneflower (use 3)
In summer, this perennial bears large daisylike flowers on stiff branched stalks above a loose clump of coarse green leaves. Flower petals are purple, centers orange. See *Echinacea purpurea,* p. 166.

Ⓕ 'Little Gem' candytuft (use 3)
An evergreen perennial, this makes a low, sprawling mass of thin glossy leaves. Covered with small white flowers in spring. See *Iberis sempervirens,* p. 173.

See pp. 44–45 for the following:

Ⓖ 'Autumn Joy' sedum (use 3)

Ⓗ 'Goldsturm' coneflower (use 3)

Ⓘ Creeping thyme (as needed)

Ⓙ Paving

Ⓚ Ornament

Plant portraits

Privacy, shade, flowers, foliage, and fragrance—these plants provide all the necessities for a relaxing backyard retreat.

● = First design, pp. 44–45
▲ = Second design, pp. 46–47

'Purpurascens' Japanese silver grass (*Miscanthus sinensis,* p. 175) ▲

Golden clematis
(*Clematis tangutica,* p. 163) ●

'Little Gem' candytuft
(*Iberis sempervirens,* p. 173) ▲

'Gomer Waterer' rhododendron
(*Rhododendron,* p. 178) ●

'Birch Hybrid' bellflower
(*Campanula,* p. 162) ●

Harry Lauder's walking stick
(*Corylus avellana* 'Contorta', p. 165) ●

Create a "Living" Room

A patio garden provides privacy and pleasure

A patio can become a true extension of your living space with the addition of plants to screen views and to create an attractive setting. Such outdoor "rooms" are particularly welcome in the Northwest with the arrival of summer after the rainy season. In this design, plants and a tall louvered fence at one end of the patio form a three-dimensional wall that changes with the seasons. The flagstone paving accommodates a family barbecue or even a large gathering that can spill out onto the lawn. Together, plants and patio nicely mingle the "indoors" with the outdoors.

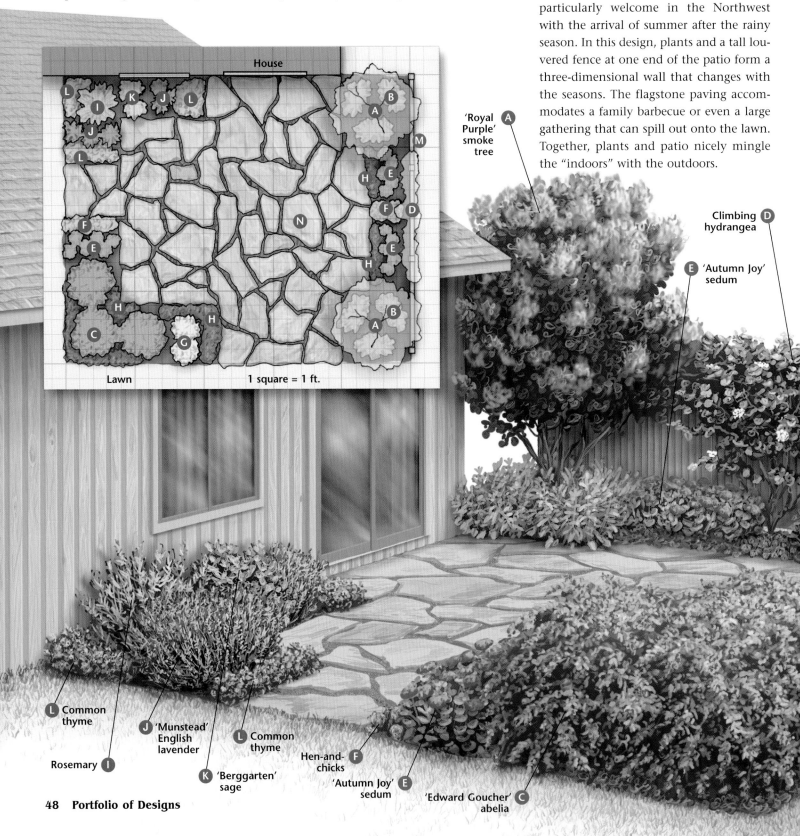

House

Lawn

1 square = 1 ft.

'Royal Purple' smoke tree Ⓐ

Climbing hydrangea Ⓓ

Ⓔ 'Autumn Joy' sedum

Ⓛ Common thyme

Ⓙ 'Munstead' English lavender

Ⓛ Common thyme

Rosemary Ⓘ

Ⓚ 'Berggarten' sage

Hen-and-chicks Ⓕ

'Autumn Joy' sedum Ⓔ

'Edward Goucher' abelia Ⓒ

From early summer through fall, the plantings provide a colorful accompaniment to your patio activities. There are flowers in pink, purple, lilac, rose, blue, and white. Foliage, much of it evergreen, is a subtle palette of silvery grays and greens accented by darker greens and purples.

Next to the house is a kitchen garden that enlivens meals as well as the patio planting. We show plants grown for seasoning and fragrance, with foliage that picks up the garden color scheme. In a warm sunny spot, you could substitute basil, tomatoes, or peppers.

Site: Sunny

Season: Summer

Concept: Planting provides privacy and a colorful setting for entertaining guests or enjoying the early-morning air on your own.

A 'Royal Purple' smoke tree

M Louvered fence

B Grey's senecio

N Paving

H 'Burgundy Glow' ajuga

G 'Silver King' artemisia

Plants & Projects

Seasonal pruning and cleanup will keep these plants looking good for years. The hydrangea vine climbs by itself, clinging to the fence. Train the smoke trees to tree form and prune them yearly, as well as the other shrubs and the vine, to maintain the desired sizes.

A 'Royal Purple' smoke tree (use 2 plants)
This small deciduous tree is eye-catching for months. The leaves are red in spring, dark purple in summer, and gold, orange, or red in fall. It displays large fluffy pink flower plumes from summer into fall. See *Cotinus coggygria*, p. 165.

B Grey's senecio (use 6)
The gray-green foliage of this evergreen shrub contrasts strikingly with the smoke tree above it. Bears yellow flowers in summer, but some people shear the flowers (as shown here) to highlight the foliage. See *Senecio greyi*, p. 181.

C 'Edward Goucher' abelia (use 3)
This shrub forms a mound of dark green foliage that has bronze tones in spring and fall. Rosy purple flowers bloom in summer and attract butterflies. See *Abelia × grandiflora* 'Edward Goucher', p. 158.

D Climbing hydrangea (use 1)
Draping the fence with large glossy leaves from early spring to late fall, this deciduous vine bears lacy clusters of white flowers in summer. The thick stem's peeling bark is attractive in winter. See *Hydrangea petiolaris*, p. 172.

E 'Autumn Joy' sedum (use 16)
Flat clusters of tiny rosy flowers perch atop this perennial's fleshy gray-green leaves in summer. In fall, flowers turn rust-colored. See *Sedum*, p. 181.

F Hen-and-chicks (use 24)
This charming little evergreen perennial makes rosettes of succulent gray-green leaves. See *Sempervivum tectorum*, p. 181.

G 'Silver King' artemisia (use 2)
A perennial that forms a handsome clump of finely divided, aromatic, woolly silver-gray leaves that turn red in fall. See *Artemisia ludoviciana* var. *albula*, p. 160.

H 'Burgundy Glow' ajuga (as needed)
This evergreen perennial edges the flagstones with purple leaves marked with white and pink. It bristles with spikes of blue flowers in spring. See *Ajuga reptans*, p. 159.

I Rosemary (use 1)
The thin gray-green leaves of this evergreen shrub are aromatic and tasty. Small blue, lilac, or white flowers bloom intermittently through the year. See *Rosmarinus officinalis*, p. 179.

J 'Munstead' English lavender (use 6)
This evergreen shrub forms a mound of fragrant gray-green leaves. Foliage is covered with spikes of fragrant pale lavender flowers in early summer. See *Lavandula angustifolia*, p. 174.

K 'Berggarten' sage (use 2)
A compact perennial with fragrant gray-green leaves that are used as a culinary seasoning. It bears spikes of small blue flowers in early summer. See *Salvia officinalis*, p. 180.

L Common thyme (use 13)
This kitchen-garden ground cover produces small, fragrant evergreen leaves that are valued as a seasoning. In summer it is covered with tiny pink, rose, or white flowers. See *Thymus vulgaris*, p. 182.

M Louvered fence
A cedar fence provides privacy while allowing air to circulate through nearby plants. See p. 129.

N Paving
Flagstones of varied size and shape make an informal patio. Stones with mottled gray tones will complement the planting's foliage. See p. 110.

Lawn   1 square = 1 ft.

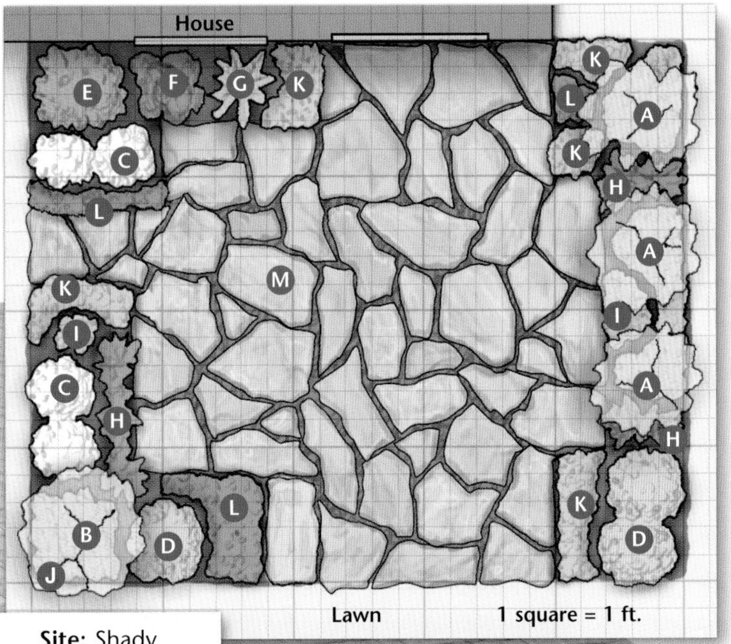

Site: Shady

Season: Spring

Concept: A mixed planting of shrubs and perennials creates privacy and ambience for a shady patio.

A patio in the shade

If your patio is already blessed with a cool canopy of afternoon shade, perhaps from a large nearby tree, consider this design. The basics are the same as on the previous pages, but here we feature a garden of shade-loving shrubs and perennials.

As before, the planting creates a sense of privacy on the patio without blocking out the surroundings. The scents of the late-winter-blooming winter hazel and daphne will draw you out of the house early in the year. As summer nears, the winter hazel leafs out to form an ethereal screen.

Bloom continues through the spring into summer in pinks, yellows, and whites. The handsome foliage of shrubs and perennials takes center stage from midsummer into winter. And the striking leaves and flower stalks of the acanthus and the remarkably twisted stems of Harry Lauder's walking stick are guaranteed to serve as conversation pieces at any gathering.

- **A** Winter hazel
- **H** Japanese painted fern
- **D** 'Bow Bells' rhododendron
- **M** Paving
- **L** 'Burgundy Glow' ajuga
- **B** Harry Lauder's walking stick
- **J** 'Pink Pewter' lamium
- **C** 'Snow Lady' rhododendron
- **I** Lungwort
- **K** Blue star creeper
- **G** Tassel fern
- **F** Bear's breeches
- **C** 'Snow Lady' rhododendron
- **E** Variegated winter daphne

Plants & Projects

A **Winter hazel** (use 3 plants)
A deciduous shrub with vase-shaped habit, it bears clusters of pendulous fragrant yellow flowers on bare branches in early spring. New leaves are pink, then turn green. See *Corylopsis pauciflora*, p. 165.

B **Harry Lauder's walking stick** (use 1)
The stems and twigs of this deciduous tree are contorted in fantastic shapes. Yellow (male) or red (female) flowers bloom in late winter before leaves appear. In fall, foliage turns yellow. See *Corylus avellana* 'Contorta', p. 165.

C **'Snow Lady' rhododendron** (use 4)
Clusters of fragrant white flowers bloom on this shrub in spring. Attractive evergreen foliage. See *Rhododendron*, p. 178.

D **'Bow Bells' rhododendron**
(use 3)
This evergreen shrub produces clusters of lovely light pink flowers in spring. New leaves are copper-colored. See *Rhododendron*, p. 178.

E **Variegated winter daphne**
(use 1)
An evergreen shrub prized for the clusters of intensely fragrant pinkish white flowers it bears in late winter and early spring. Glossy leaves are edged with yellow. See *Daphne odora* 'Aureomarginata', p. 166.

F **Bear's breeches** (use 1)
This perennial forms a mound of large, deeply lobed leaves. Spikes of white-and-purple flowers bloom in spring on stiff stalks rising above the foliage. See *Acanthus mollis*, p. 158.

G **Tassel fern** (use 1)
The upright, finely divided fronds of this evergreen fern contrast handsomely with the acanthus. See Ferns: *Polystichum polyblepharum*, p. 168.

H **Japanese painted fern** (use 17)
This small, low-growing fern offers rosettes of lacy leaves in shades of green, silver, and maroon. See Ferns: *Athyrium nipponicum* 'Pictum', p. 168.

I **Lungwort** (use 6)
Starting in early spring, this perennial bears numerous tiny pink, red, or violet flowers. Green leaves are spotted with white and look good through fall. See *Pulmonaria saccharata*, p. 178.

J **'Pink Pewter' lamium**
(as needed)
A perennial ground cover, this forms a mat of greenish gray leaves edged with silver. Clear pink flowers in late spring and early summer. See *Lamium maculatum*, p. 174.

K **Blue star creeper** (as needed)
This low, creeping perennial has tiny bright green leaves and bears sky blue, starlike flowers in late spring and then off and on during the summer. See *Pratia pedunculata*, p. 177.

See p. 49 for the following:

L **'Burgundy Glow' ajuga**
(as needed)

M **Paving**

Plant portraits

Whether you have sun or shade, these plants create a cozy patio niche with attractive flowers and foliage.

● = First design, pp. 48–49
▲ = Second design, pp. 50–51

Hen-and-chicks
(*Sempervivum tectorum*, p. 181) ●

'Berggarten' sage
(*Salvia officinalis*, p. 180) ●

Climbing hydrangea
(*Hydrangea petiolaris*, p. 172) ●

Common thyme (*Thymus vulgaris*, p. 182) ●

'Pink Pewter' lamium
(*Lamium maculatum*, p. 174) ▲

'Munstead' English lavender
(*Lavandula angustifolia*, p. 174) ●

'Silver King' artemisia
(*Artemisia ludoviciana* var. *albula*, p. 160) ●

Splash Out

Make a water garden the focus of outdoor activities

Site: Sunny

Season: Summer

Concept: A pond is at the center of a versatile and exciting outdoor living area.

A water garden adds a new dimension to a home landscape. It can be the eye-catching focal point of the entire property, a center of outdoor entertainment, or a quiet out-of-the-way retreat. A pond can be a hub of activity—a place to garden, watch birds and wildlife, raise ornamental fish, or stage an impromptu paper-boat race. It just as easily affords an opportunity for some therapeutic inactivity; a few minutes contemplating the ripples on the water's surface provides a welcome break in a busy day.

A pond can't be moved easily, so choose your site carefully. Practical considerations are outlined on pp. 112–115 (along with instructions on installation and on planting water plants). In addition to those considerations, contact local authorities to find out if you must follow code requirements. Then consider how the pond and its plantings relate to the surroundings. Before plopping a pond down in the middle of the backyard, imagine how you might integrate it, visually if not physically, with nearby plantings and structures. For example, we've shown this pond bordered by an informal crushed-rock patio.

Foliage is the star of the planting and gives it year-round appeal. Fall and winter are the most colorful seasons, with the bronzy red plume cedar and curly sedge, yellow ocher heather, tawny Japanese silver grass, and bright red dogwood stems. In spring and summer, the season shown here, flowers accent foliage that comes in a pleasing range of greens.

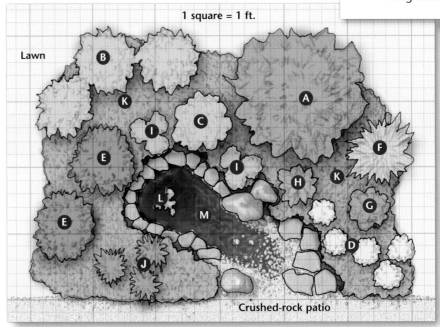

1 square = 1 ft.

Lawn

Crushed-rock patio

'Elegantissima' variegated **B** Siberian dogwood

Lenten rose **I**

Spreading **E** English yew

K 'Massachusetts' kinnikinnick

Fox red **J** curly sedge

'Massachusetts' **K** kinnikinnick

L Water plants

Plants & Projects

Installing a pond is arduous but simple work, involving several weekends of digging. The plants require only seasonal maintenance, but the pond will need regular attention to keep a healthy balance of water plants and fish (if you have them) in order to maintain adequate oxygen levels and to keep algae in check. Consult local or mail-order suppliers to help you get the right mix.

A Plume cedar (use 1 plant)
This fine-textured evergreen tree is soft gray-green in summer and bronzy red in winter. Peeling cinnamon-colored bark is attractive. See *Cryptomeria japonica* 'Elegans', p. 166.

B 'Elegantissima' variegated Siberian dogwood (use 3)
An all-season performer, this deciduous shrub displays red stems in winter, white flowers in spring, green-and-white leaves in summer, and blue berries in late summer. See *Cornus alba*, p. 164.

C Winter hazel (use 1)
A wispy open deciduous shrub, this bears yellow flowers on bare wood in early spring that are followed by bronze leaves that turn green in summer. See *Corylopsis pauciflora*, p. 165.

D 'Robert Chapman' Scotch heather (use 5)
This evergreen shrub forms a low mass of ascending stems. Tiny scalelike leaves are bright red when new and then turn golden. In summer, small white flowers bloom up and down the stems. See *Calluna vulgaris*, p. 162.

E Spreading English yew (use 2)
This low evergreen shrub has large dark green needles. Spreads to make a good ground cover. See *Taxus baccata* 'Repandens', p. 182.

F 'Morning Light' Japanese silver grass (use 1)
The slender arching leaves of this perennial are green with a white midrib that gives the clump a silvery sheen. In late summer and fall it bears tall fluffy flower and seed heads. See *Miscanthus sinensis*, p. 175.

G Bear's breeches (use 1)
This striking perennial forms a clump of large, deeply cut leaves from which arise tall spikes of white-and-purple flowers. Blooms in late spring. See *Acanthus mollis*, p. 158.

H Hosta (use 1)
A perennial grown primarily for its foliage. For this design, choose a cultivar that forms a big mound of large blue leaves. See *Hosta*, p. 171.

I Lenten rose (use 6)
An evergreen perennial that bears distinctive purple, pink, white, or green flowers in early spring. Its leathery green leaves are attractive all year. See *Helleborus orientalis*, p. 170.

J Fox red curly sedge (use 3)
This perennial makes a clump of thin reddish bronze leaf blades that keep their color year-round. The summer flowers are insignificant. See *Carex buchananii*, p. 162.

K 'Massachusetts' kinnikinnick (as needed)
Plant this tough evergreen ground cover in open spaces between other plants. Deep green leaves have a burgundy cast. The small white-to-pink spring flowers produce red berries. See *Arctostaphylos uva-ursi*, p. 160.

L Water plants (as desired)
You can grow a variety of plants in the pond. We've shown a water lily. See Water plants, p. 183.

M Pond
You can make this pond with a commercially available liner. The deep end is edged with flagstones. The other rises gradually until water and surrounding "land" are joined by a miniature shore of river rock and large stones. See p. 112.

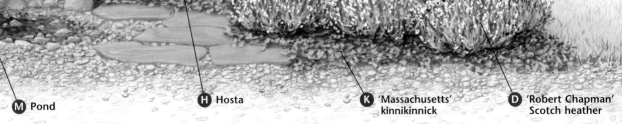

C Winter hazel

I Lenten rose

A Plume cedar

F 'Morning Light' Japanese silver grass

G Bear's breeches

M Pond

H Hosta

K 'Massachusetts' kinnikinnick

D 'Robert Chapman' Scotch heather

Plant portraits

Set off by nearby water, these plants combine fresh foliage and lovely flowers for your poolside pleasure.

● = First design, pp. 52–53
▲ = Second design, pp. 54–55

Black mondo grass (*Ophiopogon planiscapus* 'Ebony Knight', p. 175) ▲

'Morning Light' Japanese silver grass (*Miscanthus sinensis*, p.175) ●

Fox red curly sedge (*Carex buchananii*, p. 162) ●

'Robert Chapman' Scotch heather (*Calluna vulgaris*, p. 162) ●

'Sulphureum' barrenwort (*Epimedium* × *versicolor*, p. 167) ▲

Water lily (Water plants: *Nymphaea*, p. 183) ●

Sweet woodruff (*Galium odoratum*, p. 169) ▲

Mini-pond

This little pond provides the pleasures of water gardening for those without the space or energy required to install and maintain a larger pond. Within its smaller confines, you can enjoy one or more water plants and a few fish. Or you might leave it as a reflecting pool, as shown here.

Pond and plantings can stand alone in an expanse of lawn, but they will look best integrated into a larger scheme. The scale is just right for use as the focal point of a small patio, as shown here, or as part of a larger patio planting.

As in the previous design, the planting displays a delightful collection of foliage textures and colors chosen to complement or contrast with those of their neighbors. Spring is brightened by delicate flowers. And the black mondo grass and colorful pavers are a striking sight throughout the year.

Plants & Projects

Ⓐ Red-vein enkianthus
(use 1 plant)
The blue-green leaves of this slow-growing deciduous shrub turn orange-red in fall. Small white bell-shaped flowers that are veined with red bloom in late spring. See *Enkianthus campanulatus*, p. 167.

Ⓑ Soft shield fern (use 7)
This evergreen fern forms a dense mass of upright green fronds, each rising from its own brown crown. See Ferns: *Polystichum setiferum*, p. 168.

Ⓒ 'Krossa Regal' hosta (use 1)
This perennial makes a vase-shaped clump of wide, powdery blue-green leaves. Tall stalks bear pale lilac flowers in summer. See *Hosta*, p. 171.

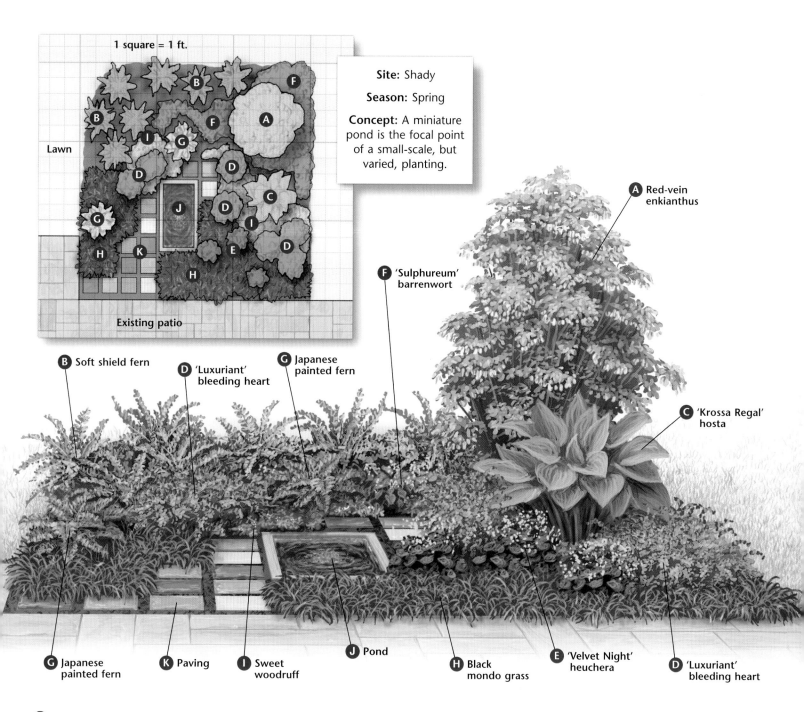

1 square = 1 ft.

Lawn

Site: Shady

Season: Spring

Concept: A miniature pond is the focal point of a small-scale, but varied, planting.

Existing patio

B Soft shield fern

D 'Luxuriant' bleeding heart

G Japanese painted fern

F 'Sulphureum' barrenwort

A Red-vein enkianthus

C 'Krossa Regal' hosta

G Japanese painted fern

K Paving

I Sweet woodruff

J Pond

H Black mondo grass

E 'Velvet Night' heuchera

D 'Luxuriant' bleeding heart

D 'Luxuriant' bleeding heart (use 7)
Lines of dainty heart-shaped pink flowers dangle from thin curving stalks above this perennial's soft, fernlike blue-green foliage. Blooms in late spring. See *Dicentra*, p. 166.

E 'Velvet Night' heuchera (use 3)
A semievergreen perennial prized for its striking purple foliage. Tiny brown-green flowers float on thin stalks above the foliage in spring. See *Heuchera americana*, p. 171.

F 'Sulphureum' barrenwort (use 12)
This evergreen perennial bears purple-tinted green leaves on wiry stems. Yellow flowers rise above the leaves in spring. See *Epimedium* × *versicolor*, p. 167.

G Japanese painted fern (use 2)
A small deciduous fern with lacy fronds of silver, green, and maroon. See Ferns: *Athyrium nipponicum* 'Pictum', p. 168.

H Black mondo grass (as needed)
This perennial ground cover spreads to form a patch of wide, grassy, purple-black leaves. See *Ophiopogon planiscapus* 'Ebony Knight', p. 175.

I Sweet woodruff (as needed)
Planted around the bleeding heart and hosta, this perennial carpets the ground with bright green foliage that is covered with tiny clusters of white flowers in spring. See *Galium odoratum*, p. 169.

J Pond
It's easy to make this shallow reflecting pond with a rectangular fiberglass shell and some elbow grease. See p. 112.

K Paving
Set bright-colored pavers on a sand-and-gravel base after you have installed the shallow pond. See p. 104.

Garden in the Round

Create a planting with several attractive faces

Plantings in residential landscapes are usually "attached" to something. Beds and borders hew to property lines, walls, or patios; foundation plantings skirt the house, garage, or deck. Most of these plantings are meant to be viewed from the front, rather like a wall-mounted sculpture in raised relief.

The planting shown here is designed to "float" like an island in the landscape. Because you can walk around the bed, plants can be displayed "in the round," presenting different scenes from different vantage points. This is an excellent option if you want to squeeze more gardening space from a small lot, add interest to a rectangular one, or divide a large area into smaller outdoor "rooms."

Without a strong connection to a structure or other landscape feature, a bed like this requires a sensitivity to scale. To be successful, the bed must neither dominate its surroundings nor be lost in them. And it must relate to other plantings and landscape features, even though it is not connected to them. Here, the large shrubs and massed plants beneath them are attractive from a distance. And there's always something to admire up close as you stroll by.

Lawn

1 square = 1 ft.

Site: Sunny

Season: Midsummer

Concept: Floating on the lawn, this planting looks good from any vantage point: at a distance, or as you stroll close by.

'Dawn' viburnum **B**

See site plan for **D**.

'Happy Returns' **G** daylily

'Little Princess' **C** spirea

Blue oat **I** grass

'Mavis Simpson' **H** geranium

Plants & Projects

The blue, green, silvery, and purple foliage of this planting set each other off, while also making an effective backdrop for the yellow and pink flowers. There's bloom in every season—even winter—with the peak in summer. Little more than seasonal pruning and maintenance will keep the planting healthy and attractive.

A 'Royal Purple' smoke tree (use 1 plant)
Very showy throughout the growing season, the leaves of this large deciduous shrub open red, turn purple in summer, and then change to gold, orange, or red in fall. Displays equally showy fluffy plumes of pink-brown flowers from summer to fall. See *Cotinus coggygria*, p. 165.

B 'Dawn' viburnum (use 1)
A deciduous shrub that bears fragrant pink flowers in late winter. Dark green leaves are tinged with red. See *Viburnum × bodnantense*, p. 182.

C 'Little Princess' spirea (use 3)
This deciduous shrub forms a mound of dark green leaves. Flat-topped clusters of tiny rosy pink flowers bloom for weeks in summer. See *Spiraea japonica*, p. 181.

D 'Silver Knight' Scotch heather (use 5)
The silvery gray foliage of this evergreen shrub complements the flowering viburnum in winter. Small mauve-pink flowers bloom in summer, dry out and remain on stems in winter. See *Calluna vulgaris*, p. 162.

E 'Flower Carpet Pink' rose (use 2)
This spreading deciduous shrub bears numerous pink flowers against shiny green leaves from spring through autumn. See *Rosa*, p. 178.

F 'Blue Star' juniper (use 5)
An evergreen shrub, it forms a low, spreading mass of striking silvery blue foliage. See *Juniperus squamata*, p. 174.

G 'Happy Returns' daylily (use 8)
This perennial bears cheerful lemon yellow, trumpet-shaped flowers from early summer into fall. Clumps of arching narrow foliage are attractive, too. See *Hemerocallis*, p. 170.

H 'Mavis Simpson' geranium (use 2)
This perennial makes a spreading patch of gray-green leaves covered in summer with pale pink flowers. See *Geranium × riversleaianum*, p. 169.

I Blue oat grass (use 10)
Grown for its pale blue foliage, this clump-forming evergreen perennial also bears thin flower spikes that turn beige or tan. See *Helictotrichon sempervirens*, p. 170.

J Cushion spurge (use 5)
This perennial forms a low mound of green leaves that turn red in fall. Yellow flowers appear in spring and last for months. See *Euphorbia polychroma*, p. 168.

K Blue star creeper (as needed)
Dotted between and at the edges of the steppingstones, this perennial makes a mat of green foliage that is speckled off and on from spring through summer with light blue starlike flowers. See *Pratia pedunculata*, p. 177.

L Path
Flagstones of irregular shapes and random sizes reflect the informality of the planting. See p. 104.

'Royal Purple' **A** smoke tree

Blue oat grass **I**

K Blue star creeper

Cushion spurge **J**

L Path

H 'Mavis Simpson' geranium

'Blue Star' **F** juniper

E 'Flower Carpet Pink' rose

G 'Happy Returns' daylily

An anchored island

People in the Northwest love their majestic trees. Builders strive to preserve at least some existing trees on new lots, and mature specimens on older properties are prized. But, like an elephant in a living room, a 50-ft. conifer in the middle of a lawn can be more than a little problematic.

This design shows one way to make a treasured, but awkward, friend more at home in your landscape. As the anchor of an island bed, the tree is no longer marooned on the lawn. And by relating its island planting to other plantings elsewhere on the property, the tree becomes part of a larger whole.

Chosen for their tolerance of dry dappled shade, these plants perform year-round. Spring, shown here, is the season of peak bloom. Foliage of varied colors and textures provides interest in the planting from summer into winter.

Plants & Projects

A **Winter hazel** (use 1 plant)
This large deciduous shrub blooms on bare wood in the early spring, displaying clusters of small yellow flowers. New leaves are bronze, turning to green. See *Corylopsis pauciflora*, p. 165.

B **Barnes' narrow male fern** (use 3)
The upright semievergreen fronds of this fern have an interesting slightly ruffled look. See Ferns: *Dryopteris filix-mas* 'Barnesii', p. 168.

C **Lungwort** (use 4)
A perennial with wide green, white-spotted leaves. In early spring, small stalks bear pink, red, or violet flowers. See *Pulmonaria saccharata*, p. 178.

D **Bigroot geranium** (use 6)
This perennial makes a bushy clump of fragrant light green leaves. Bears magenta or pink flowers in late spring. It is evergreen in mild winters. See *Geranium macrorrhizum*, p. 169.

E **'Fröhnleiten' barrenwort** (use 19)
An evergreen perennial whose leaflets turn red and purple in cold winters. Rising above the leaves in spring, long stalks bear bright yellow flowers. See *Epimedium × perralchicum*, p. 167.

F **'Velvet Night' heuchera** (use 3)
Grown for its striking deep purple leaves, this perennial also bears tiny brown-green

> **Site:** Shady
>
> **Season:** Spring
>
> **Concept:** An island bed gives a mature tree a more active role in a home landscape as well as adding interest to a lawn-dominated yard.

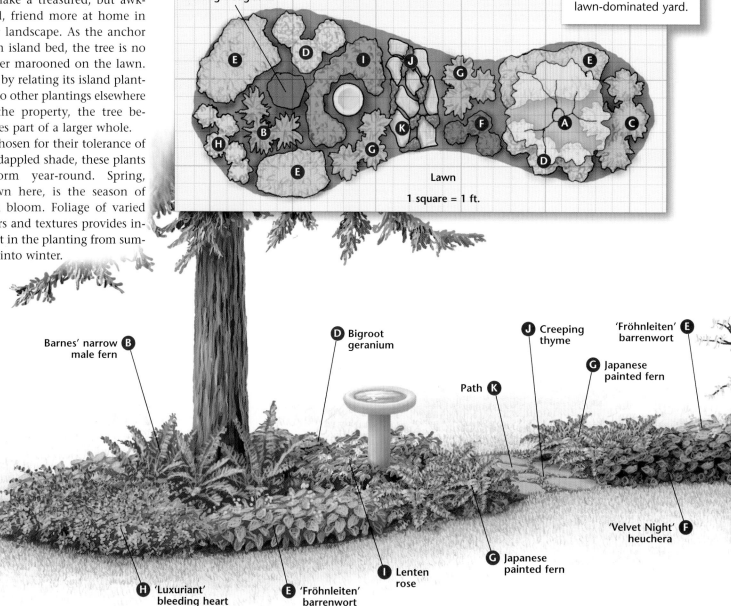

Existing Douglas fir

Lawn

1 square = 1 ft.

Barnes' narrow male fern **B**

D Bigroot geranium

J Creeping thyme

'Fröhnleiten' **E** barrenwort

Path **K**

G Japanese painted fern

H 'Luxuriant' bleeding heart

E 'Fröhnleiten' barrenwort

I Lenten rose

G Japanese painted fern

'Velvet Night' **F** heuchera

flowers in summer. Foliage is evergreen in mild winters. See *Heuchera americana*, p. 171.

G **Japanese painted fern** (use 6)
This striking deciduous fern has lacy silver-green fronds with maroon veins and stalks. The colors are almost iridescent. See Ferns: *Athyrium nipponicum* 'Pictum', p. 168.

H **'Luxuriant' bleeding heart** (use 5)
Forming clumps of soft fernlike leaves, this perennial displays charming heart-shaped pink flowers that dangle on arching stalks above the foliage in late spring. See *Dicentra*, p. 166.

I **Lenten rose** (use 3)
In late winter and early spring, the distinctive white, green, pink, or purple flowers of this perennial cluster among the shiny compound foliage at the ends of thick green stalks. See *Helleborus orientalis*, p. 170.

J **Creeping thyme** (as needed)
Planted among the flagstones, this evergreen perennial forms a mat of fragrant shiny green leaves that turn maroon in winter. See *Thymus praecox* ssp. *arcticus*, p. 182.

See p. 57 for the following:

K Path

A Winter hazel

C Lungwort

D Bigroot geranium

Plant portraits

In shade or sun, these plants make an island bed attractive when viewed from near or far.

● = First design, pp. 56–57
▲ = Second design, pp. 58–59

'Happy Returns' daylily (*Hemerocallis*, p. 170) ●

Creeping thyme (*Thymus praecox* ssp. *arcticus*, p. 182) ▲

'Fröhnleiten' barrenwort (*Epimedium* × *perralchicum*, p. 167) ▲

'Mavis Simpson' geranium (*Geranium* × *riversleaianum*, p. 169) ●

Cushion spurge (*Euphorbia polychroma*, p. 168) ●

'Luxuriant' bleeding heart (*Dicentra*, p. 166) ▲

'Little Princess' spirea (*Spiraea japonica*, p. 181) ●

A Beginning Border
Flowers and a fence offer a traditional design

A mixed border can be one of the most delightful of all gardens. Indeed, that's usually its sole purpose. Unlike many other types of landscape plantings, a traditional border is seldom yoked to any function beyond that of providing as much beauty as possible. From the first neat mounds of foliage in the spring to the fullness of summer bloom and autumn color, the mix of flowers, foliage, textures, tones, and hues brings pleasure.

This border is designed for a beginning or busy gardener, using durable plants that are easy to establish and care for. Behind the planting, screening out distraction, is a simple fence. The border is meant to be viewed from the front, so tall plants need to go at the back. There are interesting plant combinations to enjoy from every vantage point, near or close-up. It is easy to extend the planting along the fence to suit your site and energy.

The plants here provide months of bloom. To complement the spring flowers of the clematis, plant bulbs that will bloom among the emerging perennials. In summer and fall, the garden is a subtle tapestry of color, with flowers in shades of pink, violet, and blue woven among leaves in many shades of green. Attractive foliage of the grasses, heavenly bamboo, and other plants carries interest through the winter.

Site: Sunny

Season: Fall

Concept: Even a novice can make this flower border flourish. Attractive plants displayed against a simple fence will provide months of enjoyment.

Lawn

1 square = 1 ft.

'Sarabande' Japanese silver grass C

'Elsa Spath' E clematis

Fence L

'Plum Passion' B heavenly bamboo

'May Night' H salvia

'Magnus' purple G coneflower

'Hameln' dwarf I fountain grass

Plants & Projects

In early spring, cut the butterfly bush, Russian sage, and ornamental grasses close to the ground. Shear spent flowers off the salvia to promote repeat bloom. Prune the clematis to control its size.

A **'Pink Delight' butterfly bush**
(use 1 plant)
This deciduous shrub forms a clump of arching stems. From midsummer into fall, long spikes of pink flowers bloom at the ends of the stems. See *Buddleia davidii*, p. 161.

B **'Plum Passion' heavenly bamboo** (use 2)
The foliage of this evergreen shrub is purple when new, blue-green in summer, and purple in fall and winter. Fluffy clusters of white flowers bloom in summer, followed by long-lasting red berries. See *Nandina domestica*, p. 175.

C **'Sarabande' Japanese silver grass** (use 3)
This perennial forms a fountain of long thin leaves, each green with a central white stripe. Flower stalks rise above the leaves in late summer or fall, though bloom can be unreliable in the Northwest. See *Miscanthus sinensis*, p. 175.

D **'Sunset' rockrose** (use 2)
Magenta-pink flowers cover this mounded evergreen shrub for weeks in summer. Wavy-edged gray-green foliage is attractive year-round. See *Cistus × pulverulentus*, p. 163.

E **'Elsa Spath' clematis** (use 1)
A deciduous vine with dark green compound leaves. It bears large violet-blue flowers from late spring into fall. See *Clematis* hybrids, p. 163.

F **'Longin' Russian sage** (use 2)
This perennial forms an airy silver-gray clump of upright stems and small leaves. Bears spikes of lavender-blue flowers from summer into fall. See *Perovskia atriplicifolia*, p. 176.

G **'Magnus' purple coneflower** (use 7)
A perennial with tall, sturdy stalks that bear rosy pink flowers with dark centers from summer into fall. See *Echinacea purpurea*, p. 166.

H **'May Night' salvia** (use 8)
From early summer into fall, spikes of dark indigo-purple flowers rise above this perennial's heart-shaped leaves. See *Salvia × superba*, p. 180.

I **'Hameln' dwarf fountain grass** (use 11)
A clump-forming grass with thin leaves that are green in summer and gold or tan in fall.

Plumes of buff-colored flowers are borne from midsummer through fall. See *Pennisetum alopecuroides*, p. 176.

J **'Mavis Simpson' geranium** (use 1)
This sprawling perennial has light green leaves and bears small pink flowers in summer. See *Geranium × riversleaianum*, p. 169.

K **'Autumn Joy' sedum** (use 3)
A perennial with succulent gray-green foliage. Topped from summer through fall by flat flower heads that turn from greenish pink to deep russet. See *Sedum*, p. 181.

L **Fence**
This easy-to-build fence makes an attractive backdrop for the border. See p. 130.

M **Steppingstones and ornament**
Flagstones lead to an ornamental focal point and provide access for maintaining the deepest part of the planting.

C 'Sarabande' Japanese silver grass

A 'Pink Delight' butterfly bush

B 'Plum Passion' heavenly bamboo

K 'Autumn Joy' sedum

F 'Longin' Russian sage

D 'Sunset' rockrose

J 'Mavis Simpson' geranium

I 'Hameln' dwarf fountain grass

M Steppingstones and ornament

A border in the shade

If the best spot for a border on your property receives only morning sun, try this design. Like the previous design, this one arranges carefully chosen combinations of shrubs and perennials against a solid background. Here, however, the plants are proven performers in the shade.

Nearest the fence are mid-size shrubs offering a mixture of deciduous and evergreen foliage and a variety of eye-catching flowers from late winter through fall. Lower-growing perennials fill out the front of the bed with no less interesting foliage and flowers. The upright, swordlike leaves of the iris and sweet flag are particularly effective accents here.

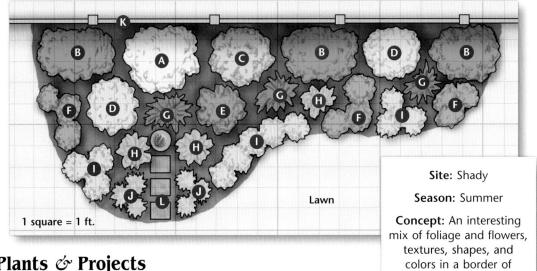

1 square = 1 ft.

Lawn

Site: Shady

Season: Summer

Concept: An interesting mix of foliage and flowers, textures, shapes, and colors in a border of shade-tolerant plants.

Plants & Projects

A Mexican orange (use 1 plant)
An evergreen shrub with shiny compound leaves. Clusters of fragrant white flowers bloom in spring and sporadically through summer. See *Choisya ternata*, p. 163.

B 'Cleopatra' camellia (use 3)
An upright, compact evergreen shrub. In late fall and winter, its glossy green leaves set off rose-pink flowers. See *Camellia sasanqua*, p. 162.

C 'Nikko Blue' hydrangea (use 1)
This deciduous shrub offers large round leaves and striking clusters of papery blue flowers in summer. See *Hydrangea macrophylla*, p. 172.

D 'Sungold' St.-Johnswort (use 2)
A vase-shaped deciduous shrub with chartreuse green leaves. It bears bright yellow flowers in summer, followed by a fall display of bright red fruit. See *Hypericum*, p. 172.

E 'Maiden's Blush' fuchsia (use 1)
An upright shrub prized for its distinctive pale pink, pendent flowers. Foliage may be evergreen in mild winters. See *Fuchsia*, p. 169.

F Lenten rose (use 9)
This perennial forms a clump of shiny green leaves with toothed edges. In late winter it

K Fence

D 'Sungold' St.-Johnswort

A Mexican orange

C 'Nikko Blue' hydrangea

B 'Cleopatra' camellia

D 'Sungold' St.-Johnswort

J Variegated sweet flag

L Steppingstones and ornament

H 'Green Gold' hosta

E 'Maiden's Blush' fuchsia

I 'Peach Blossom' astilbe

G Japanese iris

H 'Green Gold' hosta

F Lenten rose

Japanese G iris

bears white, greenish, pink, or purple flowers. See *Helleborus orientalis*, p. 170.

G **Japanese iris** (use 3)
A perennial displaying sword-like leaves and spectacular purplish blue flowers in summer. See *Iris ensata*, p. 173.

H **'Green Gold' hosta** (use 3)
This perennial makes a clump of large dark green leaves with yellow borders that fade to cream. In summer, you can remove the lavender flowers to highlight the foliage. See *Hosta*, p. 171.

I **'Peach Blossom' astilbe** (use 11)
Striking plumes of tiny flowers rise above this perennial's feathery foliage in summer. Flowers are peach-colored. See *Astilbe × japonica*, p. 161.

J **Variegated sweet flag** (use 6)
A perennial, grasslike plant with leaves striped creamy white and green. Spreads to form a patch. See *Acorus gramineus* 'Variegatus', p. 159.

See p. 61 for the following:

K **Fence**

L **Steppingstones and ornament**

B 'Cleopatra' camellia

F Lenten rose

Plant portraits

These shrubs and perennials are a welcome sight in borders in sun or shade.

● = First design, pp. 60–61
▲ = Second design, pp. 62–63

'Nikko Blue' hydrangea (*Hydrangea macrophylla*, p. 172) ▲

'Hameln' dwarf fountain grass
(*Pennisetum alopecuroides*, p. 176) ●

'Peach Blossom' astilbe
(*Astilbe × japonica*, p. 161) ▲

'Elsa Spath' clematis (*Clematis* hybrids, p. 163) ●

Japanese iris (*Iris ensata*, p. 173) ▲

A Woodland Link

Create a shrub border for nearby woods

The woodlands of the Northwest are treasured by all who live in the region. Subdivisions, both new and old, often incorporate woodland areas, with homes bordering landscapes of stately trees and large shrubs. And in some older neighborhoods, mature trees on adjacent lots create almost the same woodland feeling.

The planting shown here integrates a domestic landscape with a woodland edge, making a pleasant transition between the open area of lawn and the woods beyond. The design takes inspiration from the buffer zone of small trees and shrubs nature provides at a sunny woodland edge, and it should provide the same attraction to wildlife (and to the people who enjoy wildlife) as a natural edge does.

Trees and shrubs of various sizes mingle in the planting, larger ones toward the back, imitating natural layered growth. Narrow Serbian spruces echo the taller trees in the woods behind. Avenues of geraniums extend from the front center of the planting to each corner. In spring these areas showcase daffodils and other bulbs. From winter through fall there are flowers and attractive foliage. Whether viewed from across the yard or up close, the planting is appealing all year.

Site: Sunny

Season: Early summer

Concept: A layered planting of trees, shrubs, and perennials makes a pleasing transition between lawn and adjacent woodland.

Plants & Projects

Before planting, dig and improve the soil throughout the entire area (except under the path) with organic matter. A mulch of compost or wood chips and regular watering the first summer will speed establishment. Other than seasonal maintenance, you'll need to divide the bulbs and perennials when they become crowded.

A Chinese witch hazel
(use 3 plants)
In winter, fragrant clusters of small yellow flowers cover the bare branches of this small deciduous tree or large shrub. Leaves turn yellow in fall. See *Hamamelis mollis*, p. 170.

B Serbian spruce (use 3)
This spire-shaped conifer has short evergreen needles that are glossy green above and whitish below. See *Picea omorika*, p. 177.

C 'Valley Fire' Japanese andromeda (use 9)
A dense bushy evergreen shrub whose glossy green leaves are

B Serbian spruce

L Garden ornament

C 'Valley Fire' Japanese andromeda

Barnes' narrow male fern F

Gloriosa daisy H

K Path

See site plan for J.

I Catmint

A Chinese witch hazel

C 'Valley Fire' Japanese andromeda

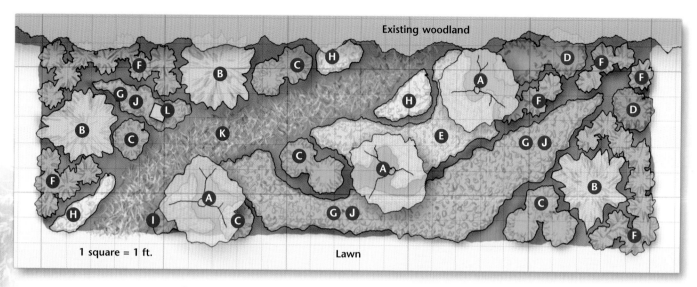

Existing woodland

1 square = 1 ft.

Lawn

bright red when new. In spring, an abundant supply of eye-catching buds produce drooping clusters of white flowers. See *Pieris japonica*, p. 177.

D Holly osmanthus (use 3)
The toothed, lustrous dark green leaves of this evergreen shrub resemble holly leaves. In spring, it is covered with small fragrant white flowers. See *Osmanthus burkwoodii*, p. 176.

E Salal (use 38)
When grown in full sun, this evergreen shrub spreads to form a low mass of dull green leaves. Bears pendulous pinkish white flowers in spring and edible blue-black fruit in fall. See *Gaultheria shallon*, p. 169.

F Barnes' narrow male fern (use 31)
Massed in spots at the edges of the planting, this semiever-green fern makes an upright clump of long narrow fronds. See Ferns: *Dryopteris filix-mas* 'Barnesii', p. 168.

G 'Johnson's Blue' geranium (use 24)
This perennial makes a wide mound of attractive foliage that is covered from late spring into summer with cup-shaped, lavender-blue flowers. See *Geranium*, p. 169.

H Gloriosa daisy (use 18)
Cheerful orange-yellow flowers with dark centers rise above this perennial's gray-green leaves for months in summer. See *Rudbeckia hirta*, p. 179.

I Catmint (use 3)
A perennial with equally attractive foliage and flowers. Pale green leaves on sprawling stems are a crinkly heart shape. From early spring into fall, tiny blue flowers line the upper portions of the stems. See *Nepeta* × *faassenii*, p. 175.

J Bulbs (as needed)
For a spectacular spring show, plant daffodils, hyacinths, and tulips among the geraniums. Choose your favorite colors and plant a lot of them—if possible, 100 or more of each. See Bulbs, p. 161.

K Path
This wood-chip path nicely complements the woodland feeling. See p. 104.

L Garden ornament
A piece of architectural salvage, such as the column shown here, or a birdbath can add interest to the planting.

A Chinese witch hazel

D Holly osmanthus

B Serbian spruce

E Salal

H Gloriosa daisy

G 'Johnson's Blue' geranium

F Barnes' narrow male fern

C 'Valley Fire' Japanese andromeda

F Barnes' narrow male fern

Link for a shadier edge

If an adjacent woodland shades your property, try this design, which features plants tolerant of shady conditions. The layout of the planting bed is similar to that of the previous design. Larger trees and shrubs are underplanted by low shrubs, perennials, and bulbs. Two "avenues" of low plants open from the front center of the planting to the corners. And a meandering path affords up-close viewing as well as access to the woods beyond.

From late winter through spring, the planting is in full bloom. Flowers in whites, pinks, and yellows fill the trees and carpet the ground, creating a lovely sight from a distance and up close, where fragrance enhances the enjoyment. Foliage textures and colors and the shapes of the plants provide interest in summer, accented by swaths of blue Carpathian bellflowers. In fall, the leaves of the serviceberry and oakleaf hydrangea impart a fiery finish to the growing season.

Plants & Projects

A **'Autumn Brilliance' serviceberry** (use 4 plants)
This deciduous tree is covered with white flowers in early spring, provides dappled shade in summer, and offers bright red-orange fall foliage. See *Amelanchier × grandiflora*, p. 160.

B **Mountain hemlock** (use 3)
This slow-growing evergreen conifer makes a handsome irregular cone of blue-green needlelike foliage. See *Tsuga mertensiana*, p. 182.

C **Oakleaf hydrangea** (use 5)
The leaves of this deciduous shrub turn from pale green, to dark green, to red and purple from spring to fall. It bears striking clusters of long-lasting papery flowers in summer. See *Hydrangea quercifolia*, p. 172.

D **Low sarcococca** (use 8)
This low, spreading evergreen shrub is a good ground cover. In late winter, small fragrant white flowers nestle at the bases of the glossy green leaves. See *Sarcococca humilis*, p. 180.

E **Leucothoe** (use 8)
A compact evergreen shrub, wider than tall, with a dense growth of shiny narrow leaves. Bears fragrant white flowers in spring. See *Leucothoe axillaris*, p. 174.

F **Carpathian bellflower** (use 30)
This perennial forms a patch of heart-shaped green leaves that are covered for most of the summer with bell-shaped light blue flowers. See *Campanula carpatica*, p. 162.

> **Site:** Shady
>
> **Season:** Late spring
>
> **Concept:** Evergreen trees and shrubs guarantee color year-round at this shady woodland edge.

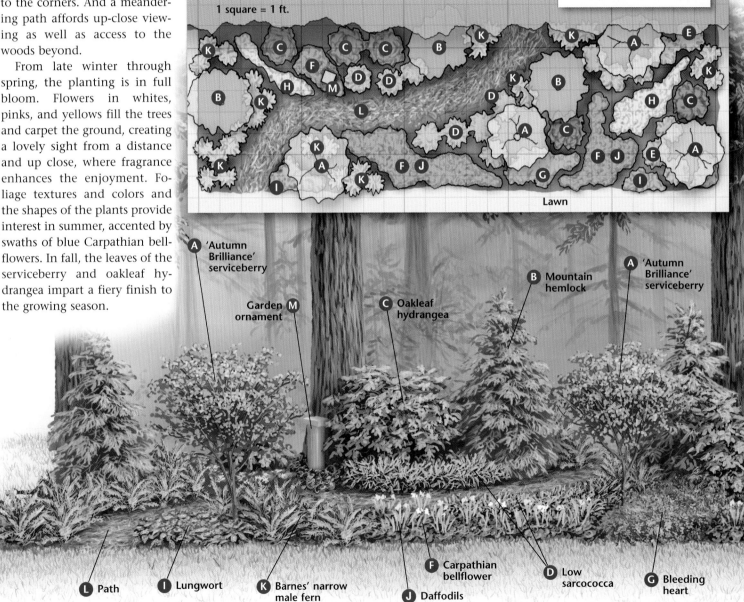

1 square = 1 ft.

Lawn

A 'Autumn Brilliance' serviceberry

M Garden ornament

C Oakleaf hydrangea

B Mountain hemlock

A 'Autumn Brilliance' serviceberry

L Path **I** Lungwort **K** Barnes' narrow male fern **F** Carpathian bellflower **J** Daffodils **D** Low sarcococca **G** Bleeding heart

G **Bleeding heart** (use 7)
A perennial with soft, blue-green, fernlike foliage. In late spring, pink heart-shaped flowers dangle from thin arching stalks. See *Dicentra spectabilis*, p. 166.

H **'Magnificum' leopard's bane** (use 24)
This perennial spreads to form a low patch of heart-shaped leaves. Yellow asterlike flowers bloom in spring. See *Doronicum orientale*, p. 166.

I **Lungwort** (use 6)
A perennial with attractive gray-green foliage spotted with white. In spring, many tiny pink, red, or violet flowers float on stalks above the leaves. See *Pulmonaria saccharata*, p. 178.

J **Daffodils** (as needed)
A mix of white and yellow daffodils planted with the Carpathian bellflowers make a lovely spring show. Plant several hundred if possible. See Bulbs: *Narcissus*, p. 161.

See p. 65 for the following:

K **Barnes' narrow male fern** (use 30)

L **Path**

M **Garden ornament**

A 'Autumn Brilliance' serviceberry

E Leucothoe

Lungwort **I**

H 'Magnificum' leopard's bane

Plant portraits

With handsome foliage and flowers, these plants are effective against a woodland backdrop.

● = First design, pp. 64–65
▲ = Second design, pp. 66–67

Gloriosa daisy
(*Rudbeckia hirta*, p. 179) ●

'Magnificum' leopard's bane
(*Doronicum orientale*, p. 166) ▲

Salal (*Gaultheria shallon*, p. 169) ●

Bleeding heart (*Dicentra spectabilis*, p. 166) ▲

Serbian spruce
(*Picea omorika*, p. 177) ●

Mountain hemlock
(*Tsuga mertensiana*, p. 182) ▲

Hyacinth
(Bulbs: *Hyacinthus*, p. 161) ●

A No-Mow Slope

A terraced planting transforms a steep site

S teep slopes can be a landscaping headache. Planted with lawn grass, they're a chore to mow, and they can present problems of erosion and maintenance if you try to establish other ground covers or plantings. One solution to this dilemma is shown here: Tame the slope with low retaining walls and steps. Then plant the resulting flat (or flatter) beds with attractive trees, shrubs, and perennials.

Steep slopes near the house are common in many Northwest communities. Here, a narrow, steeply sloping front yard has been terraced with low retaining walls and wide steps. The result transforms the home's public face and creates an enticing path to the front door.

Visitors approaching from the sidewalk or the driveway pass through colorful plantings. Shrubs and perennials bloom in whites, pinks, and purples in late winter and spring. Trees and shrubs offer fall color and handsome evergreen foliage in winter. Near the house, you can extend the foundation shrubs along the wall or tie them in to existing plantings.

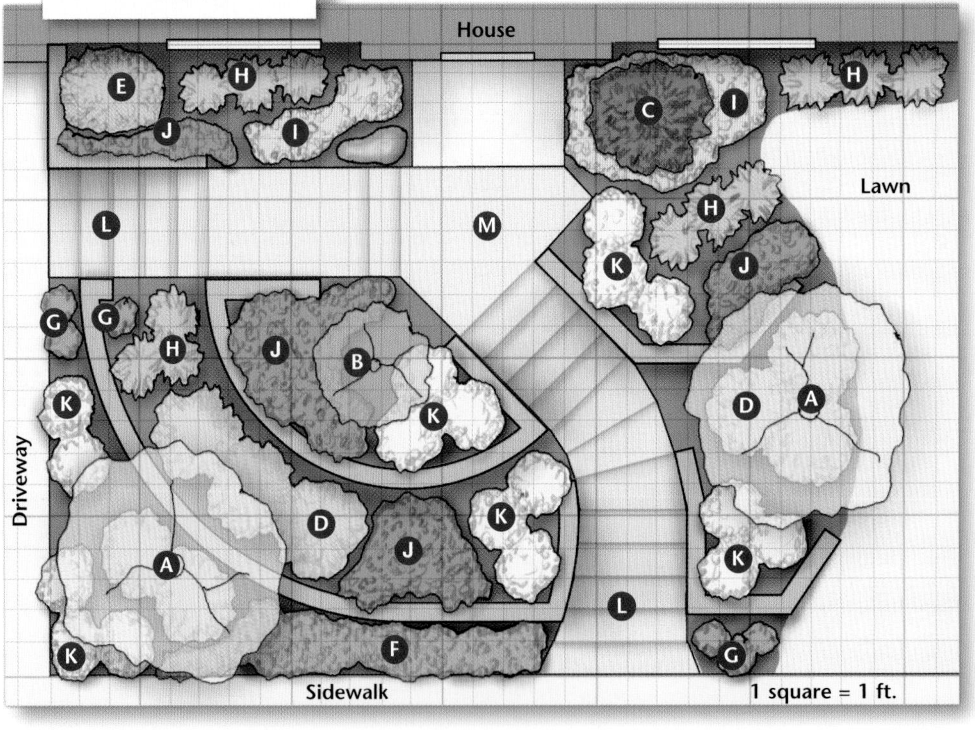

Plants & Projects

Reshaping the slope and building the retaining walls, steps, and walkways is a big job. Even if you plan to do much of the work yourself, it's best to consult a landscape contractor for advice and local building officials about regulations. Once established, the plants will give years of enjoyment and need only seasonal maintenance.

Ⓐ Japanese snowbell
(use 2 plants)
This deciduous tree is a three-season performer. Fragrant white flowers dangle from its branches in spring and green summer leaves turn yellow in fall. See *Styrax japonicum*, p. 182.

Ⓑ 'Royal Purple' smoke tree
(use 1)
This large deciduous shrub is red in spring, dark purple in summer, and gold, orange, or red in fall. In summer and fall it bears plumes of tiny pink flowers. Prune lower limbs to approximate a tree form. See *Cotinus coggygria*, p. 165.

Ⓒ Red laceleaf Japanese maple
(use 1)
An eye-catching presence by the door, this shrubby tree offers delicate lacy foliage that is

Japanese snowbell Ⓐ

'Goldflame' Ⓓ spirea

Evergreen Ⓚ candytuft

See site plan for Ⓜ.

'Vancouver Gold' Ⓕ silky leaf woadwaxen

Site: Sunny

Season: Spring

Concept: Retaining walls, steps, and attractive plants tame this slope and enhance the home's public face.

House

Lawn

Driveway

Sidewalk

1 square = 1 ft.

H 'Hidcote' English lavender

I 'Springwood Pink' heath

C Red laceleaf Japanese maple

D 'Goldflame' spirea

K Evergreen candytuft

E Variegated winter daphne

J 'Massachusetts' kinnikinnick

B 'Royal Purple' smoke tree

L Retaining wall and steps

G Dwarf rhododendron

---

red in summer and redder in fall. See *Acer palmatum* 'Dissectum Atropurpureum', p. 159.

D **'Goldflame' spirea** (use 8)
This deciduous shrub forms a mass of thin arching stems. Bright gold leaves are tinged with orange in spring and turn red in fall. Bears flat clusters of pink flowers in summer. See *Spiraea japonica*, p. 181.

E **Variegated winter daphne** (use 1)
The rosy white flowers of this evergreen shrub bloom from late winter into spring. Shiny green-and-cream leaves look good year-round. See *Daphne odora* 'Aureomarginata', p. 166.

F **'Vancouver Gold' silky leaf woadwaxen** (use 8)
This low, spreading shrub forms a mat of small, deciduous, dark green leaves. In summer, it is covered with yellow flowers. See *Genista pilosa*, p. 169.

G **Dwarf rhododendron** (use 6)
This compact evergreen shrub tucks into the spaces by the steps and sidewalk. In spring, its dark purple flowers look good against the gray-green leaves. See *Rhododendron impeditum*, p. 178.

H **'Hidcote' English lavender** (use 12)
Masses of fragrant dark purple flowers top the gray-green

leaves of this small bushy shrub in early summer. Its aromatic evergreen foliage looks good the rest of the year. See *Lavandula angustifolia*, p. 174.

I **'Springwood Pink' heath** (use 14)
This low, spreading evergreen shrub has fine needlelike leaves. A profusion of tiny pink bell-shaped flowers bloom in late winter and spring. See *Erica carnea*, p. 167.

J **'Massachusetts' kinnikinnick** (use 19)
Ideal for dry slopes, this evergreen ground cover forms a low mass of dark glossy leaves on reddish stems. Small pink-

ish white flowers bloom in spring and produce red berries in summer. See *Arctostaphylos uva-ursi*, p. 160.

K **Evergreen candytuft** (use 17)
A bushy evergreen perennial ground cover. Bright clusters of white flowers stand out against its dark glossy leaves for weeks in spring. See *Iberis sempervirens*, p. 173.

L **Retaining walls and steps**
The walls and steps are made with a precast-concrete retaining-wall system available at garden centers. See p. 116.

M **Paving**
Choose a surface that complements the house. See p. 104.

Plant portraits

These durable, low-care plants will help transform difficult hillside sites.

● = First design, pp. 68–69
▲ = Second design, pp. 70–71

Evergreen candytuft (*Iberis sempervirens*, p. 173) ●

'Caesar's Brother' Siberian iris
(*Iris sibirica*, p. 173) ▲

Red laceleaf Japanese maple
(*Acer palmatum* 'Dissectum Atropurpureum', p. 159) ●

'Sango Kaku' coralbark maple
(*Acer palmatum*, p. 159) ▲

'Goldflame' spirea
(*Spiraea japonica*, p.181) ●

Fuchsia
(*Fuchsia magellanica*, p. 169) ▲

Working with a hillside

If terracing a steep slope with retaining walls and steps does not appeal to you, or is beyond your budget, consider this design. Here we've worked with the existing hillside, replacing turfgrass with tough, easy-care ground covers. Once the plants are established, their roots will hold the hillside soil in place, and they will require little supplemental watering during the summer.

The planting is as attractive as it is durable. Mounding deciduous and evergreen shrubs contrast with the swordlike foliage of Siberian iris and airy clumps of Russian sage. Above these lower-growing plants, the striking coralbark maple provides dappled shade and a sense of separation from street and sidewalk traffic. There are months of bloom in reds, pinks, purples, and lavender, from the spikes of tiny Russian sage flowers to the exotic blossoms of fuchsia.

Plants & Projects

Ⓐ 'Sango Kaku' coralbark maple
(use 1 plant)
Colorful in all seasons, this small deciduous tree has lacy leaves that open red, turn light green, and then yellow in fall. Bare winter bark is coral red. See *Acer palmatum*, p. 159.

Ⓑ Fuchsia (use 3)
Deep red-and-purple flowers cover this small shrub all summer long. They'll invite hummingbirds to your front yard. Evergreen in mild winters and needs watering in summer. See *Fuchsia magellanica*, p. 169.

Ⓒ Spreading English yew (use 9)
An evergreen shrub with flat needlelike leaves that stay dark green all year. Left unpruned,

Site: Sunny

Season: Summer

Concept: Tough but attractive plants make a colorful, easy-care front yard on a sloping site.

Fuchsia **B**

D 'Dwarf Pavement' rose

Spreading English yew **C**

'Caesar's Brother' **G** Siberian iris

'Vancouver Gold' **I** silky leaf woadwaxen

See site plan for **H** .

E 'Newport Dwarf' escallonia

Spreading English yew **C**

A 'Sango Kaku' coralbark maple

D 'Dwarf Pavement' rose

'Caesar's **G** Brother' Siberian iris

Russian **F** sage

the shrubs will blend together to form a soft mass. See *Taxus baccata* 'Repandens', p. 182.

D 'Dwarf Pavement' rose (use 34) A tough deciduous shrub with masses of glossy green leaves and wonderfully fragrant pink flowers from spring into fall. Its stems are very thorny, so if you have small children you might consider a less prickly rose. See *Rosa rugosa*, p. 178.

E 'Newport Dwarf' escallonia (use 9) Compact and glossy-leaved, this evergreen shrub grows thick enough to hide the foundation and stays low enough to frame the windows without pruning. It bears clusters of red flowers in summer. See *Escallonia rubra*, p. 167.

F Russian sage (use 5) This perennial makes a wispy clump of small gray-green

leaves on upright stems. For many weeks in summer, lavender flower spikes appear above and among the leaves. See *Perovskia*, p. 176.

G 'Caesar's Brother' Siberian iris (use 8) A perennial with narrow grassy leaves and deep blue-purple flowers on stiff stalks in late spring. A nice splash of texture and color in front of the yews. See *Iris sibirica*, p. 173.

H 'Autumn Joy' sedum (use 7) This perennial forms a mass of thick stems and succulent gray-green leaves. Large flat flower heads turn from shades of pink to rusty red as summer progresses into autumn. See *Sedum*, p. 181.

See p. 69 for the following:

I 'Vancouver Gold' silky leaf woadwaxen (use 22)

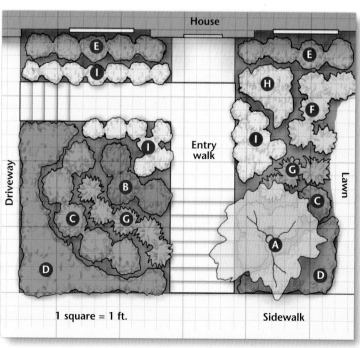

House

E

I

H

F

Driveway

I

Entry walk

B

C

G

A

D

Lawn

G

C

D

1 square = 1 ft.

Sidewalk

Angle of Repose

Make a back-door garden in a sheltered niche

Many homes offer the opportunity to tuck a garden into a protected corner. In the front yard, such spots are ideal for an entry garden or a landscaping display that enhances the view of your house from the sidewalk or the street. If the niche is in the backyard, like the site shown here, the planting can be more intimate, part of a comfortable outdoor "room" you can stroll through at leisure or enjoy from a nearby patio or window.

This design gives pleasure year-round. From spring into summer the garden is awash with flowers in whites, pinks, purple, and blue. Some attract hummingbirds and butterflies. Holly osmanthus entices family and friends to the small patio with its lovely springtime aroma. Yellow coreopsis and bold deep blue asters maintain a flowering presence from summer into fall. The showy copper-colored sepals of the abelia flowers also last into late fall.

Although flowers are lovely, they are fleeting. For lasting appeal, this planting relies on its foliage. Featuring many evergreen plants, the design combines interesting, sometimes arresting, foliage textures and colors. The leaves sport a range of green and purple hues. The shrubs are either loose and bushy or dense and mounded. Bristling near the center of the planting, New Zealand flax adds an exotic touch. At the bed edges, perennials make the transition to the lawn by picking up the green-and-purple color scheme.

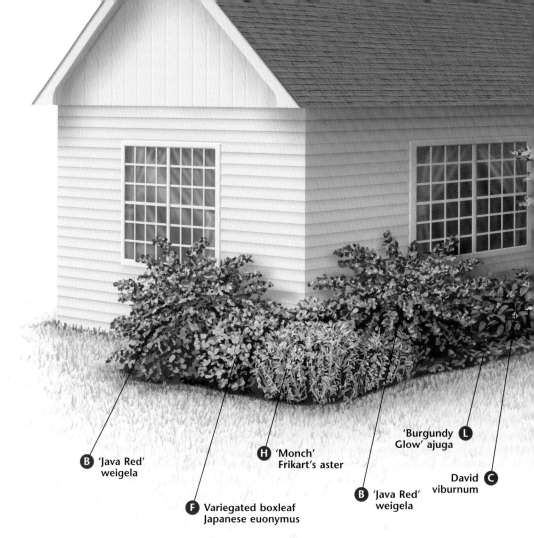

B 'Java Red' weigela

H 'Monch' Frikart's aster

F Variegated boxleaf Japanese euonymus

B 'Java Red' weigela

L 'Burgundy Glow' ajuga

C David viburnum

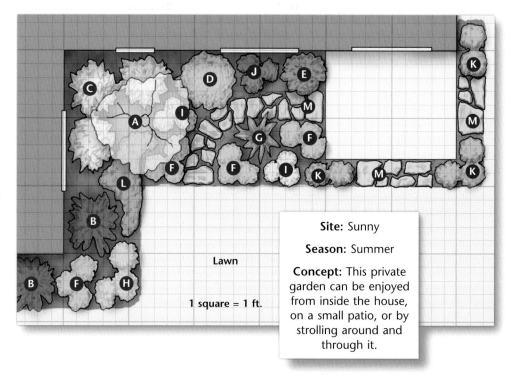

Lawn

1 square = 1 ft.

Site: Sunny

Season: Summer

Concept: This private garden can be enjoyed from inside the house, on a small patio, or by strolling around and through it.

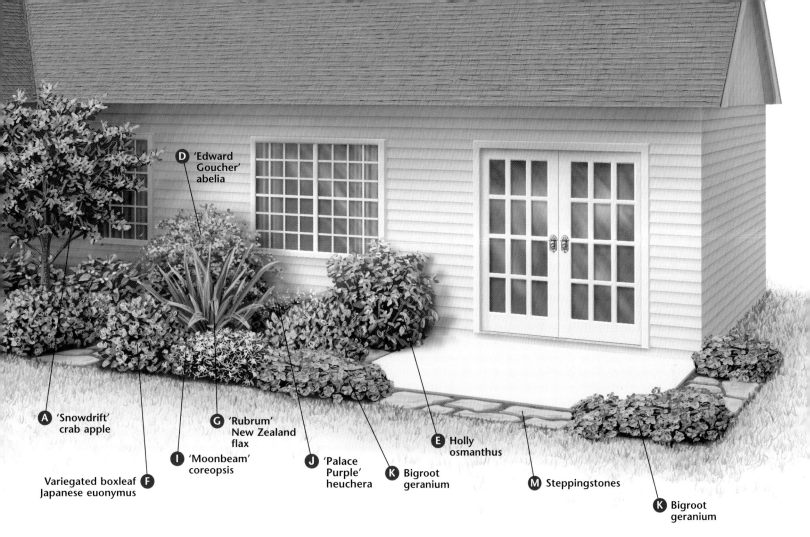

D 'Edward Goucher' abelia

A 'Snowdrift' crab apple

G 'Rubrum' New Zealand flax

I 'Moonbeam' coreopsis

F Variegated boxleaf Japanese euonymus

J 'Palace Purple' heuchera

K Bigroot geranium

E Holly osmanthus

M Steppingstones

K Bigroot geranium

Plants & Projects

Once established, the crab apple and shrubs will require seasonal pruning to keep them healthy and the right size. Divide the perennials when they become crowded.

A 'Snowdrift' crab apple
(use 1 plant)
In spring this small deciduous tree bears red buds and showy white flowers. Small orange-red fruits ripen in fall and last all winter, if the birds don't get them. See *Malus*, p. 174.

B 'Java Red' weigela (use 2)
This deciduous shrub makes a fountain of dark green leaves with a purple tint. In early summer, hummingbirds are attracted to nectar in the tubular deep pink flowers. See *Weigela*, p. 183.

C David viburnum (use 3)
An evergreen shrub, this has bold, leathery dark green

leaves. Clusters of white flowers blushed with pink bloom in late spring and produce metallic blue fruit in autumn. See *Viburnum davidii*, p. 182.

D 'Edward Goucher' abelia
(use 1)
This shrub's evergreen leaves turn from bronzy green, to dark green, to purple-bronze from spring through winter. It bears masses of small rosy purple flowers in summer. See *Abelia × grandiflora*, p. 158.

E Holly osmanthus (use 1)
A slow-growing evergreen shrub with toothed, dark green leaves. Small fragrant white flowers perfume the patio in spring. See *Osmanthus burkwoodii*, p. 176.

F Variegated boxleaf Japanese euonymus (use 12)
This evergreen shrub has tiny white-and-green leaves. Massed

in three places, it helps tie the planting together. See *Euonymus japonicus* 'Microphyllus Variegatus', p. 168.

G 'Rubrum' New Zealand flax
(use 1)
This perennial makes a striking display of saberlike purple-red leaves. Its reddish purple summer flowers are undependable in the region. See *Phormium tenax*, p. 177.

H 'Monch' Frikart's aster (use 3)
From late summer through fall, this perennial bears striking deep blue flowers with bright golden centers. Foliage looks good the rest of the season. See *Aster × frikartii*, p. 160.

I 'Moonbeam' coreopsis (use 6)
Abundant sunny yellow flowers cover this perennial's mound of lacy green foliage in summer. See *Coreopsis verticillata*, p. 164.

J 'Palace Purple' heuchera
(use 3)
This perennial is grown primarily for its deep purple, maple-like leaves. It bears feathery spikes of tiny white flowers from spring into summer. See *Heuchera*, p. 171.

K Bigroot geranium (use 7)
This perennial forms a mass of fragrant semievergreen foliage. Magenta or pink flowers bloom in late spring. See *Geranium macrorrhizum*, p. 169.

L 'Burgundy Glow' ajuga (use 7)
A low-growing perennial with rosettes of leaves shaded purple, green, and white. In spring, it bears spikes of blue flowers. See *Ajuga reptans*, p. 159.

M Steppingstones
Irregular flagstone steppingstones allow up-close viewing and access for maintenance. See p. 104.

A touch of the Orient

Chosen for a shady site, these plants provide a subtle flavor of the Far East. The Japanese stewartia, heavenly bamboo, andromeda, camellia, enkianthus, and Japanese painted fern all suggest an Asian woodland.

Attractive throughout the year, the planting is particularly effective in late winter and early spring, the season shown here. As winter moves to spring, buds and flowers, colorful foliage, and interesting patterns of bare branches entice viewers inside the house to get back outdoors. Interplant spring-flowering bulbs with the hosta for even more color. As in the previous design, handsome foliage, accented by the flowers of the stewartia, hydrangeas, and geraniums, provides enjoyment in the summer and fall.

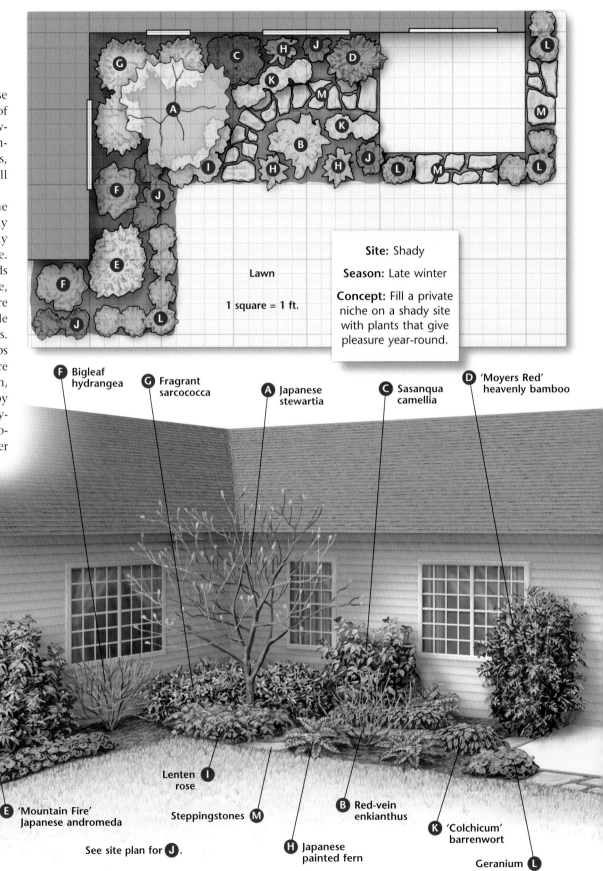

Lawn

1 square = 1 ft.

Site: Shady

Season: Late winter

Concept: Fill a private niche on a shady site with plants that give pleasure year-round.

F Bigleaf hydrangea

G Fragrant sarcococca

A Japanese stewartia

C Sasanqua camellia

D 'Moyers Red' heavenly bamboo

F Bigleaf hydrangea

L Geranium

E 'Mountain Fire' Japanese andromeda

See site plan for **J**.

Lenten rose **I**

Steppingstones **M**

H Japanese painted fern

B Red-vein enkianthus

K 'Colchicum' barrenwort

Geranium **L**

Plants & Projects

Ⓐ Japanese stewartia
(use 1 plant)
This deciduous tree offers attractive bark and silky buds in winter and spring, white flowers in summer, and colorful fall foliage. See *Stewartia pseudocamellia*, p. 181.

Ⓑ Red-vein enkianthus (use 1)
An upright deciduous shrub with small blue-green leaves that turn orange-red in fall. Bears pinkish flowers in late spring. See *Enkianthus campanulatus*, p. 167.

Ⓒ Sasanqua camellia (use 1)
Large flowers bloom on this shrub from late fall into winter. Evergreen foliage looks good year-round. There are many cultivars to choose from. See *Camellia sasanqua*, p. 162.

Ⓜ Steppingstones

Ⓓ 'Moyers Red' heavenly bamboo (use 1)
This large multistemmed shrub is a striking presence by the patio. Feathery evergreen foliage turns red in fall and winter. See *Nandina domestica*, p. 175.

Ⓔ 'Mountain Fire' Japanese andromeda (use 1)
This evergreen shrub forms a dense mound of glossy foliage. New leaves are bright red and appear after clusters of pink flowers bloom in late winter. See *Pieris japonica*, p. 177.

Ⓕ Bigleaf hydrangea (use 2)
Large clusters of papery blue, pink, or white flowers bloom on this deciduous shrub for months in the summer. See *Hydrangea macrophylla*, p. 172.

Ⓖ Fragrant sarcococca (use 3)
The glossy green leaves of this evergreen shrub are a good backdrop for the fragrant white flowers borne in late winter. See *Sarcococca ruscifolia*, p. 180.

Ⓗ Japanese painted fern (use 3)
Evergreen in mild winters, the lacy fronds of this fern are an iridescent mix of green, silver, and maroon. See Ferns: *Athyrium nipponicum* 'Pictum', p. 168.

Ⓘ Lenten rose (use 3)
This evergreen perennial has shiny green, toothed leaves and distinctive flowers in pink, purple, white, or green. Blooms late winter into spring. See *Helleborus orientalis*, p. 170.

Ⓙ Hosta (use 7)
A perennial grown for its attractive foliage. Choose a midsize cultivar with green leaves for this design. See *Hosta*, p. 171.

Ⓚ 'Colchicum' barrenwort (use 5)
This evergreen perennial has heart-shaped leaves that turn from copper to green to maroon during the year. It bears small yellow flowers in spring. See *Epimedium pinnatum*, p. 167.

Ⓛ Geranium (use 12)
This perennial bears light purple flowers on light green foliage in summer. See *Geranium × cantabrigiense*, p. 169.

See p. 73 for the following:

Ⓜ Steppingstones

Plant portraits

Evergreen and deciduous plants provide interest all year in a colorful planting.

● = First design, pp. 72–73
▲ = Second design, pp. 74–75

'Snowdrift' crab apple (*Malus*, p. 174) ●

'Java Red' weigela (*Weigela*, p. 183) ●

'Mountain Fire' Japanese andromeda (*Pieris japonica*, p. 177) ▲

Variegated boxleaf Japanese euonymus (*Euonymus japonicus* 'Microphyllus Variegatus', p. 168) ●

A Pleasant Passage

Reclaim a narrow side yard for a stroll garden

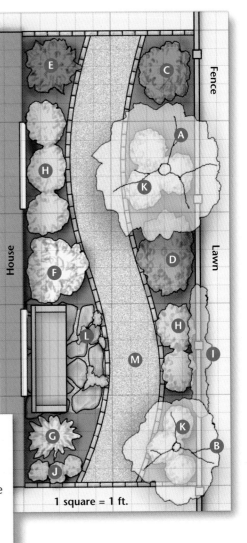

1 square = 1 ft.

Many residential lots include a slim strip of land between the house and a property line. Usually overlooked by everyone except children and dogs racing between the front yard and the back, this often shady corridor can become a valued addition to the landscape. In this design, a lovely little stroll garden invites adults, and even children, to linger as they move from one part of the property to another.

The wall of the house and a fence on the property line give the space an enclosed feeling, like a narrow room. A gently curving gravel path widens the passage visually and lengthens the stroll through it. A wooden bench set on flagstones offers a comfortable place for a pause.

On both sides of the path, evergreen and deciduous shrubs and trees provide color all year. Pink rhododendron blossoms line the path in spring. Flowering clematis on the fence is a focal point from the bench in summer. The red and purple foliage of the hydrangea and maple catches the eye in fall. Fragrant yellow witch hazel flowers brighten the passage in winter.

Plants & Projects

Lay out and install the path and edging. Then prepare and plant the beds. As the maple grows, you'll need to prune it to provide headroom for strollers. To encourage the witch hazel to grow as a small tree rather than a shrub, prune the suckers after it flowers. Once established, the plants require seasonal care as well as pruning to maintain size and shape.

A Japanese maple (use 1 plant)
This deciduous tree has a delicate open habit that offers dappled shade along the path. We've shown a seed-grown plant with green summer foliage and red fall color, but you can choose a favorite cultivar. See *Acer palmatum*, p. 159.

B Chinese witch hazel (use 1)
A small deciduous tree or shrub with large bold gray-green leaves that turn yellow in fall. It's striking in winter when fragrant yellow flowers bloom on bare wood. See *Hamamelis mollis*, p. 170.

C 'Nana Gracilis' dwarf Hinoki cypress (use 1)
A narrow, naturally sculpted conifer. Its glossy emerald foliage is a bright spot at one end of the path. See *Chamaecyparis obtusa*, p. 163.

D Silk-tassel bush (use 1)
Showy gray-green flower tassels dangle from this evergreen shrub in the winter months. Leaves are gray-green and have wavy margins. See *Garrya elliptica*, p. 169.

E 'Shirobana' spirea (use 1)
Another little gem at path's end, this deciduous shrub has dark green leaves and flat clusters of white, pink, and rose flowers all summer. See *Spiraea japonica*, p. 181.

F Oakleaf hydrangea (use 1)
This deciduous shrub has large lobed leaves, lacy flowers from spring through fall, and good fall color. The peeling reddish bark looks good in winter. See *Hydrangea quercifolia*, p. 172.

G 'Hidcote' St.-Johnswort (use 1)
An attractive benchside shrub. Dark green leaves are evergreen in mild winters. Gold flowers bloom all summer. See *Hypericum* 'Hidcote', p. 172.

H 'Cilpinense' evergreen rhododendron (use 5)
Small leaves and a compact habit make this evergreen shrub ideal for narrow spaces. It bears light pink flowers very early in spring. See *Rhododendron*, p. 178.

I Small-flowered clematis (use 1)
A vigorous climber, this deciduous vine becomes a focal point from the bench in summer and fall when its dark green leaves are covered with flowers. Many cultivars are available. See *Clematis* hybrids, p. 163.

J Frikart's aster (use 3)
Tough and carefree, this perennial bears clusters of purple flowers that last for many weeks starting in late summer. See *Aster × frikartii*, p. 160.

K Geranium (use 6)
An evergreen perennial that forms a leafy mound with clusters of pale purple flowers in summer. See *Geranium × cantabrigiense*, p. 169.

L Mother-of-thyme (use 6)
In summer, this shrubby perennial bears small purple flowers on a mat of tiny aromatic evergreen leaves. See *Thymus serpyllum*, p. 182.

M Path
Curving gently through the planting is a gravel path edged by cobblestones. See p. 104.

N Seating area
Random-sized flagstones laid on a sand-and-gravel base support a comfortable bench of your choice. See p. 104.

A Japanese maple

B Chinese witch hazel

See site plan for E.

F Oakleaf hydrangea

G 'Hidcote' St.-Johnswort

C 'Nana Gracilis' dwarf Hinoki cypress

N Seating area

D Silk-tassel bush

L Mother-of-thyme

J Frikart's aster

M Path

H 'Cilpinense' evergreen rhododendron

K Geranium

I Small-flowered clematis

A shady corridor

If a side of your house has a shady exposure, try this design. Here, shade-loving trees, shrubs, perennials, and ground covers create a pleasing mix of textures and colors.

A curved path of flagstones opens at one end into a terrace that allows room for seating and a potted camellia. Along the path, the large bold leaves of aucuba, bear's breeches, and hostas mingle with the lacy leaves of heavenly bamboo, astilbes, and ferns.

Spring is the season of peak bloom. For many months, the seating area will be filled with pleasant scents. Sweet-smelling sarcococca blooms in early spring. Summer brings the fragrance of leucothoe flowers. And almost any time of year you can reach down from your chair and rub a bigroot geranium leaf to savor its scent.

Plants & Projects

A Stripebark maple (use 1 plant)
A narrow deciduous tree with a wide repertoire: yellow clusters of flowers in spring; a dark green leaf canopy in summer; yellows, reds, and purples in fall; and bark that shows off green and white stripes in winter. See *Acer davidii*, p. 158.

B Heavenly bamboo (use 2)
This evergreen shrub has slender stems and lacy leaves that turn from bronze to green to red over the year. It bears white flower clusters in summer and off and on all year. The berries range from orange to red. See *Nandina domestica*, p. 175.

C 'Rainbow' drooping leucothoe (use 1)
An evergreen shrub with shiny cream, pink, and green leaves. Fragrant white flower clusters appear under the drooping leaves in spring. See *Leucothoe fontanesiana*, p. 174.

D Fragrant sarcococca (use 1)
This small evergreen shrub with glossy leaves and very fragrant white flowers will scent

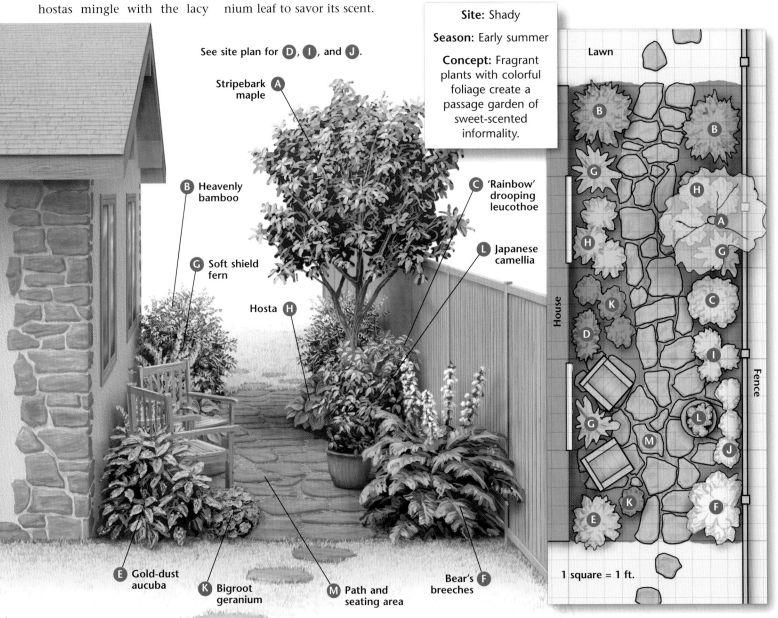

See site plan for **D**, **I**, and **J**.

Stripebark **A** maple

B Heavenly bamboo

G Soft shield fern

Hosta **H**

C 'Rainbow' drooping leucothoe

L Japanese camellia

E Gold-dust aucuba

K Bigroot geranium

M Path and seating area

Bear's **F** breeches

Site: Shady

Season: Early summer

Concept: Fragrant plants with colorful foliage create a passage garden of sweet-scented informality.

Lawn

House

Fence

1 square = 1 ft.

the seating area in early spring. See *Sarcococca ruscifolia*, p. 180.

E **Gold-dust aucuba** (use 1)
The large, yellow-speckled, glossy leaves of this evergreen shrub make an attractive background for the small maroon flowers in spring. See *Aucuba japonica* 'Variegata', p. 161.

F **Bear's breeches** (use 1)
A perennial with very large leaves and vigorous growth. In late spring, spikes of white-and-purple flowers rise high above the foliage. See *Acanthus mollis*, p. 158.

G **Soft shield fern** (use 3)
A dense evergreen fern with lovely soft fronds and upright growth. See Ferns: *Polystichum setiferum*, p. 168.

H **Hosta** (use 6)
Carefree, shade-tolerant perennial prized for its leaves. There are many colors and shapes to choose from. A blue-leaved cultivar works well here. See *Hosta*, p. 171.

I **Astilbe** (use 3)
Plumes of tiny flowers rise on stalks above the lacy leaves of this shade-loving perennial in early summer. Choose one of the many pink cultivars. See *Astilbe*, p. 161.

J **Bishop's hat** (use 3)
An outstanding ground cover, this evergreen perennial forms a low mass of heart-shaped leaves that are tinged red and purple in summer. In early spring it bears sprays of small white to pinkish flowers. See *Epimedium grandiflorum*, p. 167.

K **Bigroot geranium** (use 4)
A perennial with attractive semievergreen leaves that are aromatic when crushed. Its pink to magenta flowers bloom in late spring. See *Geranium macrorrhizum*, p. 169.

L **Japanese camellia** (use 1)
Planted in a pot, this glossy evergreen shrub bears large white, pink, or red flowers in spring. You can choose from many cultivars. See *Camellia japonica*, p. 162.

M **Path and seating area**
A curved path widens into a cozy terrace. Both are made of flagstones laid on a sand-and-gravel base. See p. 104.

Plant portraits

Eye-catching plants for an overlooked spot: here are flowers, foliage, and fragrance to make your side-yard stroll garden a favorite.

● = First design, pp. 76–77
▲ = Second design, pp. 78–79

Japanese camellia
(*Camellia japonica*, p. 162) ▲

Stripebark maple
(*Acer davidii*, p. 158) ▲

Heavenly bamboo (*Nandina domestica*, p. 175) ▲

Gold-dust aucuba
(*Aucuba japonica* 'Variegata', p. 161) ▲

'Hidcote' St.-Johnswort (*Hypericum*, p. 172) ●

Astilbe (*Astilbe*, p. 161) ▲

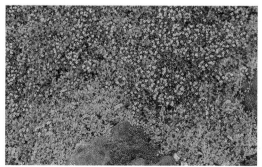

Mother-of-thyme (*Thymus serpyllum*, p. 182) ●

Down to Earth

Harmonize your deck with its surroundings

Japanese stewartia **A**

Site: Sunny

Season: Summer

Concept: A pleasing mix of durable, often fragrant plants integrates a low deck with its hillside surroundings.

Compact **E**
Korean spice
viburnum

'Spring Bouquet' **D**
viburnum

'Springwood **F**
White' heath

A backyard deck is a perfect spot for enjoying the outdoors. Too often, however, the deck offers little connection to its outdoor surroundings. Perched on skinny posts above a patch of lawn, it is a lonely outpost rather than an inviting gateway into the garden.

In this design, a low deck nestles in a planting that provides flowers and foliage for year-round enjoyment. Conceived for a site with a backyard that slopes down from the deck, the planting turns an area that is impractical for play or difficult to maintain as a lawn into a lovely border of foliage and flowers that you can enjoy from house, deck, or yard below. (The planting can be adapted for sites that are steeper or more level than the gradual slope shown.)

The plants are chosen and placed to minimize erosion and to make the most of color, texture, form, and fragrance. Flowering trees frame the bed at both ends, providing blossoms in spring, shade in summer, colorful foliage in fall, and attractive bark in winter. Evergreen and deciduous shrubs, vines, perennials, and grasses extend the colors and textures, as well as sweet scents, from one end of the deck to the other.

Plants & Projects

You'll need to water young plants to get them established. But after a year or two, these durable perennials, trees, and shrubs will require infrequent supplemental watering and a minimum of care. Prune the shrubs to keep them from overgrowing their neighbors. Shear the heath each spring. Divide any perennials that become crowded.

A Japanese stewartia (use 1 plant)
This deciduous tree is striking in every season. Silky buds and fresh green leaves appear in spring, followed by large white camellia-like flowers in summer, bronze-to-purple foliage in fall, and attractive bare branches with flaking bark in winter. See *Stewartia pseudo-camellia*, p. 181.

B Japanese snowbell (use 1)
This deciduous tree provides dappled summer shade and yellow foliage in fall. Fragrant white flowers will dangle over the deck in spring. See *Styrax japonicum*, p. 182.

C Mexican orange (use 5)
A dense, glossy, evergreen shrub that makes an informal and aromatic hedge along the deck. The light green leaves are pungent in the hot sun, and the clusters of white flowers that bloom off and on all year look like orange blossoms and smell just as sweet. See *Choisya ternata*, p. 163.

D 'Spring Bouquet' viburnum (use 4)
Beautiful all year, this evergreen shrub has dark green, red-tinted leaves. Clusters of burgundy-white buds form in fall and last through winter, opening into sweet-scented white flowers in spring. Blue berries appear in late summer. See *Viburnum tinus*, p. 182.

E Compact Korean spice viburnum (use 2)
A deciduous shrub with clusters of white flowers that add a sweet spicy scent near the steps in spring. Leaves may turn red in fall. See *Viburnum carlesii* 'Compactum', p. 182.

F 'Springwood White' heath (use 20)
This evergreen shrub spreads to form a fine-textured but tough edge along the lawn. Small needlelike foliage is covered with white flowers in early spring. See *Erica carnea*, p. 167.

G 'Comtesse de Bouchard' clematis (use 2)
Vigorous as well as beautiful, this deciduous vine will cover the rails of the deck with dark green leaves from spring through fall. Large rose-pink flowers bloom in summer. See *Clematis* hybrids, p. 163.

H Peony hybrid (use 3)
A bushy perennial with dark green glossy leaves that turn shades of purple and gold in autumn. It bears large fragrant flowers in late spring in colors that range from white to pink to rose. See *Paeonia*, p. 176.

I Fountain grass (use 12)
This perennial forms a graceful mound of slender arching green leaves. Plumes of pink or purple flowers rise above the foliage in midsummer and last while the leaves turn gold or tan in fall. See *Pennisetum setaceum*, p. 176.

J 'Monch' Frikart's aster (use 6)
A carefree perennial with eye-catching, yellow-centered, deep blue daisylike flowers above dark green foliage. It blooms with the fountain grass from late summer through fall. See *Aster × frikartii*, p. 160.

K 'Bright Star' purple coneflower (use 6)
A summer-blooming perennial that looks fabulous alongside the fountain grass. It forms a mound of dark green leaves. Tall, sturdy stalks bear large burgundy daisylike flowers above the foliage. See *Echinacea purpurea*, p. 166.

L 'Stella d'Oro' daylily (use 15)
Sunny yellow flowers bloom among the arching grassy leaves of this compact perennial from early summer to late fall. See *Hemerocallis*, p. 170.

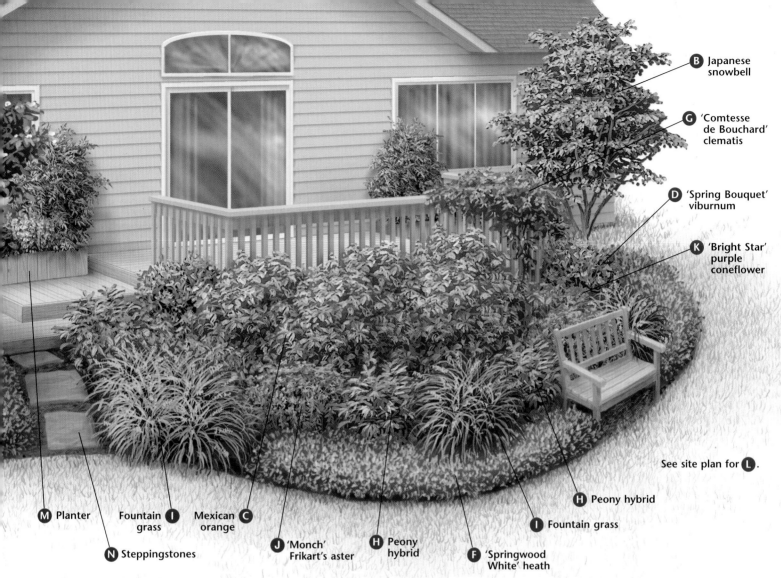

B Japanese snowbell

G 'Comtesse de Bouchard' clematis

D 'Spring Bouquet' viburnum

K 'Bright Star' purple coneflower

See site plan for **L**.

H Peony hybrid

I Fountain grass

F 'Springwood White' heath

H Peony hybrid

J 'Monch' Frikart's aster

M Planter

I Fountain grass

C Mexican orange

N Steppingstones

M Planters

Large wooden containers on the pads leading to the deck are planted with evergreen shrubs and perennials. One each of the following is shown per box: 'Plum Passion' heavenly bamboo (see *Nandina domestica*, p. 175) is an upright shrub with purple new growth and winter color. At its feet are Grey's senecio (see *Senecio greyi*, p. 181), a mounding shrub with woolly leaves, and 'Palace Purple' heuchera (see *Heuchera*, p. 171), a perennial with dark purplish, maple-shaped leaves.

N Steppingstones

A few flagstones are planted among the flowers for quick access to the yard. See p. 104.

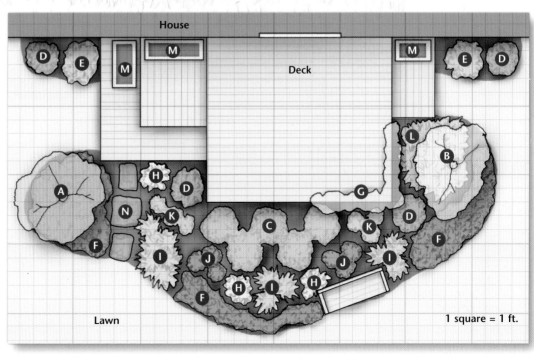

House

Deck

Lawn

1 square = 1 ft.

Site: Shady

Season: Spring

Concept: On a shady site, colorful flowers and foliage brighten the view from the deck.

A Red-vein enkianthus

G Akebia

D Variegated winter daphne

M Japanese stewartia

L Planter

C Leucothoe

H Sword fern

I Lenten rose

N Steppingstones

J Variegated hosta

E 'Bow Bells' rhododendron

F 'Debutante' Japanese andromeda

B Mountain laurel

K 'Snow Queen' barrenwort

House

Deck

C D L L L I D C

H J

M D A

F G C

B F K

N I F

E I

J E F

K

Lawn   1 square = 1 ft.

Skirting a shady deck

This design also integrates the deck with its surroundings, but it does so in a shadier environment, produced by large trees or the house.

Evergreen shrubs, ferns, and perennials form a lush skirt flowing down the hill from the deck. Flowers in shades of pink bloom from late winter through summer, brightening this shady site. The foliage is as colorful as the flowers, and much of it lasts all year. There are variegated leaves, leaves tinted when new, and leaves that blaze with color in fall. Planters offer possibilities for seasonal displays.

Like the previous design, this one catches the eye when viewed from the house, the deck, or the lawn.

Plants & Projects

A Red-vein enkianthus (use 1 plant)
A large deciduous shrub with tiered branches and small blue-green leaves that turn bright orange-red in fall. Clusters of red-veined white flowers bloom in late spring. See *Enkianthus campanulatus*, p. 167.

B Mountain laurel (use 5)
An evergreen shrub with glossy leaves and showy pink flowers in early summer. (Cultivar on facing page has red buds, too.) See *Kalmia latifolia*, p. 174.

C Leucothoe (use 3)
Clusters of sweet-scented white flowers line the stems of this evergreen shrub in spring. See *Leucothoe axillaris*, p. 174.

D Variegated winter daphne (use 3)
A compact shrub with gold-edged evergreen leaves. In late winter, purple buds open into very sweet-smelling small white flowers with a rosy tint. See *Daphne odora* 'Aureomarginata', p. 166.

E 'Bow Bells' rhododendron (use 4)
This delightful evergreen shrub nestles by the bench. Light pink bell-shaped flowers bloom in spring. New leaves start out coppery and turn green. See *Rhododendron*, p. 178.

F 'Debutante' Japanese andromeda (use 4)
In spring, this evergreen shrub bears abundant bell-shaped white flowers, and bright gold or red new leaves mingle with glossy green leaves. See *Pieris japonica*, p. 177.

G **Akebia** (use 2)
This fast-growing vine will cover the deck railings with dark green foliage for most of the year. In spring, look for small purple flowers sprinkled among the leaves. See *Akebia quinata,* p. 159.

H **Sword fern** (use 19)
Native to the Northwest, this dependable fern has long dark shiny fronds that look good all year. See Ferns: *Polystichum munitum,* p. 168.

I **Lenten rose** (use 8)
Large white, pink, purple, or greenish flowers bloom very early in spring on this handsome perennial with leathery evergreen leaves. See *Helleborus orientalis,* p. 170.

J **Variegated hosta** (use 9)
Perennials grown primarily for their foliage, hostas also bear white, lavender, or purple flowers in summer on stalks above the leaves. A cultivar with variegated green-and-white leaves will complement the nearby Lenten rose and barrenwort. See *Hosta,* p. 171.

K **'Snow Queen' barrenwort** (use 16)
One of the best shade-loving ground covers, this perennial has attractive heart-shaped foliage that changes color over the seasons. In spring, airy sprays of small white flowers show up among leaves, which have deep red margins. See *Epimedium* × *rubrum,* p. 167.

L **Planters**
Fill these with shade-loving shrubs and ferns. One per planter of the following are shown: 'Valley Fire' Japanese andromeda (see *Pieris japonica,* p. 177) is an evergreen shrub with glossy red leaves and drooping clusters of white flowers. Fragrant sarcococca (see *Sarcococca ruscifolia,* p. 180) is an evergreen shrub with very fragrant flowers in early spring. Japanese painted fern (see Ferns: *Athyrium niponicum* 'Pictum', p. 168) has fronds in shades of green, silver, maroon.

See pp. 80–81 for the following:

M Japanese stewartia (use 1)

N Steppingstones

Plant portraits

These plants can enhance a deck with lovely foliage textures and colors, as well as pretty flowers.

● = First design, pp. 80–81
▲ = Second design, pp. 82–83

'Debutante' Japanese andromeda (*Pieris japonica*, p. 177) ▲

Akebia (*Akebia quinata*, p. 159) ▲

Mountain laurel (*Kalmia latifolia*, p. 174) ▲

Fountain grass (*Pennisetum setaceum*, p. 176) ●

Variegated hosta (*Hosta*, p. 171) ▲

Compact Korean spice viburnum (*Viburnum carlesii* 'Compactum', p. 182) ●

Gateway Garden
Arbor, fence, and plantings make a handsome entry

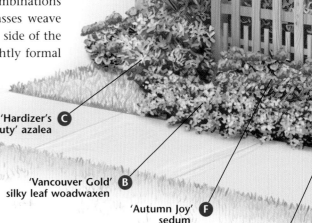

Saucer magnolia **A**

'Hardizer's Beauty' azalea **C**

'Vancouver Gold' silky leaf woadwaxen **B**

'Autumn Joy' sedum **F**

'Goldsturm' coneflower **G**

Entrances are an important part of any landscape. They can welcome visitors onto your property; highlight a special feature, such as a rose garden; or mark the passage between two areas with different character or function. The design shown here can serve any of these purposes.

A contemporary version of the old picket fence makes a friendly and attractive barrier, just enough to signal the confines of the front yard or contain the family dog. The simple vine-covered arbor provides welcoming access.

In this design the fence is stepped back on both sides of the arbor to create planting niches for small trees, shrubs, and perennials. The picketed enclosures help showcase the blossoms of azaleas and magnolias, which send fragrance over the walkway in spring. Imaginative combinations of shrubs, perennials, and grasses weave through the planting on either side of the fence. The overall effect is slightly formal but comfortable.

Plants & Projects

For many people, a picket fence and vine-covered arbor represent old-fashioned neighborly virtues. You can extend the fence and plantings as needed. The shrubs require no more than seasonal pruning to maintain size and shape.

A **Saucer magnolia** (use 2 plants) In early spring, this deciduous tree puts on a glorious display of large fragrant flowers in white, pinks, or purples. Leaves come out after the flowers fade and are large, attractive, and shiny green. The bare branches are handsome in winter. See *Magnolia × soulangiana*, p. 174.

B **'Vancouver Gold' silky leaf woadwaxen** (use 11) Tiny dark green leaves on this low-growing deciduous shrub make a pretty edge along the pavement. Masses of sunny yellow flowers will brighten the entry in early summer. Gray-green stems give an evergreen look in winter. See *Genista pilosa*, p. 169.

C **'Hardizer's Beauty' azalea** (use 8) A striking evergreen shrub beneath the magnolias. Bright pink flowers bloom in spring against a background of dark green leaves. See *Rhododendron*, p. 178.

D **Dwarf rhododendron** (use 5) This evergreen shrub forms a neat low mound of small blue-gray leaves. In spring, it bears clusters of beautiful deep purple flowers. See *Rhododendron impeditum*, p. 178.

E **'The President' clematis** (use 2) This fast-growing deciduous vine will cover the arbor with a profusion of large violet-blue flowers in early summer. See *Clematis* hybrids, p. 163.

F **'Autumn Joy' sedum** (use 8) A favorite perennial for foliage and fall flowers. It forms an attractive mass of succulent leaves topped in late summer with flat flower heads that start out pink and slowly turn rusty red. See *Sedum*, p. 181.

G **'Goldsturm' coneflower** (use 5) This perennial forms a large clump of deep green leaves. In summer and into fall, dark-eyed, daisylike gold flowers provide sunny color by the arbor. See *Rudbeckia*, p. 179.

H **'Moonshine' yarrow** (use 7) Another bright spot along the fence, this perennial bears clusters of tiny lemony yellow flowers above a mass of gray-green fernlike foliage all summer long. See *Achillea*, p. 159.

I **Dragonfly columbine** (use 6) This perennial forms a lovely mound of blue-green leaves with scalloped margins. In spring, large flowers with long spurs dangle on slender stalks above the leaves. See *Aquilegia*, p. 160.

J **'Elijah Blue' blue fescue grass** (use 14) Tucked between the woadwaxen and yarrow, bright blue blades of this clump-forming perennial offer a striking contrast in texture and color. Narrow flower spikes rise above the leaves in summer and turn tan in fall. See *Festuca ovina* var. *glauca*, p. 168.

K **'Alba' thrift** (use 12) This evergreen perennial forms a neat cushion of narrow green leaves. In spring, it sends up many stiff green stalks ending in pom-poms of pure white flowers. Scattered blooms appear through summer and fall. See *Armeria maritima*, p. 160.

L **'Birch Hybrid' bellflower** (use 23) This perennial spreads to form a low mass of heart-shaped leaves covered for most of the summer in purple-blue bell-like flowers. See *Campanula*, p. 162.

M **Fence and arbor** Made of standard dimension lumber, the fence and arbor are easy to build. A simple ladder trellis runs up the sides and over the top of the arbor to support the vines. See p. 132.

N **Paving** Flagstone, shown here, is ideal for a high-traffic entry. Choose a material to suit your site and needs. See p. 104.

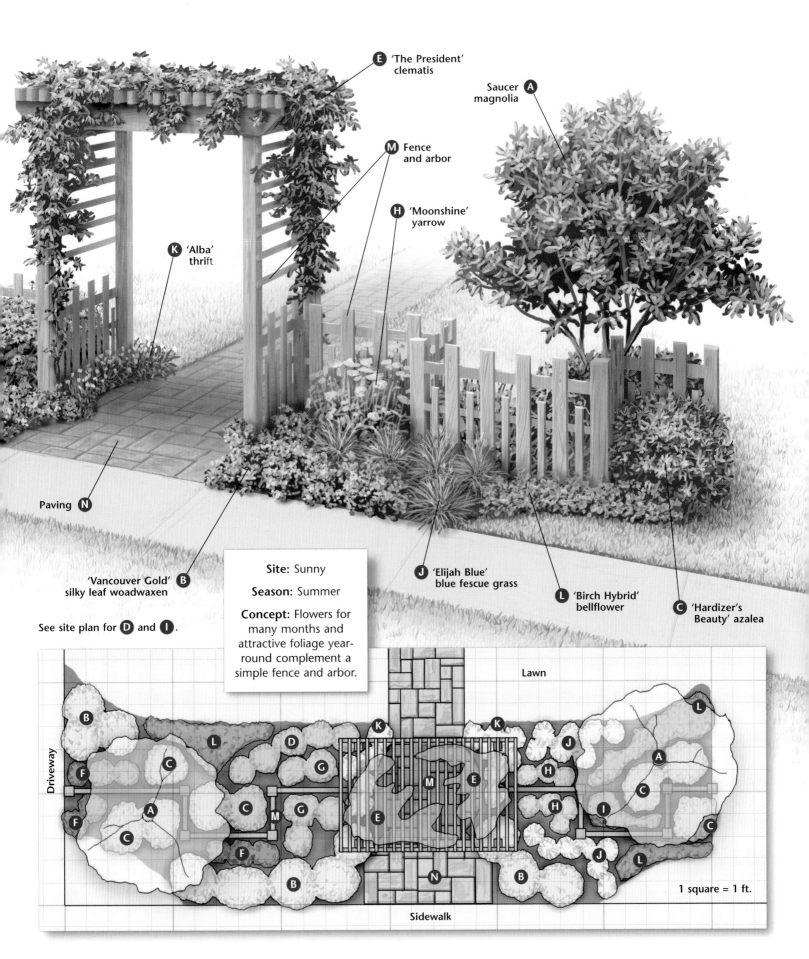

E 'The President' clematis

A Saucer magnolia

M Fence and arbor

H 'Moonshine' yarrow

K 'Alba' thrift

Paving **N**

'Vancouver Gold' silky leaf woadwaxen **B**

See site plan for **D** and **I**.

Site: Sunny

Season: Summer

Concept: Flowers for many months and attractive foliage year-round complement a simple fence and arbor.

J 'Elijah Blue' blue fescue grass

L 'Birch Hybrid' bellflower

C 'Hardizer's Beauty' azalea

Lawn

Driveway

Sidewalk

1 square = 1 ft.

Plant portraits

Combining enticing fragrance, lovely flowers, and handsome foliage, these plants create a distinctive entry.

● = First design, pp. 84–85
▲ = Second design, pp. 86–87

'Alba' thrift
(*Armeria maritima*, p. 160) ●

Saucer magnolia
(*Magnolia × soulangiana*, p. 174) ●

'Hardizer's Beauty' azalea (*Rhododendron*, p. 178) ●

'The President' clematis (*Clematis* hybrids, p. 163) ●

'Elijah Blue' blue fescue grass
(*Festuca ovina* var. *glauca*, p. 168) ●

'Springwood Pink' heath (*Erica carnea*, p. 167) ▲

Site: Sunny

Season: Early summer

Concept: Evergreen shrubs and swaying grasses replace the fence to make an engaging but effective barrier.

'Riccarrtonii' **D** fuchsia

F 'Hidcote' English lavender

A welcoming border

Not every entry calls for a fence. In this simple design, waist-high evergreen shrubs, perennials, and grasses create a deep garden bed that serves as an attractive barrier on either side of a vine-covered entry arbor.

An abundance of evergreen foliage ensures that the planting looks good year-round. The rhododendrons put on a glorious floral show in spring. Their foliage provides a handsome backdrop for the summer blossoms of fuchsias and bellflowers, the fall foliage and plumes of Japanese silver grass, and the winter blooms of the heath.

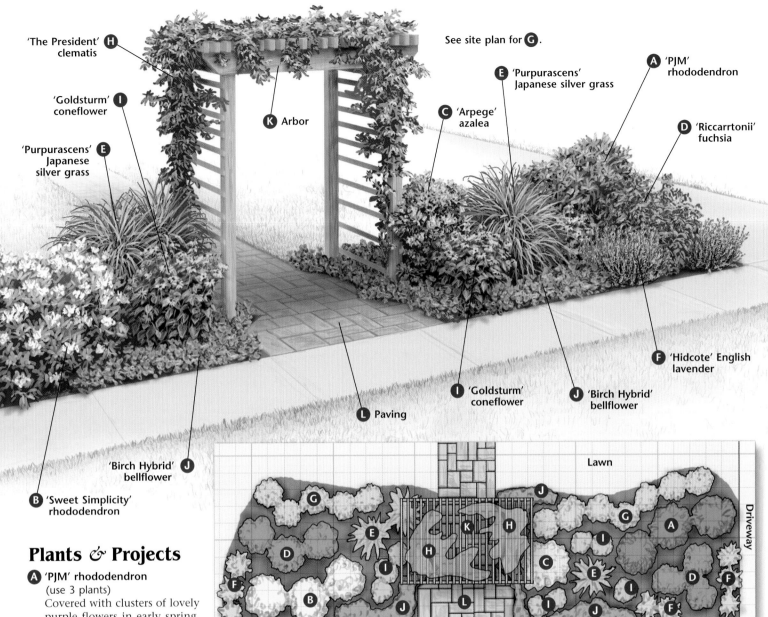

'The President' clematis **H**

'Goldsturm' coneflower **I**

'Purpurascens' Japanese silver grass **E**

See site plan for **G**.

E 'Purpurascens' Japanese silver grass

A 'PJM' rhododendron

C 'Arpege' azalea

D 'Riccarrtonii' fuchsia

K Arbor

F 'Hidcote' English lavender

I 'Goldsturm' coneflower

J 'Birch Hybrid' bellflower

L Paving

J 'Birch Hybrid' bellflower

B 'Sweet Simplicity' rhododendron

Lawn

Driveway

1 square = 1 ft.

Sidewalk

Plants & Projects

A **'PJM' rhododendron**
(use 3 plants)
Covered with clusters of lovely purple flowers in early spring, the dark green foliage of this compact evergreen shrub looks good all winter. See *Rhododendron*, p. 178.

B **'Sweet Simplicity' rhododendron** (use 3)
White blossoms edged in pink will spill over the walk when this evergreen shrub blooms in late spring. Leaves are dark green and shiny all year. See *Rhododendron*, p. 178.

C **'Arpege' azalea** (use 1)
In spring, the sweet-scented deep yellow flowers of this shrub are a treat near the walkway. Leaves are deciduous and dark green. See *Rhododendron viscosum*, p. 178.

D **'Riccarrtonii' fuchsia** (use 6)
Like a hanging basket without the fuss, this upright shrub bears a profusion of small, bright pink-and-purple flowers all summer long. Leaves are dark green with a bronzy cast. See *Fuchsia*, p. 169.

E **'Purpurascens' Japanese silver grass** (use 3)
This graceful arching perennial has purplish green leaves that turn orange-red in fall. Flower plumes may rise above the leaves in late summer and turn

to fluffy seed heads in winter. See *Miscanthus sinensis*, p. 175.

F **'Hidcote' English lavender** (use 8)
A small evergreen shrub with fragrant gray-green leaves. Masses of scented, deep purple flowers rise on long stalks above the leaves in early summer. See *Lavandula angustifolia*, p. 174.

G **'Springwood Pink' heath** (use 12)
From winter to spring this evergreen shrub makes a carpet

of pink blooms along the lawn edge. Very small, green, needle-like foliage brightens the edge of the planting the rest of the year. See *Erica carnea*, p. 167.

See p. 84 for the following:

H **'The President' clematis** (use 2)

I **'Goldsturm' coneflower** (use 8)

J **'Birch Hybrid' bellflower** (use 32)

K **Arbor**

L **Paving**

A Green Space for Recycling

Screen off bins with a fence, foliage, and flowers

Sometimes the simplest landscaping project packs a surprisingly big punch. This design hides recycling bins, an increasingly common residential feature, from view, while making access easy and recycling chores more enjoyable. The paving, screen, and plantings can be installed in a weekend. With this small investment of time and money you can turn one of the most frequently visited parts of your property into an eye-catching feature.

A wooden screen angles around a paved area that is roomy enough for several bins, yard-waste containers, and trash cans. Made of thin vertical slats, the screen obscures the area from view yet allows ventilation. It opens at the driveway, where the bins are most likely to be wheeled out. Against the screen, a simple planting of shrubs, vines, and perennials makes a bold year-round display.

Foliage, flowers, and fruit display warm colors all year. The planting's cheeriness will be especially appreciated during the dreary winter months. As shown here, it offers sweet-scented yellow blossoms of Chinese witch hazel, the oranges and reds of the Scotch heather, and the bright red twigs of the dogwood.

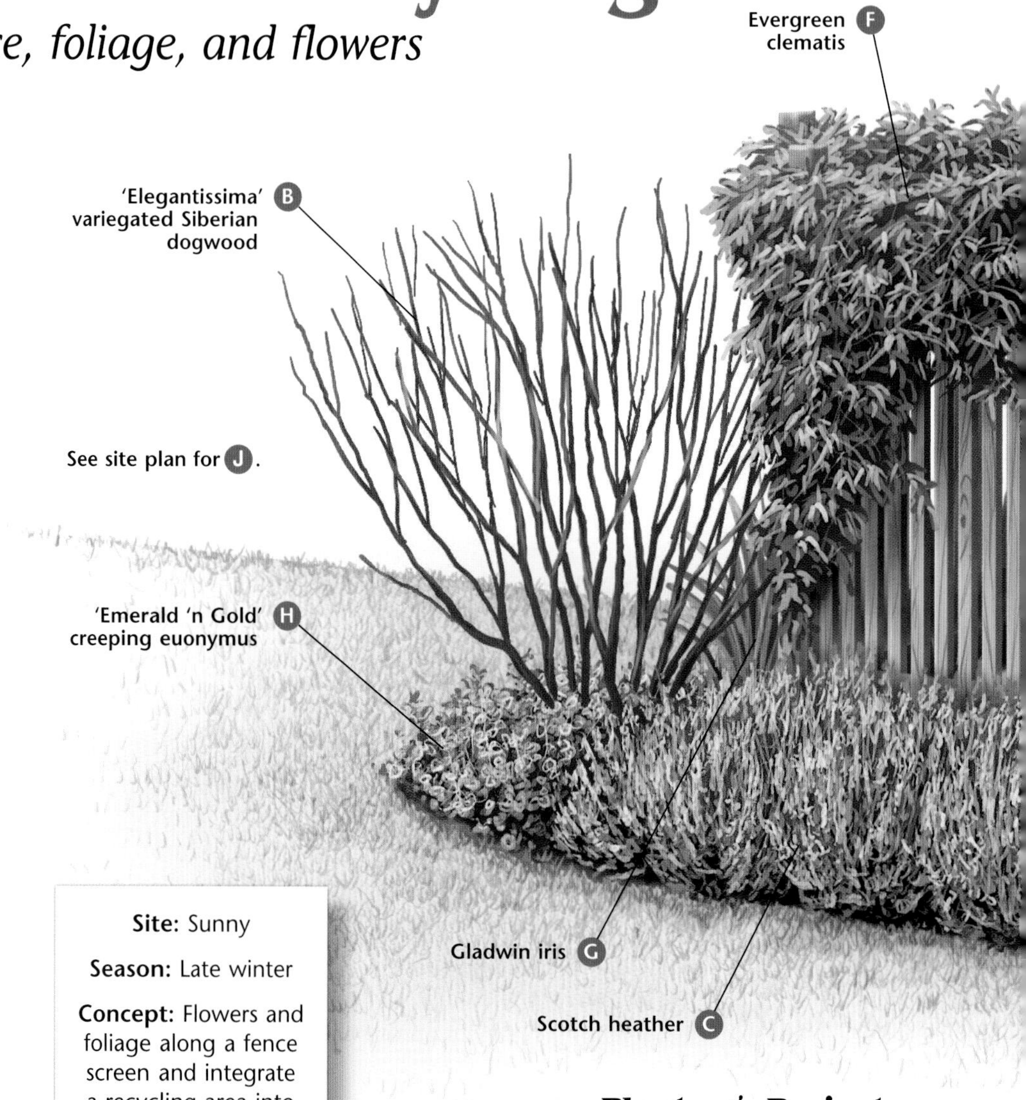

Evergreen clematis **F**

'Elegantissima' variegated Siberian dogwood **B**

See site plan for **J**.

'Emerald 'n Gold' creeping euonymus **H**

Gladwin iris **G**

Scotch heather **C**

Site: Sunny

Season: Late winter

Concept: Flowers and foliage along a fence screen and integrate a recycling area into the backyard.

Plants & Projects

Spend a weekend installing this project. Then keep it looking good with just seasonal care. The clematis can be left alone to cover the screen or pruned to concentrate the foliage on the top. Shear the spent flowers off the heather in late winter, and prune the euonymus to keep it from climbing the dogwood.

A **Chinese witch hazel**
(use 1 plant)
A small deciduous tree or large shrub with gray-green leaves that turn yellow in fall. In winter, before leaves appear, it bears very fragrant flowers with

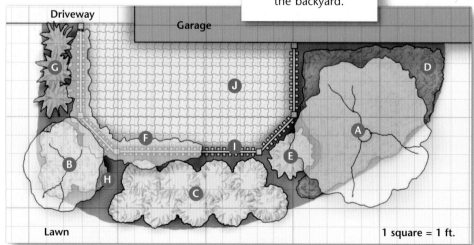

Driveway · Garage · G · J · D · F · I · A · B · H · E · C · Lawn · 1 square = 1 ft.

I Screen **E** 'Harbour Dwarf' heavenly bamboo **A** Chinese witch hazel **D** Foxberry

yellow straplike petals. See *Hamamelis mollis*, p. 170.

B **'Elegantissima' variegated Siberian dogwood** (use 1)
Colorful all year, this deciduous shrub has white flowers in spring, green-and-white leaves through fall, and bright red bark in winter. See *Cornus alba*, p. 164.

C **Scotch heather** (use 9)
This evergreen shrub forms a mass of tiny green scalelike leaves that turn red, orange, or yellow in winter. In summer, it bears small white, pink, or purple flowers. The colors of foliage and flower vary with the cultivar. The one shown has warm winter tones. See *Calluna vulgaris*, p. 162.

D **Foxberry** (use 15)
A Northwest native, this evergreen shrub will fill the space under the tree with glossy dark green foliage. Clusters of small pinkish white flowers in late spring are followed by sour red berries that you can share with the birds. See *Vaccinium vitis-idaea*, p. 182.

E **'Harbour Dwarf' heavenly bamboo** (use 1)
This compact, bushy evergreen shrub forms a clump of slender stems and lacy leaves, bronze to green in spring and summer, bright crimson in winter. See *Nandina domestica*, p. 175.

F **Evergreen clematis** (use 1)
A fast-growing evergreen vine with lustrous dark green leaves. White flowers will cover the foliage and perfume the air in early spring. See *Clematis armandii*, p. 163.

G **Gladwin iris** (use 3)
A perennial with glossy, lance-shaped leaves. Clusters of purple flowers in summer are followed by interesting seedpods that split to reveal striking bright orange seeds. See *Iris foetidissima*, p. 173.

H **'Emerald 'n Gold' creeping euonymus** (use 3)
This spreading shrub makes a tough, good-looking ground cover. Small shiny evergreen leaves are gold and green and have a pink tinge in winter. See *Euonymus fortunei*, p. 167.

I **Screen**
A simple structure with narrow vertical "pickets," this screen is as easy to construct as it is attractive to the eye. See p. 130.

J **Paving**
Interlocking precast pavers laid on sand and gravel will accommodate rolling bins and make sweeping up easy. See p. 104.

Screen for a shady site

The concept here is similar to that in the preceding design—screen your recycling center from view with just a few hours' installation labor. The difference is that the plants in this design will do all the screening and thrive in dappled shade.

The foliage makes an effective and attractive screen all year, providing subtle contrasts and complements in color and texture in every season.

Starting in winter, the planting also offers flowers for many months of the year. In mild years the Christmas rose may be blooming by the drive when you make the trip to recycle holiday wrappings. It may still be in flower when the rhododendrons blossom in spring. There's another show in summer, when the foxberry, bunchberry, and heavenly bamboo bloom together.

See site plan for **I** and **J**.

Plants & Projects

A Vine maple (use 1 plant)
Anchoring one end of the planting, this small native tree (or large shrub) has lovely gray bark and light green deciduous leaves that put on a show in fall when they turn yellow, red, and purple. See *Acer circinatum*, p. 158.

B 'Moyers Red' heavenly bamboo (use 7)
A beautiful natural screen, this slender-stemmed shrub has fine-textured evergreen foliage that is red when young and turns red again in fall and winter. Fluffy clusters of white flowers decorate the "screen" in summer. See *Nandina domestica*, p. 175.

C Fragrant sarcococca (use 3)
This evergreen shrub has glossy green leaves and small white

> **Site:** Shady
>
> **Season:** Midsummer
>
> **Concept:** A living screen of lustrous foliage and fragrant flowers greens up a recycling center.

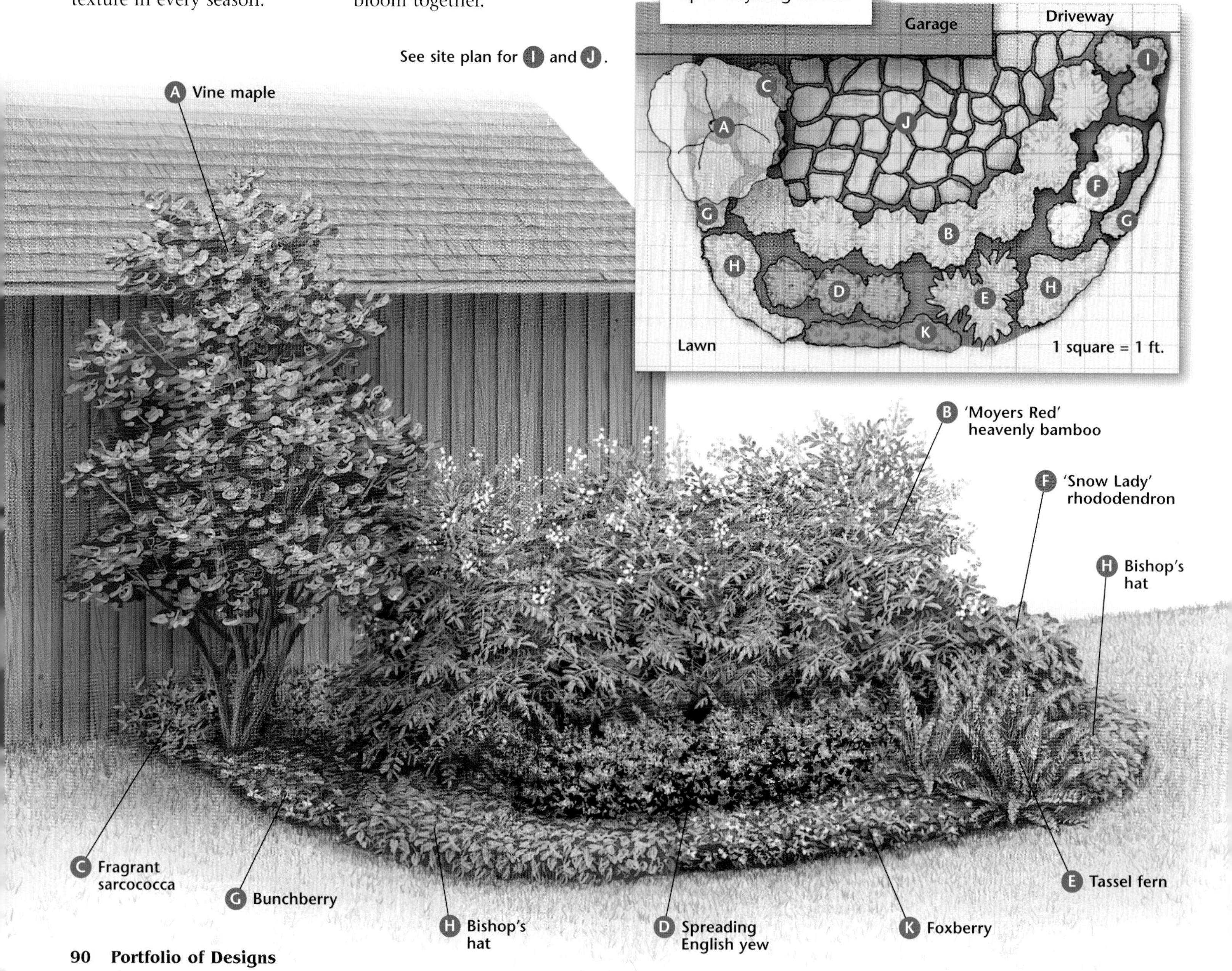

A Vine maple

Garage   Driveway

Lawn   1 square = 1 ft.

B 'Moyers Red' heavenly bamboo

F 'Snow Lady' rhododendron

H Bishop's hat

C Fragrant sarcococca

G Bunchberry

H Bishop's hat

D Spreading English yew

K Foxberry

E Tassel fern

flowers with a welcome sweet scent in late winter. See *Sarcococca ruscifolia*, p. 180.

D **Spreading English yew** (use 3)
Naturally compact and low-growing in front of the heavenly bamboo, this evergreen shrub is distinguished by large, flat, needlelike leaves that stay dark green all year. See *Taxus baccata* 'Repandens', p. 182.

E **Tassel fern** (use 3)
Stiff, lustrous evergreen fronds add fine texture and contrasting form to the rhododendrons and yews on each side of them. See Ferns: *Polystichum polyblepharum*, p. 168.

F **'Snow Lady' rhododendron** (use 3)
This evergreen shrub bears showy white, fragrant blossoms that stand out in spring against its fuzzy green foliage and the red leaves of the heavenly bamboo. See *Rhododendron*, p. 178.

G **Bunchberry** (use 14)
A native perennial ground cover, this spreads to form a very low mass of erect stems topped with shiny dark green leaves that turn red in fall. Small white, dogwoodlike flowers cover the plant from late spring into summer. See *Cornus canadensis*, p. 164.

H **Bishop's hat** (use 13)
One of the best perennial ground covers for shade. The lovely heart-shaped evergeen leaves turn from coppery to green to maroon over the summer. In spring, they are topped with sprays of small, pale pink or white flowers. See *Epimedium grandiflorum*, p. 167.

I **Christmas rose** (use 3)
This evergreen perennial forms a clump of handsome dark, shiny leaves. In winter, large white flowers open at the ends of the stems and last for weeks. See *Helleborus niger*, p. 170.

J **Paving**
Irregular flagstones in the storage area are easy to install, and they complement the free-form screen. See p. 104.

See p. 89 for the following:

K **Foxberry** (use 6)

Plant portraits

A mix of carefree plants creates or complements a colorful screen in all seasons.

● = First design, pp. 88–89
▲ = Second design, pp. 90–91

Scotch heather (*Calluna vulgaris*, p. 162) ●

Foxberry (*Vaccinium vitis-idaea*, p. 182) ● ▲

Christmas rose (*Helleborus niger*, p. 170) ▲

'Emerald 'n Gold' creeping euonymus (*Euonymus fortunei*, p. 167) ●

Evergreen clematis (*Clematis armandii*, p. 163) ●

Elegant Symmetry

Make a formal garden for your backyard

Formal landscaping often lends dignity to the public areas around a home (see pp. 24–25). Formality can also be rewarding in a more private setting. There, the groomed plants, geometric lines, and symmetrical layout of a formal garden can help to organize the surrounding landscaping, provide an elegant area for entertaining, or simply be enjoyed for their own sake.

"Formal" need not mean elaborate. This elegant design is really no more than a little perennial border in the shape of a wheel. A small decorative tree at the center and a holly hedge around the edge establish the shapes. Opposing beds of perennials are laid out along the curved hedge in mirror images of each other.

The garden will be in its glory in late summer and fall (as shown here) with a vibrant palette of foliage in reds and purples and flowers in blues, purple, rust, yellows, and golds. The show lasts a long time before the perennials die back. In winter the holly hedge and the maple will maintain the garden's structure.

Even more than other types of landscaping, formal gardens work well only when carefully correlated with other elements in the landscape, including structures and plants. A round garden can be difficult to integrate. Relate it to rectilinear elements, such as a fence or hedges. And repeat plants used in the design elsewhere in your landscape to tie things together.

Plants & Projects

Of all gardens, a formal garden most obviously reflects the efforts of its makers. After the hedge has filled in, this garden requires attention mostly to keep it looking neat—shearing the hedge, pruning, and seasonal cleanup. Cut the mums back by one-half in June to control their height. Replace them every 3 or 4 years. For more spring color, plant bulbs among the hostas and other perennials.

A **'Bloodgood' Japanese maple**
(use 1 plant)
A fine filagree of deep red leaves makes this deciduous tree a beautiful centerpiece. Foliage stays red from spring through fall. Smooth gray bark and a delicate branching habit are attractive in winter. See *Acer palmatum*, p. 159.

B **'Green Island' Japanese holly**
(use 32)
This compact evergreen shrub forms a mass of dense twigs and dark green leaves that are

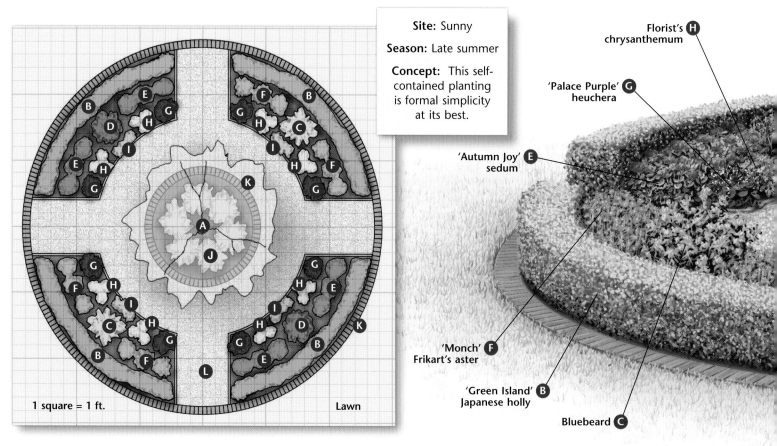

Site: Sunny

Season: Late summer

Concept: This self-contained planting is formal simplicity at its best.

1 square = 1 ft.

Lawn

Florist's **H** chrysanthemum

'Palace Purple' **G** heuchera

'Autumn Joy' **E** sedum

'Monch' **F** Frikart's aster

'Green Island' **B** Japanese holly

Bluebeard **C**

ideal for formal shearing. See *Ilex crenata*, p. 173.

C Bluebeard (use 2)
This loose, open shrub makes a perfect mound of gray-green stems and foliage. In late summer, the upper parts of the stems are lined with blue flowers that last for many weeks. See *Caryopteris × clandonensis*, p. 163.

D New England aster (use 2)
This perennial forms a stout clump of dark leaves topped from late summer through fall with masses of pink, purple, or violet flowers. See *Aster novae-angliae*, p. 160.

E 'Autumn Joy' sedum (use 12)
A standout in the fall garden, this perennial has succulent gray-green leaves and bears unusual flat clusters of flowers that start out light pink in late summer and deepen to rusty red. See *Sedum*, p. 181.

F 'Monch' Frikart's aster (use 12)
Deep blue flowers with bright golden centers cover the dark green leaves of this carefree perennial and last for many weeks from late summer on. See *Aster × frikartii*, p. 160.

G 'Palace Purple' heuchera (use 8)
Showy mounds of large, bronzy purple, maple-shaped foliage echo the Japanese maple. Leaves may survive mild winters on these semievergreen perennials. Airy sprays of small white flowers rise on thin stalks above the foliage in summer. See *Heuchera*, p. 171.

H Florist's chrysanthemum (use 24)
Autumn wouldn't be as colorful without these old-time favorite perennials, which bear masses of daisylike flowers in fall. Shown here are a mix of purples, oranges, and golds that complement the other fall colors in this scheme. When the plant isn't in bloom, dark green, lobed leaves are attractive. See *Chrysanthemum × morifolium*, p. 163.

I 'Vera Jameson' sedum (use 8)
Succulent purple-gray leaves cover the short stems of this carefree perennial, topped in late summer with flat clusters of pink flowers that last through fall. See *Sedum*, p. 181.

J 'Krossa Regal' hosta (use 6)
This long-lived perennial will fill the inner circle with vase-shaped mounds of lovely powdery blue-green leaves that contrast beautifully with the red maple. See *Hosta*, p. 171.

K Edging
The inner and outer circles are made of bricks laid perpendicular to the beds. See p. 104.

L Walkway
Crushed stone is easy to install and suits the simple lines of this design. See p. 104.

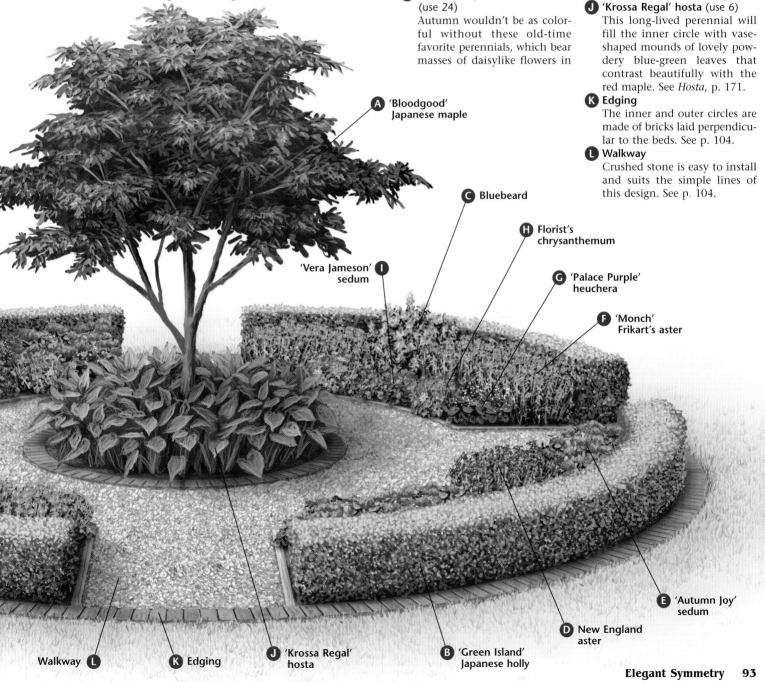

A 'Bloodgood' Japanese maple

C Bluebeard

H Florist's chrysanthemum

I 'Vera Jameson' sedum

G 'Palace Purple' heuchera

F 'Monch' Frikart's aster

E 'Autumn Joy' sedum

D New England aster

L Walkway

K Edging

J 'Krossa Regal' hosta

B 'Green Island' Japanese holly

A formal patio

In this design, a terrace large enough to accommodate a table and chairs is framed by formal beds, creating a lovely spot for an intimate lunch or a restful hour with a favorite book.

A few of the perennials are the same as in the preceding design, but the basic layout has a different look and feel. Four flowering hydrangea trees anchor the corners and provide a sense of enclosure.

White and blue are the dominant colors here, enlivened by the peach, apricot, and orange tones of tea roses, daylilies, and potted marigolds. The blooms will be at their peak in midsummer, when Northwesterners are most likely to linger on the patio. But the roses will treat you to delicious scents and sights all season.

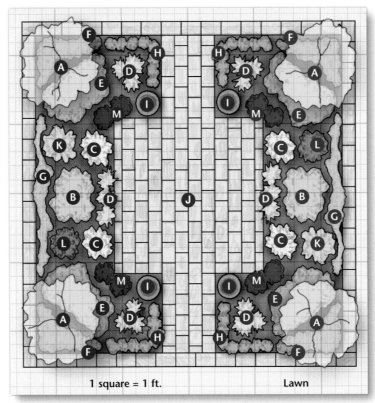

1 square = 1 ft. Lawn

Plants & Projects

Ⓐ Peegee hydrangea
(use 4 plants)
A deciduous shrub trained to grow as a small single-trunk tree. In midsummer, branch tips burst with huge clusters of creamy flowers that turn pink and age to tan in late fall. Many nurseries sell these shrubs already trained to a single trunk. See *Hydrangea paniculata* 'Grandiflora', p. 172.

Ⓑ 'Just Joey' rose (use 2)
A large robust shrub, this rose has glossy deciduous leaves and a profusion of very large fragrant flowers from spring through fall. Frilly-edged, orangy pink petals fade to white. See *Rosa*, p. 178.

Site: Sunny

Season: Late summer

Concept: A formal setting for an intimate gathering, enhanced by small trees and scented flowers.

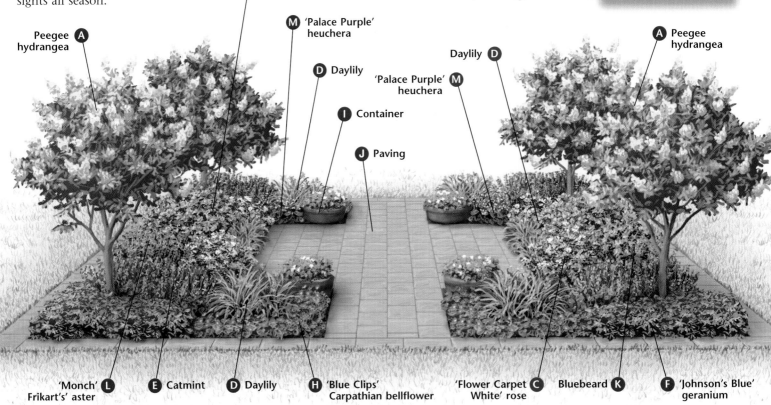

Ⓑ 'Just Joey' rose

Ⓜ 'Palace Purple' heuchera

See site plan for Ⓖ.

Peegee hydrangea Ⓐ

Ⓓ Daylily

Ⓘ Container

Ⓙ Paving

Daylily Ⓓ

'Palace Purple' heuchera Ⓜ

Ⓐ Peegee hydrangea

'Monch' Ⓛ Frikart's' aster

Ⓔ Catmint

Ⓓ Daylily

Ⓗ 'Blue Clips' Carpathian bellflower

'Flower Carpet White' rose Ⓒ

Bluebeard Ⓚ

Ⓕ 'Johnson's Blue' geranium

(C) 'Flower Carpet White' rose
(use 4)
Clusters of lightly scented white flowers will blanket the low, arching branches of this deciduous shrub from spring to fall. See *Rosa,* p. 178.

(D) Daylily (use 18)
Graceful perennial with grassy leaves and large lilylike flowers in many colors and bloom times. For months of color, plant early-, midseason-, and late-blooming varieties. See *Hemerocallis,* p. 170.

(E) Catmint (use 20)
This perennial forms soft mounds of light green foliage covered with small violet-blue flowers in early summer and off and on through fall. See *Nepeta × faassenii,* p. 175.

(F) 'Johnson's Blue' geranium
(use 24)
A perennial with handsome jagged-edged leaves and clusters of blue flowers. It blooms from early summer to fall. See *Geranium,* p. 169.

(G) Ajuga (use 38)
This evergreen perennial spreads to form a thick carpet of foliage that is covered in early spring with vivid blue flowers. Cultivars offer green or purple-bronze leaves. See *Ajuga reptans,* p. 159.

(H) 'Blue Clips' Carpathian bellflower (use 32)
This perennial forms a delicate mound of heart-shaped evergreen leaves. Small, sky blue flowers bloom most of the summer. See *Campanula carpatica,* p. 162.

(I) Containers
For bright accents on the terrace, fill the pots with long-blooming annuals. Marigolds and dahlias in bright oranges and whites are shown here.

(J) Paving
Although flagstone is shown here, choose the paving material that complements your home. See p. 104.

See p. 93 for the following:

(K) Bluebeard (use 2)

(L) 'Monch' Frikart's aster (use 2)

(M) 'Palace Purple' heuchera
(use 8)

Plant portraits

These well-behaved, low-care trees, shrubs, and perennials bring form, texture, flowers, and scent to a formal garden.

● = First design, pp. 92–93
▲ = Second design, pp. 94–95

'Blue Clips' Carpathian bellflower
(*Campanula carpatica,* p. 162) ▲

Ajuga
(*Ajuga reptans,* p. 159) ▲

Bluebeard (*Caryopteris × clandonensis,* p. 163) ● ▲

New England aster (*Aster novae-angliae,* p. 160) ●

Florist's chrysanthemum
(*Chrysanthemum × morifolium,* p. 163) ●

'Bloodgood' Japanese maple
(*Acer palmatum,* p. 159) ●

Guide to Installation

In this section, we introduce the hard but rewarding work of landscaping. Here you'll find the information you need about all the tasks required to install any of the designs in this book, organized in the order in which you'd most likely tackle them. Clearly written text and numerous illustrations help you learn how to plan the job; clear the site; construct paths, patios, ponds, fences, arbors, and trellises; prepare the planting beds; and install and maintain the plantings. Roll up your sleeves and dig in. In just a few weekends you can create a landscape feature that will provide years of enjoyment.

Organizing Your Project

If your gardening experience is limited to mowing the lawn, pruning the bushes, and growing some flowers and vegetables, the thought of starting from scratch and installing a whole new landscape feature might be intimidating. But in fact, adding one of the designs in this book to your property is completely within reach, if you approach the job the right way. The key is to divide the project into a series of steps and take them one at a time. This is how professional landscapers work. It's efficient and orderly, and it makes even big jobs seem manageable.

On this and the facing page, we explain how to think your way through a landscaping project and anticipate the various steps. Subsequent topics in this section describe how to do each part of the job. Detailed instructions and illustrations cover all the techniques you'll need to install any design from start to finish.

The step-by-step approach
Choose a design and adapt it to your site. The designs in this book address parts of the home landscape. In the most attractive and effective home landscapes, all the various parts work together. Don't be afraid to change the shape of beds; alter the number, kinds, and positions of plants; or revise paths and structures to bring them into harmony with their surroundings.

To see the relationships with your existing landscape, you can draw the design on a scaled plan of your property. Or you can work on the site itself, placing wooden stakes, pots, or whatever is handy to represent plants and structures.

Lay out the design on site. Once you've decided what you want to do, you'll need to lay out the paths and structures and outline the beds. Some people are comfortable pacing off distances and relying on their eye to judge sizes and relative positions. Others prefer to transfer the grid from the plan full size onto the site, using garden lime (a white powder available at nurseries) like chalk on a blackboard to "draw" a grid or outlines of planting beds.

Digging postholes

Amending soil

16-16-16

COMPOST

Clear the site. (See pp. 100–101.) Sometimes you have to work around existing features — a nice big tree, a building or fence, a sidewalk — but it's usually easiest to start a new landscaping project by removing unwanted structures or pavement and killing, cutting down, or uprooting all the plants. This can generate a lot of debris to dispose of, but it's often worth the trouble to make a fresh start.

Make provisions for water. (See pp. 102–103.) While water is in plentiful supply during the rest of the year, summer in the Northwest is usually a time of extended drought. Newly installed plantings will require regular summer irrigation for a year or two. Although drought-tolerant plants are increasingly popular, many plantings often require some summer watering even after the plants are well established. To grow healthy plants and conserve water during summer droughts, plan for irrigation from the start of your project.

Build the "hardscape." (See pp. 104–133.) Hardscape includes landscape structures such as fences, trellises, arbors, retaining walls, walkways, edging, and outdoor lighting. Install these elements before you start any planting.

Prepare the soil. (See pp. 134–137.) On most properties, it's uncommon to find soil that's as good as it should be for growing plants. Typically, the soil around a new house is shallow, compacted, and infertile. Some plants tolerate such poor conditions, but they don't thrive. To grow healthy, attractive plants, you need to improve the quality of the soil throughout the entire area that you're planning to plant.

Do the planting and add mulch. (See pp. 138–143.) Putting plants in the ground gives instant gratification. Mulching the soil helps control weeds and retain moisture, and it makes the area look neat even while the plants are still small.

Maintain the planting. (See pp. 143–155.) Most plantings need regular watering and occasional weeding for the first year or two. After that you'll have to do some routine maintenance — watering, pruning, shaping, cutting back, and cleaning up — to keep the plants looking their best. Depending on the design you've chosen, this may take as little as a few hours a year or as much as an hour or two every week throughout the growing season.

Planting

Setting flagstones

Clearing the Site

The site you've chosen for a landscaping project may or may not need to be cleared of fences, old pavement, construction debris, and other objects. Unless your house is newly built, the site will almost certainly be covered with plants.

Before you start cutting plants down, try to find someone to identify them for you. As you walk around together, make a sketch that shows which plants are where, and attach labels to the plants, too. Determine if there are any desirable plants worth saving—mature shade trees that you should work around, large shrubs that could be pruned to complement the design. You can move or give away plants that don't fit into the new scheme. Smaller shrubs can be dug up and relocated, worthwhile perennials and ground covers

can be divided and replanted, healthy sod can be lifted and laid elsewhere. Likewise, decide which plants have to go—diseased or crooked trees, straggly or overgrown shrubs, weedy brush, invasive ground covers, tattered lawn.

You can clear small areas yourself, bundling the brush for pickup and tossing soft-stemmed plants on the compost pile, but if you have lots of woody brush or any trees to remove, you might want to hire someone else to do the job. A crew armed with power tools can turn a thicket into a pile of wood chips in just a few hours. Have them pull out the roots and grind the stumps, too. Save the chips; they're good for surfacing paths, or you can use them as mulch.

Working around a tree

If there are any large, healthy trees on your site, be careful as you work around them. It's okay to prune off some of a tree's limbs, as shown on the facing page, but respect its trunk and its roots. Keep heavy equipment from beneath the tree's canopy, and don't lower the level of the soil there or raise it more than a few inches. Try never to cut or wound the bark on the trunk (don't nail things to a tree), because that exposes the tree to disease organisms.

Killing perennial weeds

Some common weeds that sprout back from perennial roots or runners are dandelion, bindweed, blackberry, dock, plantain, and creeping buttercup. Garden plants that can become weedy include bamboo, English ivy, creeping St.-Johnswort, pampas grass, broom, and mint. Once they get established, perennial weeds are hard to eliminate. You can't just cut off the tops, because the plants keep sprouting back. You need to dig the weeds out, smother them, or kill them with an herbicide, and it's better to do this before you plant a bed.

Digging. You can often do a good job of removing a perennial weed if you dig carefully at the base of the stems, find the roots, and follow them as far as possible through the soil, pulling out every bit of root that you find. This is relatively easy with taprooted plants such as dandelions. Plants with roots that go deeper than you can dig or those that spread by runners are difficult to eradicate all at once. Most plants will resprout from the bits that you miss, but these sprouts are easy to pull.

Smothering. This technique is easier than digging, particularly for eradicating large infestations, but much slower. First mow or cut the tops of the weeds as close to the

Smothering weeds

❶ Smothering kills weeds by depriving them of light. Cut the tops off close to the ground.

❷ Cover with thick newspaper or cardboard.

❸ Top with several inches of mulch. Wait a few months to be sure weeds are dead; then till rotted newspaper and mulch into the soil.

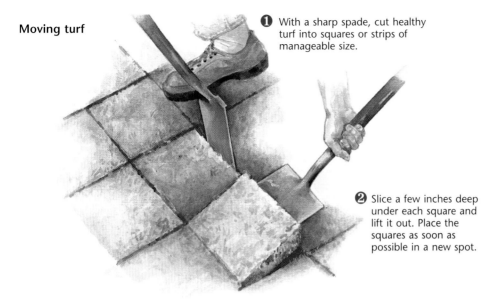

Moving turf

❶ With a sharp spade, cut healthy turf into squares or strips of manageable size.

❷ Slice a few inches deep under each square and lift it out. Place the squares as soon as possible in a new spot.

ground as possible (see ❶ on the facing page). Then cover the area with sections from the newspaper, overlapped like shingles ❷, or flattened-out cardboard boxes. Top with a layer of mulch, such as compost, straw, grass clippings, or wood chips, spread several inches deep ❸.

Smothering works by excluding light, which stops photosynthesis. If any shoots reach up through the covering and produce green leaves, pull them out immediately. Wait a few months, until you're sure the weeds are dead, before you dig into the smothered area and plant there.

Spraying. Herbicides are chemicals that kill weeds. They can be fast and effective but must be chosen and applied with care. Ask at the nursery for those that break down quickly into less toxic substances, and make sure the weed you're trying to kill is listed on the product label. Apply all herbicides exactly as directed by the manufacturer. Take care to keep herbicides off desirable plants. After spraying, you usually have to wait from one to four weeks for the weed to die completely, and some weeds need to be sprayed a second or third time before they give up. Some weeds just "melt away" when they die, but if there are tough or woody stems and roots, you'll need to dig them up and discard them.

Replacing turf

If you're planning to add a landscape feature where you now have lawn, you can "recycle" the turf to repair or extend the lawn elsewhere on your property.

The drawing above shows a technique for removing relatively small areas of strong healthy turf for replanting elsewhere. First, with a sharp spade, cut it into squares or strips about 1 to 2 ft. square (these small pieces are easy to lift) ❶. Then slice a few inches deep under each square and lift the squares, roots and all, like brownies from a pan ❷. Quickly transplant the squares to a previously prepared site. If necessary, level the turf with a water-filled roller from a rental business. Water well until the roots are established. You can rent a sod-cutting machine for larger areas.

If you don't need the turf anywhere else, or if it's straggly or weedy, leave it in place and kill the grass. One way to kill grass is to cover it with a tarp or a sheet of black plastic for about four weeks during the heat of summer. A single application of herbicide kills some grasses, but you may need to spray vigorous turf twice. After you've killed the grass, dig or till the bed, shredding the turf, roots and all, and mixing it into the soil. This is hard work if the soil is dry but less so if the ground has been softened by watering or a recent rain.

Removing large limbs

If there are large trees on your property now, you may want to remove some of the lower limbs so you can walk and see underneath them and so more light can reach plantings you're planning beneath them. Major pruning of large trees is a job for a professional arborist, but you can remove limbs smaller than 4 in. in diameter and less than 10 ft. above the ground yourself with a simple bow saw or pole saw.

Use the three-step procedure shown below to remove large limbs safely and without harming the tree. First, saw partway through the bottom of the limb, approximately 1 ft. out from the trunk ❶. This keeps the bark from tearing down the trunk when the limb falls. Then make a corresponding cut an inch or so farther out down through the limb ❷. Finally, remove the stub ❸. Undercut it slightly or hold it as you finish the cut, so it doesn't fall away and peel bark off the trunk. Note that the cut is not flush with the trunk but is just outside the thick area at the limb's base, called the branch collar. Leaving the branch collar helps the wound heal quickly and naturally. Wound dressing is considered unnecessary today.

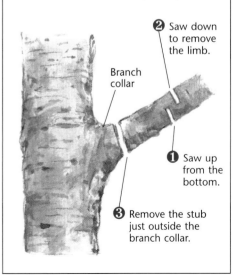

❷ Saw down to remove the limb.

Branch collar

❶ Saw up from the bottom.

❸ Remove the stub just outside the branch collar.

Water for Your Plants

The rainy season in the Northwest is usually followed by a drought that can last from mid-July through October. This dry period makes watering a critical concern of gardeners. Though some plants will survive long dry periods once established, almost all plants will need regular watering the first few years after planting. And some will need summer watering their entire life to look their best.

But there is more at stake than just the survival of plants. Conservation of water in summer is a growing concern in the region. Because outdoor landscapes use a large portion of urban water, efficient home watering systems can play an important role in conservation efforts.

So make water conservation part of your landscape planning from the beginning. The box below outlines effective water-saving practices for home landscapes. (See pp. 146–147 for more on when and how much to water.) You can also consult your local water district for advice about watering gardens and lawns.

Watering systems

One of the best ways to conserve water is to use an efficient delivery system. The simplest watering systems — watering cans and handheld hoses — are also the most limited and inefficient. They can be adequate for watering new transplants, containers, or widely separated individual plants. But sprinkling plants in an entire bed with a hose and nozzle for even an hour may provide less water than half an inch of rainfall. And wetting just the top few inches of soil this way encourages shallow root growth, making it necessary to water more frequently. To provide enough water to soak the soil to a depth of a foot or more, you need a system that can run untended for extended periods.

Hose-end sprinklers are easy to set up and leave to soak an area. But they're also inefficient: Water is blown away by wind. It runs off sloped or paved areas. It is applied unevenly, or it falls too far away from individual plants to be of use to them. And because sprinklers soak leaves as well as soil, the damp foliage may breed fungal diseases.

Low-volume irrigation. For landscape plantings like those in this book, low-volume irrigation systems are the most efficient and offer the most flexibility and control. Frequently called "drip" irrigation systems, they deliver water at low pressure through a network of plastic pipes, hoses, and tubing and a variety of emitters and microsprinklers. Such systems are designed to apply water slowly and directly to the roots of targeted plants, so very little water is lost to runoff and evaporation or wasted on plants that don't need it. Because water is usually applied at soil level, the risk of foliar diseases is reduced. And because less soil is watered, weeds are also discouraged.

Simple low-volume systems can be attached to ordinary outdoor faucets or garden hoses and controlled manually, just like a sprinkler. You can set up such a system in less than an hour. Sophisticated systems include (1) their own attachment to your main water supply, (2) a network of valves and buried pipes that allow you to divide your property into zones, and (3) an electronic control device that can automatically water each zone at preset times for preset durations. Such systems often incorporate sprinkler systems for lawns.

A person with modest mechanical skills and basic tools can plan and install a low-volume irrigation system. Extensive multi-zoned systems (particularly those with

Water-Wise Practices

Choose plants carefully. Many plants that do well in the Northwest's wet winters and dry summers are marked as "water-wise" plants at local nurseries and garden centers. Also, look for plants native to the region—they're adapted by nature for conditions here.

Group plants with similar water needs. Position plants that require the most water near the house, where they can be more easily tended and served by watering systems. Use drought-tolerant plants farther from the house.

Plant in fall. This way, new plants will have the cooler, wetter winter and spring seasons to become established before facing the summer drought.

Mulch plantings. A 2- to 3-in. layer of mulch reduces evaporation by keeping the soil cool and sheltering it from wind.

Create water-retaining basins. Use these to direct irrigation water to large plants. Make a low soil mound around the plant's perimeter, at its drip line. (Basins aren't necessary in drip-irrigated beds.)

Limit lawn size. Lawns demand lots of water. Reduce the size of your lawn by planting beds, borders, and less-thirsty ground covers.

Water in the morning. Lower morning temperatures and less wind mean less water is lost to evaporation.

Adjust watering to conditions. Water less during cool weather in the spring and fall. During the rainy season, turn off automatic timers.

Install, monitor, and maintain an irrigation system. Even a simple drip system conserves water. Once it's installed, check and adjust the equipment regularly.

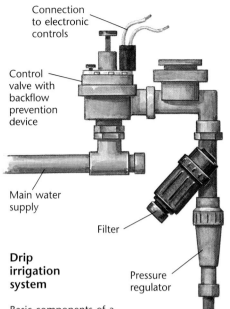

Connection to electronic controls

Control valve with backflow prevention device

Main water supply

Filter

Pressure regulator

Drip irrigation system

Basic components of a drip irrigation system are shown here. Individual systems will vary. Several common types of emitters are shown; systems can incorporate others.

their own attachment to the main water supply) are more difficult to design and install. If you tackle one, have a professional review your plans before you start. You can buy kits or individual system components from garden centers, nurseries, or specialty suppliers. (The main components of low-volume systems are outlined below.) Although most manufacturers provide helpful instructions, good criteria for choosing among different local suppliers are their knowledge of system design and installation and their ability to help you with both. A supplier may charge for this service, but good advice is worth the money.

Low-volume-system components. Any irrigation system connected to a domestic water supply needs a **backflow prevention device** (also called an antisiphon device) at the point of connection to the water supply to protect drinking water from contamination. Backflow devices are often mandated by building codes, so check with

local health or building officials to determine if a specific type of backflow prevention device is required.

Install a **filter** to prevent minerals and flakes that slough off metal water pipes from clogging the emitters. You'll need to clean the filter regularly. Between the filter and emitters, all hoses and tubing should be plastic, not metal.

Pressure regulators reduce the main's water pressure to levels required by the system's low-volume emitters.

Supply lines deliver water from the source to the emitters. Some systems incorporate buried lines of rigid plastic pipe to carry water to plantings anywhere on the property. For aboveground use, you'll need flexible tubing designed specifically for low-volume irrigation.

Emitters and **soaker hoses** deliver the water to the plants. A wide range of emitters are available for different kinds of plants and garden situations. Various drip fittings, bubblers, and microsprinklers can

be plugged into the flexible plastic tubing. A single emitter or a group of emitters might serve individual or groups of plants. Soaker hoses and "ooze" tubes seep or drip water along their length. Consult with your supplier about which delivery systems best meet your plants' needs.

A **timer** or **electronic controller** helps ensure efficient water use. Unlike you, a controller won't forget and leave the water on too long. (It may also water during a rainstorm, however.) Used in conjunction with zoned plantings, these devices provide control and flexibility to deal with the specific water needs of groups of plants or even individual specimens. They also allow you to go on vacation confident that your plants will get enough water.

Installation. Permanent irrigation equipment should be installed early in any landscaping project. Lay underground piping that crosses paths, patios, or similar landscape features after the site is cleared but before installing any of these permanent features. It is best to lay pipes in planting areas, including lawns, after you have prepared the soil. That way, you won't damage the piping when digging or rototilling. Install underground pipe in trenches dug to the appropriate depth. Then temporarily cap the ends. Hook up the aboveground tubing and position emitters after planting.

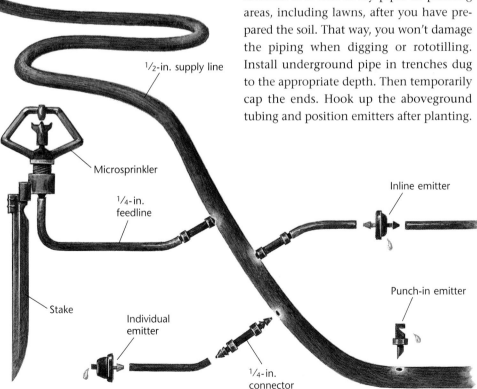

½-in. supply line

Microsprinkler

¼-in. feedline

Inline emitter

Stake

Individual emitter

¼-in. connector

Punch-in emitter

Making Paths and Walkways

Every landscape needs paths and walkways if for no other reason than to keep your feet dry as you move from one place to another. A path can also divide and define the spaces in the landscape, orchestrate the way the landscape is viewed, and even be a key element enhancing its beauty.

Whether it is a graceful curving garden path or a utilitarian slab leading to the garage, a walk has two main functional requirements: durability and safety. It should hold up through seasonal changes. It should provide a well-drained surface that is easy to walk on and to maintain.

A path's function helps determine its surface and its character. In general, heavily trafficked walkways leading to a door, garage, or shed need hard, smooth (but not slick) surfaces and should take you where you want to go fairly directly. A path to a backyard play area could be a strip of soft wood bark, easy on the knees of rambunctious children. A relaxed stroll in the garden might require only a hopscotch collection of flat stones meandering from one prized plant to another.

Before laying out a walk or path, spend some time observing existing traffic patterns. If your path makes use of a route people already take (particularly children), they'll be more likely to stay on the path and off the lawn or flowers. Avoid areas that are slow to drain. When determining path width, consider whether the path must accommodate rototillers and wheelbarrows or two strollers walking abreast, or just provide steppingstone access for maintaining the plants.

Dry-laid paths

You can make a path simply by laying bricks or spreading wood chips on top of bare earth. While quick and easy, this method has serious drawbacks. Laid on the surface, with no edging to contain them, loose materials are soon scattered, and solid materials are easily jostled out of place. If the earth base doesn't drain very well, the path will be a swamp after a rainstorm. Where winter temperatures dip below freezing and then warm up, the cycles of freezing and thawing expand and contract the soil, moving path and walkway materials laid on it. The effect of this "frost heaving" is minimal on loose materials such as wood chips or gravel, but it can shift brick and stone significantly out of line, making the path unsightly and potentially dangerous.

The method we recommend—laying surface material on an excavated base of sand or gravel, or both—minimizes these problems. Water moves through sand and gravel quickly, and such a base "cushions" the surface materials from any freeze-thaw movement of the underlying soil. Excavation can place the path surface at ground level, where the surrounding soil or an edging can contain loose materials and keep solid materials from shifting.

All styles, from a wood-bark path to a cut-stone entry walk, and all the materials discussed in this section can be laid on an excavated base of sand or gravel, alone or in combination.

Drainage

Few things are worse than a path dotted with puddles or icy patches. To prevent

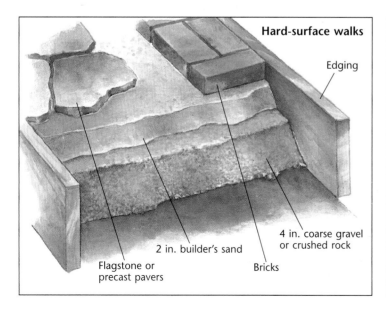

Hard-surface walks

Edging

2 in. builder's sand

Flagstone or precast pavers

Bricks

4 in. coarse gravel or crushed rock

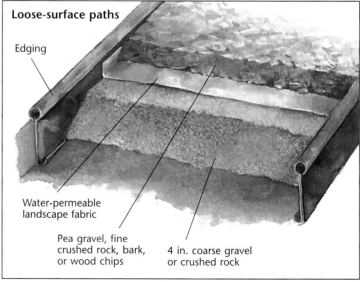

Loose-surface paths

Edging

Water-permeable landscape fabric

Pea gravel, fine crushed rock, bark, or wood chips

4 in. coarse gravel or crushed rock

Choosing a surface

Walkways and paths can be made of either solid or loose material. Your choice of material will depend on the walkway's function, your budget, and your personal preferences.

Loose materials, including bark, wood chips, crushed rock, and gravel, are best for informal and low-traffic areas. Inexpensive and simple to install, they settle, scatter, or decompose and must be replenished or replaced every few years.

Solid materials, such as brick, flagstone, and concrete pavers, are more expensive and time-consuming to install, but they are permanent, requiring only occasional maintenance. (Compacted crushed rock can also make a hard-surface walk.) Durable and handsome, they're ideal for high-traffic, "high-profile" areas.

Bark and wood chips

Perfect for a "natural" look or a quick temporary path, these loose materials can be laid directly on the soil or, if drainage is poor, on a gravel bed. Bagged materials from a nursery or garden center will be cleaner, more uniform, and considerably more expensive than bulk supplies bought by the cubic yard. In many areas, specialty suppliers of bark and sawdust offer bulk supplies at reasonable prices.

Gravel and crushed rock

Loose rounded pea gravel gives a bit underfoot, creating a "soft" but somewhat messy path. The angular facets of crushed rock and decomposed granite eventually compact into a harder, tidier path that can, if the surrounding soil is firm enough, be laid without an edging or base. Gravel and rock vary from area to area. Buy these materials by the ton or cubic yard.

Concrete pavers

Precast concrete pavers are versatile, readily available, and often the least expensive hard-surface material. They come in a range of colors and shapes, including interlocking patterns. Precast edgings are also available. Most home and garden centers carry a variety of precast pavers, which are sold by the piece.

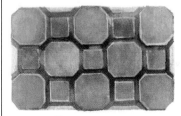

Precast pavers

Brick

Widely available in a range of sizes, colors, and textures, brick complements many design styles, both formal and informal. When carefully laid on a well-prepared sand-and-gravel base, brick provides an even, safe, and long-lasting surface. If you buy used brick, pick the densest and hardest. Avoid brick with glazed faces; the glaze traps moisture and salts, which eventually damage the brick. If you live where it regularly freezes and thaws, buy bricks rated to withstand the weather conditions.

Running bond

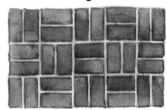

Two-brick basket weave

Herringbone

Diagonal herringbone

Flagstone

"Flagstone" is a generic term for stratified stone that can be split to form pavers. Limestone and sandstone are common paving materials. The surfaces of marble and slate are typically too smooth to make safe paving because they are slippery when wet. Cut into squares or rectangles, flagstone can be laid as individual steppingstones or in interesting patterns. Flags with irregular outlines present other patterning opportunities. Flagstones come in a range of colors, textures, and sizes. Flags for walks should be at least 2 in. thick; thinner stones fracture easily. Purchased by weight, surface area, or pallet load, flagstones are usually the most expensive paving choice.

Cut flagstone

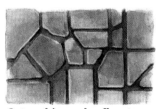

Cut and irregular flagstone

Irregular flagstone

Edgings

All walk surfaces need to be contained in some fashion along their edges. Where soil is firm or tightly knit by turf, neatly cut walls of the excavation can serve as edging. An installed edging often provides more effective containment, particularly if the walk surface is above grade. It also prevents damage to bricks or stones on the edges of paths. Walkway edgings are commonly made of 1- or 2-in.-thick lumber, thicker landscaping timbers, brick, or stone, as shown below. For a hidden edging, garden centers sell specially designed plastic edging strips that install on top of the gravel base and are covered by the adjacent soil.

Wood edging

Wood should be rot-resistant cedar or some other wood pressure-treated for ground-contact use. If you're working in loose soils, fix a deep wooden edging to support stakes with double-headed nails. When the path is laid, pull the nails, and fill and tamp behind the edging. Then drive the stakes below grade. In firmer soils, or if the edging material is not wide enough, install it on top of the gravel base. Position the top of the edging at the height of the path.

Treated dimensional lumber with support stakes

Landscape timbers with crossties laid on gravel base

Brick and stone edging

In firm soil, a row of bricks laid on edge and perpendicular to the length of the path adds stability. For a more substantial edging, stand bricks on end on the excavated soil surface, add the gravel base, and tamp earth at the base of the bricks on the outside of the excavation. Set stone edgings laid on end in the same way.

Bricks on edge, laid on gravel base

Bricks on end, laid on soil

(Continued from p. 104)

these from forming, the soil around and beneath the path should drain well. The path's location and construction should ensure that rainwater does not collect on the surface. Before you locate a path, observe runoff and drainage on your property during and after heavy rains. Avoid routing a path through areas where water courses, collects, or is slow to drain.

While both loose and solid paving can sometimes be successfully laid directly on well-drained compacted soil, laying surface materials on a base of sand and gravel will help improve drainage and minimize frost heaving. For most situations, a 4-in. gravel bed topped with 2 in. of sand will work well. Very poorly drained soils may require more gravel, an additional layer of coarse rock beneath the gravel, or even drain tiles. If you suspect that your site has serious drainage problems, consult a landscape contractor.

Finally, keep water from pooling on a walk by making its surface higher in the center than at the edges. The center of a 4-ft.-wide walk should be at least $1/2$ in. higher than its edges. If you're using a drag board to level the sand base, curve its lower edge to create this "crown." Otherwise crown the surface by eye.

Preparing the base

Having decided on location and materials, you can get down to business. The initial steps of layout and base preparation are much the same for all surface materials. Before you construct paths or walkways, check your irrigation and landscape lighting plans. If underground water or electical lighting lines will cross any paths, be sure to lay the lines first.

Layout

Lay out straight sections with stakes and string ❶. You can plot curves with stakes and "fair" the curve with a garden hose, or you can outline the curve with the hose alone, marking it with lime or sand.

Preparing the base

❶ Lay out the path with stakes, string, garden hose, and lime.

❷ Dig out path between layout string and lime lines.

❸ Install the edging.

❹ Rake out gravel base.

Lay out free-form curved sections with garden hose and mark with lime.

Mark straight sections with 1x2 stakes and string.

Drag board
Edging

❺ Level sand base with a drag board.

Excavation

The excavation depth depends on how much sand-and-gravel base your soil's drainage calls for, the thickness of the surface material, and its position above or below grade ❷. Mark the depth on a stake or stick and use this to check depth as you dig. Walking surfaces are most comfortable if they are reasonably level across their width. Check the bottom of the excavation with a level as you dig. If the walk cuts across a slope, you'll need to remove soil from the high side and use it to fill the low side to produce a level surface. If you've added soil or if the subsoil is loose, compact it by tamping.

Edging installion

Some edgings can be installed immediately after excavation; others are placed on top of the gravel portion of the base ❸. (See the sidebar "Edgings" on the facing page.) If the soil's drainage permits, you can lay soft materials, loose gravel, or crushed rock now on the excavated, tamped, and edged soil base. To control weeds, and to keep bark or chips from mixing with the subsoil, you can spread water-permeable landscape fabric over the excavated soil base.

Laying the base

Now add gravel (if required), rake it level, and compact it ❹. Use gravel up to 1 in. in diameter or $1/4$- to $3/4$-in. crushed rock, which drains and compacts well. You can rent a hand tamper (a heavy metal plate on the end of a pole) or a machine compactor if you have a large area to compact.

If you're making a loose-gravel or crushed-rock walk, add the surface material on top of the base gravel. (See "Loose materials" below.) For walks of brick, stone, or pavers, add a 2-in. layer of builder's sand, not the finer sand masons use for mixing mortar.

Rake the sand smooth with the back of a level-head rake. You can level the sand with a wooden drag board ❺. Nail together two 1x4s or notch a 1x6 to place the lower edge at the desired height of the sand, and run the board along the path edging. To settle the sand, dampen it thoroughly with a hose set on fine spray. Fill any low spots, rake or drag the surface level, and then dampen it again.

Laying the surface

Whether you're laying a loose or solid material, take time to plan your work. Provide access so delivery trucks can place material close to the worksite.

Loose materials

Install water-permeable landscape fabric over the gravel base to prevent gravel from mixing with the surface material. Spread bark or wood chips 2 to 4 in. deep. Spread loose pea gravel or crushed rock about 2 in. deep. For a harder, more uniform surface, add $1/2$ in. of fine crushed rock on top of the gravel or coarser rock. You can let traffic compact crushed-rock surfaces, or compact them by hand or with a machine.

Bricks and precast pavers

Take time to figure out the pattern and spacing of the bricks or pavers by laying them out on the lawn or driveway, rather than disturbing your carefully prepared sand base. When you're satisfied, begin in a corner, laying the bricks or pavers gently on the sand so the base remains even ❶. Lay full bricks first; then cut bricks to fit as needed at the edges. To produce uniform joints, space bricks with a piece of wood cut to the joint width. You can also maintain alignment with a straightedge or with a string stretched across the path between nails or stakes. Move the string as the work proceeds.

As you complete a row or section, bed the bricks or pavers into the sand base with several firm raps of a rubber mallet or a hammer on a scrap 2x4. Check with a level or straightedge to make sure the surface is even ❷. (You'll have to do this by feel or eye across the width of a crowned path.) Lift low bricks or pavers carefully and fill beneath them with sand; then reset them. Don't stand on the walk until you've filled the joints.

When you've finished a section, sweep fine, dry mason's sand into the joints, working across the surface of the path in all directions ❸. Wet thoroughly with a fine spray and let dry; then sweep in more sand if necessary. If you want a "living" walk, sweep a loam-sand mixture into the joints and plant small, tough, ground-hugging plants, such as thyme, in them.

Rare is the brick walk that can be laid without cutting something to fit. To cut brick, mark the line of the cut with a dark pencil all around the brick. With the brick resting firmly on sand or soil, score the entire line by rapping a wide mason's

Loose materials

Cover gravel base with water-permeable landscape fabric and add 2 to 3 in. of bark or wood chips.

❶ Begin laying in a corner.

Bricks and precast pavers

To turn square corners, align the edging board with a carpenter's square.

❷ Check the surface with a level or straightedge. Fill under low bricks; tamp down high ones. Use a plank to distribute your weight if you must work on the path.

❸ Sweep fine, dry sand into the joints to fix the bricks or pavers in place.

Cutting bricks

Wear safety glasses.

Scored line

Brickset chisel

chisel called a "brickset" with a heavy wooden mallet or a soft-headed steel hammer as shown on these pages. Place the brickset in the scored line across one face and give it a sharp blow with the hammer to cut the brick.

If you have a lot of bricks to cut, or if you want greater accuracy, consider renting a masonry saw. Whether you work by hand or by machine, always wear safety glasses.

Flagstones

Install cut stones of uniform thickness as described for bricks and pavers. Working out patterns beforehand is particularly important — stones are too heavy to move around more than necessary. To produce a level surface with cut or irregular stones of varying thickness, you'll need to add or remove sand for each stone. Set the stone carefully on sand; then move it back and forth to work it into place ❶. Lay a level or straightedge over three or four stones to check the surface's evenness ❷. When a section is complete, fill the joints with sand or with sand and loam as described for bricks and pavers.

You can cut flagstone with a technique similar to that used for bricks. Score the line of the cut on the top surface with a brickset and hammer. Prop the stone on a piece of scrap wood, positioning the line of cut slightly beyond the edge of the wood. Securing the bottom edge of the stone with your foot, place the brickset on the scored line and strike sharply to make the cut.

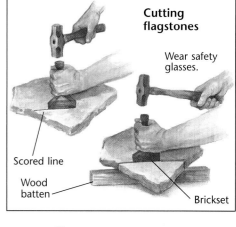

Cutting flagstones

Wear safety glasses.

Scored line

Wood batten

Brickset

❶ Set flagstones in place carefully to avoid disturbing the sand base.

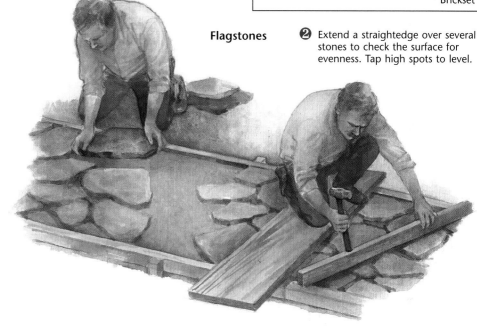

Flagstones

❷ Extend a straightedge over several stones to check the surface for evenness. Tap high spots to level.

Steppingstones

A steppingstone walk set in turf creates a charming effect and is very simple to lay. You can use cut or irregular flagstones or fieldstone, which is irregular in thickness as well as in outline. Arrange the stones on the turf; then set them one by one. Cut into the turf around the stone with a sharp flat spade or trowel, and remove the stone; then dig out the sod with the spade. Placing stones at or below grade will keep them away from mower blades. Fill low spots beneath the stone with earth or sand so the stone doesn't move when stepped on.

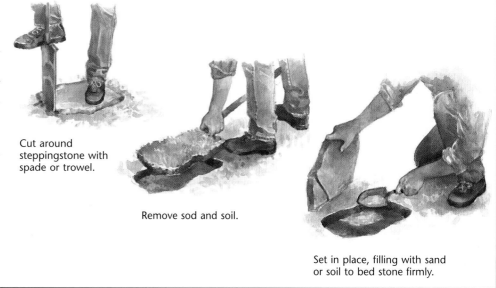

Cut around steppingstone with spade or trowel.

Remove sod and soil.

Set in place, filling with sand or soil to bed stone firmly.

Laying a Patio

You can make a simple patio using the same techniques and materials we have discussed for paths. To ensure good drainage, an even surface, and durability, lay solid surfaces such as brick, flagstone, and pavers on a well-prepared base of gravel, sand, and compacted soil. (Crushed-rock and gravel surfaces likewise benefit from a sound base.) Make sure the surface drains away from any adjacent structure (house or garage); a drop-off of 1/4 in. per foot is usually adequate. If the patio isn't near a structure, make it higher in the center to avoid puddles forming on the surface.

Establish the outline of the patio as described for paths; then excavate the area roughly to accommodate 4 in. of gravel, 2 in. of sand, and the thickness of the paving surface. (Check with your paver supplier or a landscape contractor to find out if local conditions require alterations in the type or amounts of base material.) Now grade the rough excavation to provide drainage, using a simple 4-ft. grid of wooden stakes as shown in the drawings.

Drive the first row of stakes next to the house (or in the center of a freestanding patio), leveling them with a 4-ft. builder's level or a smaller level resting on a straight 2x4. The tops of these stakes should be at the height of the eventual sand base (finish grade of the patio less the thickness of the surface material) ❶. Working from this row of stakes, establish another row about 4 to 5 ft. from the first. Make the tops of these stakes 1 in. lower than those of the first row, using a level and spacer

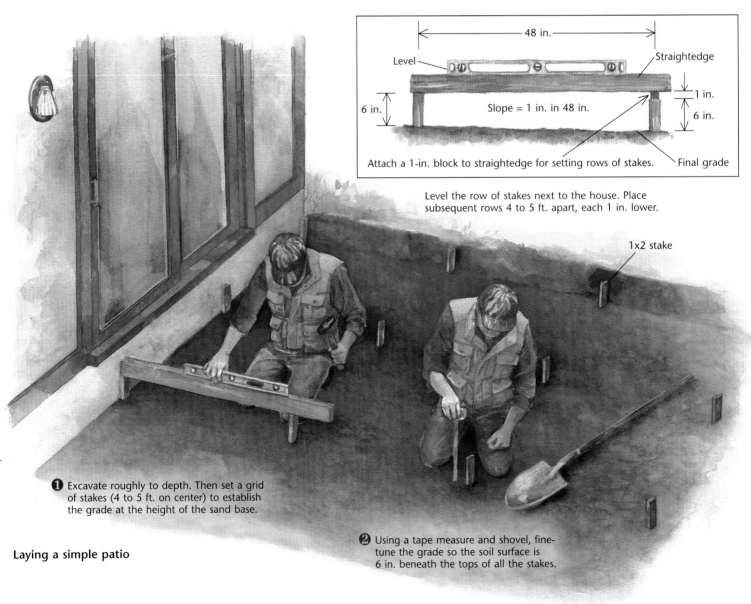

48 in.

Level

Straightedge

6 in.

Slope = 1 in. in 48 in.

1 in.

6 in.

Attach a 1-in. block to straightedge for setting rows of stakes.

Final grade

Level the row of stakes next to the house. Place subsequent rows 4 to 5 ft. apart, each 1 in. lower.

1x2 stake

❶ Excavate roughly to depth. Then set a grid of stakes (4 to 5 ft. on center) to establish the grade at the height of the sand base.

❷ Using a tape measure and shovel, fine-tune the grade so the soil surface is 6 in. beneath the tops of all the stakes.

Laying a simple patio

block, as shown on the facing page. Continue adding rows of stakes, each 1 in. lower than the previous row, until the entire area is staked. Then, with a tape measure or ruler and a shovel, fine-tune the grading by removing or adding soil until the excavated surface is 6 in. (the thickness of the sand-and-gravel base) below the tops of all the stakes ❷.

When installing the sand-and-gravel base, you'll want to maintain the drainage grade you've just established and produce an even surface for the paving material. If you have a good eye or a very small patio, you can do this by sight. Otherwise, you can use the stakes to install a series of 1x3 or 1x4 "leveling boards," as shown in the drawing below. (Before adding gravel, you may want to cover the soil with water-permeable landscape fabric to keep perennial weeds from growing; just cut slits to accommodate the stakes.)

Add a few inches of gravel ❸. Then set leveling boards along each row of stakes, with the boards' top edges even with the top of the stakes ❹. Drive additional stakes to sandwich the boards in place (don't use nails). Distribute the remaining inch or so of gravel and compact it by hand or machine; then add the 2 in. of sand. Dragging a straight 2x4 across two adjacent rows of leveling boards will produce a precise grade and an even surface ❺. Wet the sand and fill low spots that settle.

You can install the patio surface as previously described for paths, removing the leveling boards as the bricks or pavers reach them ❻. Disturbing the sand surface as little as possible, slide the boards out from between the stakes and drive the stakes an inch or so beneath the level of the sand. Cover the stakes and fill the gaps left by the boards with sand, tamped down carefully; then continue laying the paving. Finally, sweep fine sand into the joints.

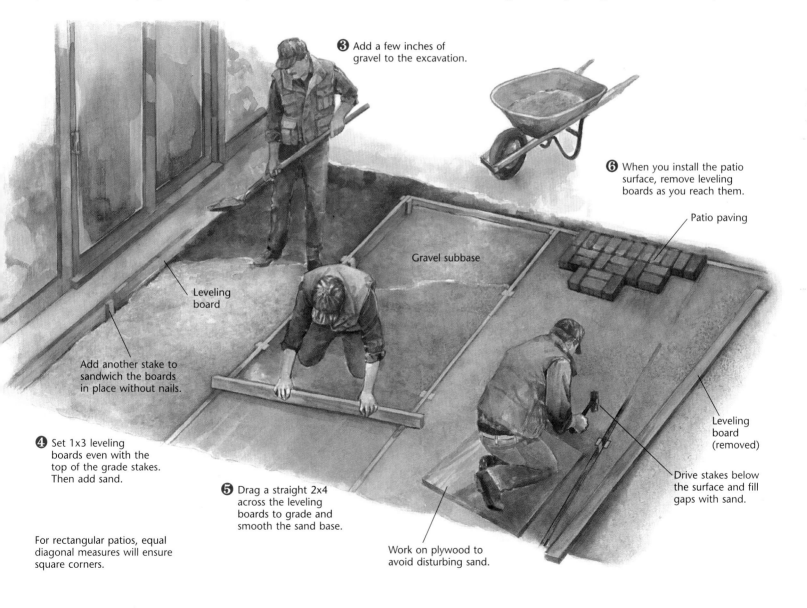

❸ Add a few inches of gravel to the excavation.

❻ When you install the patio surface, remove leveling boards as you reach them.

Patio paving

Gravel subbase

Leveling board

Add another stake to sandwich the boards in place without nails.

❹ Set 1x3 leveling boards even with the top of the grade stakes. Then add sand.

❺ Drag a straight 2x4 across the leveling boards to grade and smooth the sand base.

For rectangular patios, equal diagonal measures will ensure square corners.

Work on plywood to avoid disturbing sand.

Leveling board (removed)

Drive stakes below the surface and fill gaps with sand.

Installing a Pond

It wasn't so long ago that garden ponds like the ones in this book required yards of concrete, an expert mason, and deep pockets. Today's strong, lightweight, and long-lasting synthetic liners and rigid fiberglass shells have put garden pools in reach of every do-it-yourselfer. Installation does require some hard labor but little expertise: just dig a hole, spread the liner or seat the shell, install edging, and plant. We'll discuss installation of a linered pond in the main text; see the box below for details on installing a smaller, fiberglass pool.

Liner notes

More and more nurseries and garden centers are carrying flexible pond liners, and you can also buy them from mail-order suppliers specializing in water gardens. Synthetic rubber liners are longer lasting but more expensive than PVC liners. And both are much cheaper than rigid fiberglass shells. Buy only liners specifically made for garden ponds—don't use ordinary plastic sheeting. To many people, black liners look better than blue liners, which tend to make the pond look like a swimming pool.

Before you dig

First, make sure you comply with local codes about water features. Then keep the following ideas in mind when locating your pond. Avoid trees whose shade keeps sun-loving water plants from thriving; whose roots make digging a chore; and whose flowers, leaves, and seeds clog the water, making it unsightly and inhospitable to plants or fish. Avoid low spots on your property; otherwise your pond will become a catch basin for runoff. Select a reasonably level spot. Use a carpenter's level on a straight board much like that shown on p. 110 to determine level, adding or removing soil as necessary.

Using graph paper, enlarge the outline of the pond provided on the site plan on p. 52, altering it as you wish. If you change the size of the pond, or are interested in growing a wider variety of water plants or adding fish, remember that a healthy pond must achieve a balance between the plants and fish and the volume, depth, and temperature of the water. Even if you're not altering the size of the pond, it's a good idea to consult with a knowledgeable person at a nursery or pet store specializing in water-garden plants and animals.

Calculate the liner width by adding twice the maximum depth of the pool plus an additional 2 ft. to the width. Use the same formula to calculate the length. So, for instance, for a pond 2 ft. deep, 7 ft. wide, and 15 ft. long, the liner width would be 4 ft. plus 7 ft. plus 2 ft. (or 13 ft.). The length would be 4 ft. plus 15 ft. plus 2 ft. (or 21 ft.).

Excavation

If your soil isn't too compacted or rocky, a good-size pond can be excavated with a shovel or two in a weekend ❶. (Energetic teenagers are a marvelous pool-building resource.) If the site isn't level, you can grade it using a stake-and-level system adapted from the one described on pp. 110–111 for grading the patio.

Outline the pond's shape with garden lime, establishing the curves with a garden hose or by staking out a large grid and plotting from the graph-paper plan. Many garden ponds have two levels. One end, often the widest, is 2 ft. deep to accommodate water lilies and other plants requiring deeper water, as well as fish. The other end is 12 to 16 in. deep for plants requiring shallower submersion. (You can also put plant pots on stacks of bricks to vary heights.) The walls will be less likely to crumble as you dig, and the liner will install more easily, if you slope the walls in about 3 to 4 in. for each foot of depth. Make them smooth, removing roots, rocks, and other sharp protrusions.

Excavate a shallow relief around the perimeter of the hole to contain the liner

Small fiberglass pool

A fiberglass shell or agricultural tank 2 ft. wide, 4 ft. long, and 2 to 3 ft. deep is ideal for the small pool on p. 55. Garden centers often stock pond shells in a variety of shapes.

Dig a hole about 6 in. wider on all sides than the shell. Hole depth should equal that of the shell plus 1 in. for a sand base. Compact the bottom of the hole and spread the sand; then lower the shell into place. Add temporary wedges or props if necessary to orient and level the shell. Slowly fill the shell with water, backfilling around it with sand or sifted soil so the fill keeps pace with the rising water level. You can edge the pool with colored pavers as shown on p. 55, or overlap the edge of the shell with flagstones.

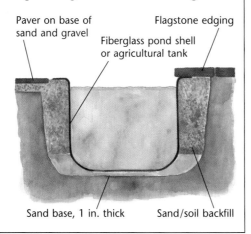

Paver on base of sand and gravel

Flagstone edging

Fiberglass pond shell or agricultural tank

Sand base, 1 in. thick

Sand/soil backfill

Section through pond

The pond on pp. 52–53 incorporates a gently sloping river-rock "shore" at its shallow end. This helps create a more "natural" transition to the planting. The liner rests on a sand base (as described in the main text) and is covered with several inches of sand to cushion, and prevent damage from, the river rock.

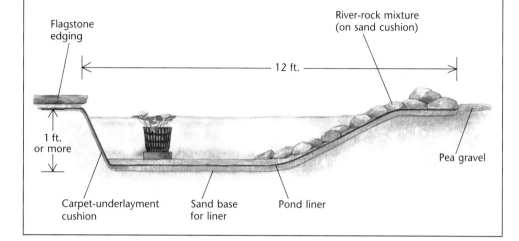

Flagstone edging

River-rock mixture (on sand cushion)

12 ft.

1 ft. or more

Pea gravel

Carpet-underlayment cushion

Sand base for liner

Pond liner

overlap and the width and thickness of the stone edging. To receive runoff after a heavy rain, create an overflow channel, as shown in the drawing on p. 114. This can simply be a 1- to 2-in. depression a foot or so wide spanned by one of the edging stones. Lengths of PVC pipe placed side by side beneath the stone will keep the liner in place. Position the overflow channel to open onto a lower area of lawn or garden adjacent to the pond or to a rock-filled dry well.

Fitting the liner

Once the hole is complete, cushion the surfaces to protect the liner ❷. The drawing shows an inch-thick layer of sand on the bottom surfaces and carpet underlay-

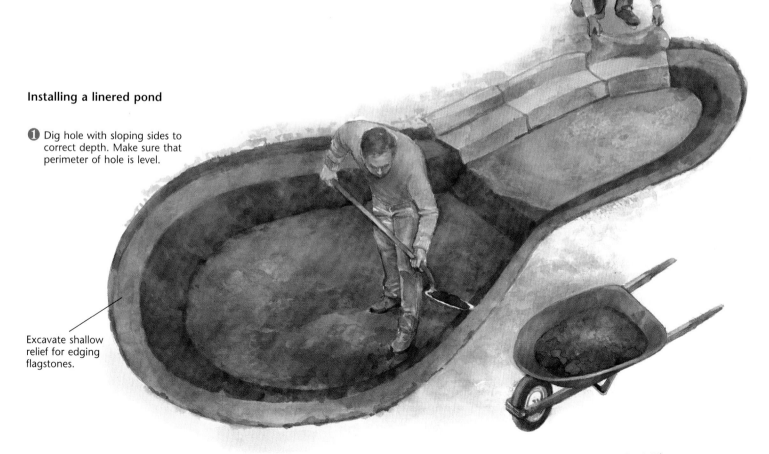

❷ Cushion walls with carpet underlayment after spreading sand on horizontal surfaces.

Installing a linered pond

❶ Dig hole with sloping sides to correct depth. Make sure that perimeter of hole is level.

Excavate shallow relief for edging flagstones.

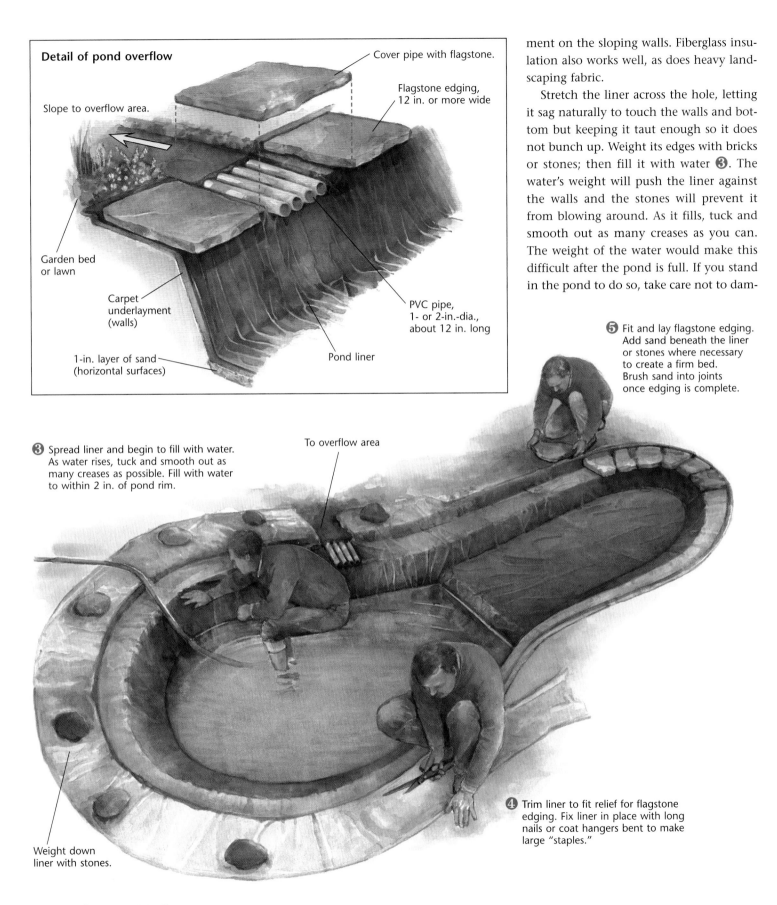

Detail of pond overflow

Cover pipe with flagstone.

Flagstone edging, 12 in. or more wide

Slope to overflow area.

Garden bed or lawn

Carpet underlayment (walls)

1-in. layer of sand (horizontal surfaces)

Pond liner

PVC pipe, 1- or 2-in.-dia., about 12 in. long

ment on the sloping walls. Fiberglass insulation also works well, as does heavy landscaping fabric.

Stretch the liner across the hole, letting it sag naturally to touch the walls and bottom but keeping it taut enough so it does not bunch up. Weight its edges with bricks or stones; then fill it with water ❸. The water's weight will push the liner against the walls and the stones will prevent it from blowing around. As it fills, tuck and smooth out as many creases as you can. The weight of the water would make this difficult after the pond is full. If you stand in the pond to do so, take care not to dam-

❺ Fit and lay flagstone edging. Add sand beneath the liner or stones where necessary to create a firm bed. Brush sand into joints once edging is complete.

❸ Spread liner and begin to fill with water. As water rises, tuck and smooth out as many creases as possible. Fill with water to within 2 in. of pond rim.

To overflow area

❹ Trim liner to fit relief for flagstone edging. Fix liner in place with long nails or coat hangers bent to make large "staples."

Weight down liner with stones.

age the liner. Don't be alarmed if you can't smooth all the creases. Stop filling when the water is 2 in. below the rim of the pond, and cut the liner to fit into the overlap relief ❹. Hold it in place with a few long nails or large "staples" made from coat hangers while you install the edging.

Edging the pond

Finding and fitting flagstones so there aren't wide gaps between them is the most time-consuming part of this task. Cantilevering the stones an inch or two over the water will hide the liner somewhat.

The stones can be laid directly on the liner, as shown ❺. Add sand where necessary under the liner to level the surface so that the stones don't rock. Such treatment will withstand the occasional gingerly traffic of pond maintenance but not the wear and tear of young children or large dogs regularly running across the edging. If you anticipate such traffic, you can bed the stones in 2 to 3 in. of mortar. It's prudent to consult with a landscape contractor about whether your intended use and soil require a footing for mortared stones.

Water work

Unless you are a very tidy builder, you'll need to siphon or pump dirty water out of the pond, clean the liner, and refill the pond. If you're adding fish and using chlorinated water, you'll need to let the water stand for a week or so to allow the chlorine (which is deadly to fish) to dissipate. Check with local pet stores to find out if your water contains chemicals that require commercial conditioners to make it safe for fish.

Installing the pond and plants is only the first step in water gardening. It takes patience, experimentation, and usually some consultation with experienced water gardeners to achieve a balance among plants, fish, waterborne oxygen, nutrients, and waste that will sustain plants and fish happily while keeping algae, diseases, insects, and predators at acceptable levels.

Growing pond plants

One water lily, a few upright-growing plants, and a bundle of submerged plants (which help keep the water clean) are enough for a medium-size pond. An increasing number of nurseries and garden centers stock water lilies and other water plants. For a larger selection, your nursery or garden center may be able to recommend a specialist supplier.

These plants are grown in containers filled with heavy garden soil (*not* potting soil, which contains ingredients that float). You can buy special containers designed for aquatic plants, or simply use plastic pails or dishpans. Line basket-like containers with burlap to keep the soil from leaking out the holes. A water lily needs at least 5 to 10 gal. of soil; the more, the better. Most other water plants, such as dwarf papyrus, need 1 to 2 gal. of soil.

After planting, add a layer of gravel on the surface to keep soil from clouding the water and to protect roots from marauding fish. Soak the plant and soil thoroughly; then set the container in the pond, positioning it so the water over the soil is 6 to 18 in. deep for water lilies, 0 to 6 in. for most other plants.

For maximum bloom, push a tablet of special water-lily fertilizer into the pot once or twice a month throughout the summer. Most water plants are easy to grow and carefree, although many are tropicals that die after hard frost, so you may need to replace these each spring.

Planting water plants

Set water plants in a container of heavy garden soil. Cover soil surface with gravel to keep soil from floating away.

Gravel

1- to 5-gal. dishpan or special container lined with burlap and filled with heavy garden soil

Building a Retaining Wall

Contours and sloping terrain can add considerable interest to a home landscape. But you can have too much of a good thing. Two designs in this book employ retaining walls to alter problem slopes. The wall shown on p. 36 eliminates a small but abrupt grade change, producing two almost level surfaces and the opportunity to install attractive plantings on them. On p. 68 retaining walls help turn a steep slope into a showpiece.

Retaining walls can be handsome landscape features in their own right. Made of cut stone, fieldstone, brick, landscape timbers, or concrete, they can complement the materials and style of your house or nearby structures. However, making a stable, long-lasting retaining wall of these materials can require tools and skills many homeowners do not possess.

For these reasons we've instead chosen retaining-wall systems made of precast concrete for designs in this book. Readily available in a range of sizes, surface finishes, and colors, these systems require few tools and no special skills to install. They have been engineered to resist the forces that soil, water, freezing, and thawing bring to bear on a retaining wall. Install these walls according to the manufacturer's specifications, and you can be confident that they will do their job for many years.

A number of systems are available in the Northwest through nurseries, garden centers, and local contractor suppliers (check the Yellow Pages). But they all share basic design principles. Like traditional dry-stone walls, these systems rely largely on weight and friction to contain the soil. In many systems, interlocking blocks or pegs help align the courses and increase the wall's strength. In all systems, blocks must rest on a solid, level base. A freely draining backfill of crushed stone is essential to avoid buildup of water pressure in the retained soil, which can buckle even a heavy wall. (In hilly terrain or where drainage is a concern, experts often recommend installing drainage pipe to remove excess water from behind retaining walls.)

The construction steps shown here are typical of those recommended by most system manufacturers for retaining walls up to 3 ft. tall; be sure to follow the manufacturer's instructions for the system you choose. For higher walls, walls on loose soil or heavy clay soils, and walls retaining very steep slopes, it is prudent to consult with local building authorities before beginning work. (Some cities and counties have regulations for placement and construction of retaining walls and landscape steps. Be sure to check with local authorities.)

Building a wall

Installing a wall system is just about as simple as stacking up children's building blocks. The most important part of the job is establishing a firm, level base. Start by laying out the wall with string and hose (for curves) and excavating a base trench.

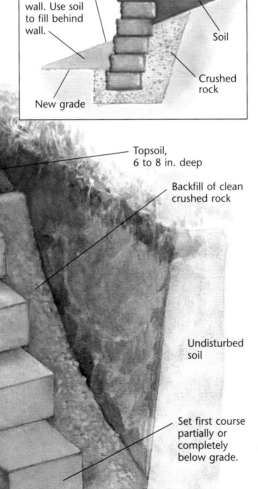

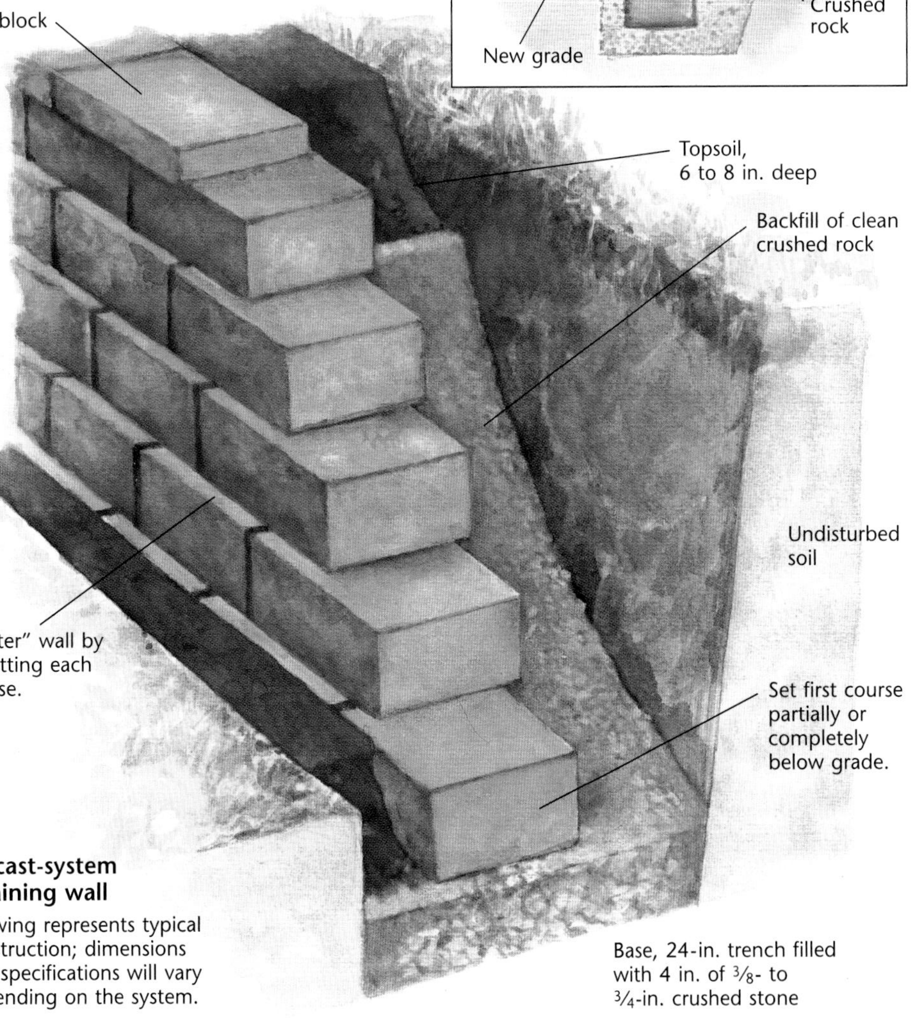

Original slope — New grade level

Excavate for wall. Use soil to fill behind wall.

Soil

New grade

Crushed rock

Cap block

Topsoil, 6 to 8 in. deep

Backfill of clean crushed rock

Undisturbed soil

"Batter" wall by offsetting each course.

Set first course partially or completely below grade.

Precast-system retaining wall

Drawing represents typical construction; dimensions and specifications will vary depending on the system.

Base, 24-in. trench filled with 4 in. of 3/8- to 3/4-in. crushed stone

As the boxed drawing on the facing page shows, the position of the wall in relation to the base of the slope determines the height of the wall, how much soil you move, and the leveling effect on the slope. Unless the wall is very long, excavate along the entire length and fine-tune the line of the wall before beginning the base trench. When excavating, remember that most systems recommend a foot of crushed-rock backfill behind the blocks.

Systems vary in the width and depth of the trench and type of base material, but in all of them, the trench must be tamped firm and be level across its width and along its length. We've shown a 4-in. layer of $3/8$- to $3/4$-in. crushed rock (blocks can slip sideways on rounded gravel, which also does not compact as well). Depending on the system and the circumstances, a portion or all of the first course lies below grade, so the soil helps hold the blocks in place.

Add crushed rock to the trench, level it with a rake, and compact it with a hand tamper or mechanical compactor. Lay the first course of blocks carefully ❶. Check frequently to make sure the blocks are level across their width and along their length.

Stagger vertical joints as you stack subsequent courses. Set back the faces of the courses so the wall angles back into the retained soil. Some systems design this "batter" into their blocks; others allow you to choose from several possible setbacks.

As the wall rises, shovel backfill behind the blocks ❷. Clean, crushed rock drains well; some systems suggest placing a barrier of landscaping fabric between the rock and the retained soil to keep soil from migrating into the fill and impeding drainage.

Thinner cap blocks finish the top of the wall ❸. Some manufacturers recommend

Building a wall

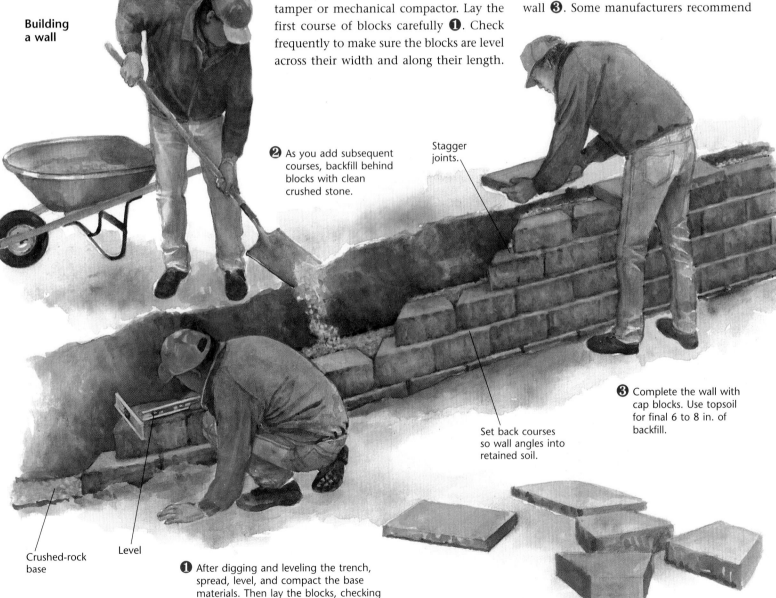

❷ As you add subsequent courses, backfill behind blocks with clean crushed stone.

Stagger joints.

Set back courses so wall angles into retained soil.

❸ Complete the wall with cap blocks. Use topsoil for final 6 to 8 in. of backfill.

Crushed-rock base

Level

❶ After digging and leveling the trench, spread, level, and compact the base materials. Then lay the blocks, checking frequently to see that they are level across their width and length.

Wall parallel to a slope: Stepped base

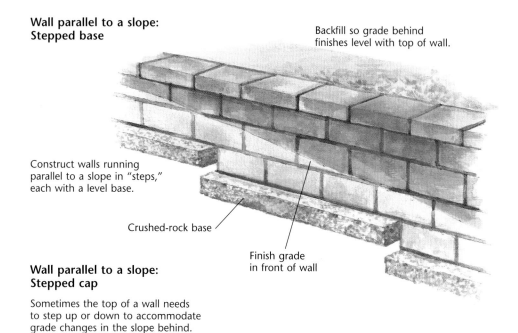

Backfill so grade behind finishes level with top of wall.

Construct walls running parallel to a slope in "steps," each with a level base.

Crushed-rock base

Finish grade in front of wall

Wall parallel to a slope: Stepped cap

Sometimes the top of a wall needs to step up or down to accommodate grade changes in the slope behind.

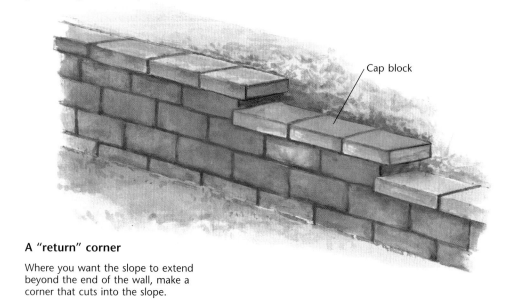

Cap block

A "return" corner

Where you want the slope to extend beyond the end of the wall, make a corner that cuts into the slope.

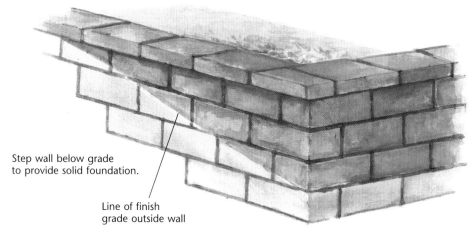

Step wall below grade to provide solid foundation.

Line of finish grade outside wall

cementing these blocks in place with a weatherproof adhesive. The last 6 to 8 in. of the backfill should be topsoil, firmed into place and ready for planting.

If your slope runs parallel to the length of the wall, you can "step" the bottom of the wall and make its top surface level, as shown in the top drawing at left. Create a length of level trench along the lowest portion of the site. Then work up the slope, creating steps as necessary. Add fill soil to raise the grade behind the wall to the level of the cap blocks.

Alternatively, you can step the top of the wall, as shown in the center drawing at left. Here, the base of the wall rests on level ground, but the top of the wall steps to match the slope's decreasing height. This saves money and labor on materials and backfill, while producing a different look.

Retaining walls (such as the ones shown on p. 36 and p. 68) are frequently placed perpendicular to the run of a slope. If you want to alter just part of the slope or if the slope continues beyond your property, you'll need to terminate the wall. A corner that cuts back into the slope (shown at bottom left) is an attractive and structurally sound solution to this problem.

Constructing curves and corners

Wall-system blocks are designed so that curves (such as the one in the design on p. 68) are no more difficult to lay than straight sections. Corners may require that you cut a few blocks or use specially designed blocks, but they are otherwise uncomplicated. If your wall must fit a prescribed length between corners, consider working from the corners toward the middle (after laying a base course). Masons use this technique, which also helps to avoid exposing cut blocks at the corners.

You can cut blocks with a mason's chisel and mallet or rent a mason's saw. Chiseling works well where the block faces are rough textured, so the faces you cut blend right in. A saw is best for smooth-faced blocks and projects requiring lots of cutting.

Steps

Steps in a low retaining wall are not difficult to build, but they require forethought and careful layout. Precast systems differ in construction details. The drawing below shows a typical design where the blocks and stone base rest on "steps" cut into firm subsoil. If your soil is less stable or is recent fill, excavate the entire area beneath the steps to the same depth as the wall base and build a foundation of blocks, as shown in the boxed drawing.

These steps are independent of the adjacent "return" walls, which are vertical, not battered (stepped back). In some systems, steps and return walls are interlocked. To match a path, you can face the treads with the same stone, brick, or pavers, or you can use the system's cap blocks or special treads.

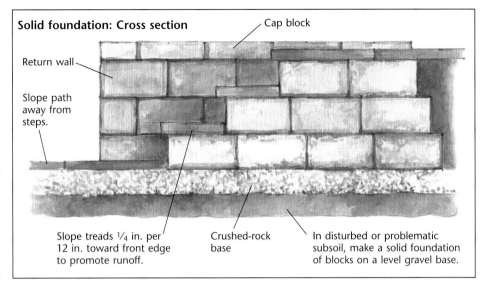

Solid foundation: Cross section

Cap block

Return wall

Slope path away from steps.

Slope treads $1/4$ in. per 12 in. toward front edge to promote runoff.

Crushed-rock base

In disturbed or problematic subsoil, make a solid foundation of blocks on a level gravel base.

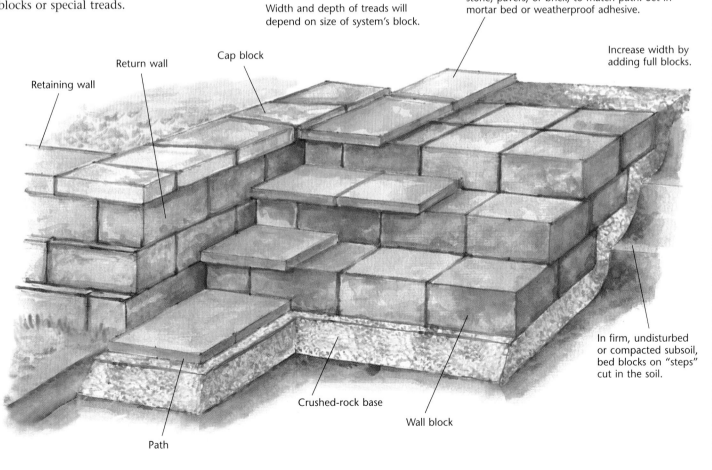

"Stepped" foundation

Width and depth of treads will depend on size of system's block.

Surface steps with system-provided treads or stone, pavers, or brick, to match path. Set in mortar bed or weatherproof adhesive.

Increase width by adding full blocks.

Retaining wall

Return wall

Cap block

In firm, undisturbed or compacted subsoil, bed blocks on "steps" cut in the soil.

Path

Crushed-rock base

Wall block

Fences, Arbors, and Trellises

Novices who have no qualms about tackling a simple flagstone path often hesitate when it comes time to erect a fence, an arbor, or even a trellis. While such projects can require more skill and resources than others in the landscape, projects in this book were designed with less-than-confident do-it-yourself builders in mind. The designs are simple, the materials are readily available, and the tools and skills will be familiar to anyone accustomed to ordinary home maintenance.

First we'll introduce you to the materials and tools needed for the projects. Then we'll present the small number of basic operations you'll employ when building them. Finally, we'll provide drawings and comments on each of the projects.

Materials

Of the materials offering strength, durability, and attractiveness in outdoor settings, wood is the easiest to work and affords the quickest results. While almost all commercially available lumber is strong enough for landscape structures, most types decay quickly in prolonged contact with soil and water. Cedar, however, contains natural preservatives and is excellent for landscape use. Alternatively, a range of softwoods (such as pine, fir, and hemlock) are pressure-treated with preservatives and will last for many years. Parts of structures that do not come in contact with soil or are not continually wet can be made of ordinary construction-grade lumber, but unless they're regularly painted or stained, they will not last as long as treated or naturally decay-resistant wood.

In addition to dimension lumber, landscape structures often incorporate lattice, which is thin wooden strips crisscrossed to form patterns of diamonds or squares. Premade lattice is widely available in sheets 4 ft. by 8 ft. and smaller. Lattice comes in decay-resistant woods as well as in treated and untreated softwoods. The strips are typically from $1/8$ to $3/8$ in. thick and about $1^1/2$ in. wide, overlapped to form squares ranging from 1 to 3 in. or more on a side. Local supplies vary, and you may find lattice made of thicker or narrower material. Lattice can be tricky to cut; if you're uneasy about this task, many suppliers will cut it for you for a small fee.

Fasteners

For millennia, basic structures like those in this section would have been assembled with complicated joints, the cutting and fitting of which required long training to master. Today, with simple nailed, bolted, or screwed joints, a little practice swinging a hammer or wielding a cordless electric screwdriver is all the training necessary.

All these structures can be assembled entirely with nails. But screws are stronger and, if you have a cordless screwdriver, make assembly easier. Buy common or box nails (both have flat heads) hot-dipped galvanized to prevent rust. Self-tapping screws ("deck" screws) require no pilot holes. For rust resistance, buy galvanized screws or screws treated with zinc dichromate.

Galvanized metal connectors are available to reinforce the joints used in these projects. (See the joinery drawings on pp. 124–125.) For novice builders, connectors are a great help in aligning parts and making assembly easier. (Correctly fastened with nails or screws, the joints are strong enough without connectors.)

Finishes

Cedar is handsome when left unfinished to weather, when treated with clear or colored stains, or when painted. Pressure-treated lumber is best painted or stained to mask the brown or green cast of the preservatives; if allowed to weather it turns a rather unattractive gray-brown.

Outdoor stains are becoming increasingly popular. Clear or lightly tinted stains can preserve or enhance the rich reddish browns of cedar. Stains also come in a range of colors that can be used like paint. Because they penetrate the wood rather than forming a film, stains don't impart an opaque surface—you'll still need paint to make a picket fence white. On the other hand, stains won't peel or chip like paint and are therefore easier to touch up and refinish.

When choosing a finish, consider what plants are growing on or near the structure. Repainting can be arduous if you need to remove yards of vines from a trellis or squeeze between a large shrub and a fence. Consider an unfinished decay-resistant wood or a stain that you allow to weather instead of repainting.

Tools

Even the least-handy homeowner is likely to have most of the tools needed for these projects: claw hammer, crosscut handsaw, brace-and-bit or electric drill, adjustable wrench, combination square, tape measure, carpenter's level, and sawhorses. You may even have an old posthole digger. A hand-held power circular saw makes faster (though noisier) work of cutting parts to length. A cordless drill/screwdriver is invaluable if you're substituting screws for nails. If you have more than a few holes to dig, consider renting a gas-powered posthole digger. An 8- to 12-in.-diameter hole will serve for 4x4 posts; if possible, rent a larger-diameter digger for 6x6 posts.

Setting posts

Most of the projects are anchored by firmly set, vertical posts. In general, the taller the structure, the deeper the posts should be set. To avoid post movement caused by expansion and contraction of the soil during freeze-thaw cycles, set all posts below the frost line. Check with local building authorities to determine frost-line depths where you live. If frost heaving isn't a concern, for best support set all arbor and fence posts at least 3 ft. deep.

The length of the posts you buy depends, of course, on the depth at which they are set and their finished heights. When calculating lengths of arbor posts, remember that the tops of the posts must be level. The easiest method of achieving this is to cut the posts to length after installation. For example, buy 12-ft. posts for an arbor finishing at 8 ft. above grade and set 3 ft. in the ground. The convenience is worth the expense of the foot or so you cut off. You can do the same for fence posts or buy them cut to length and add or remove fill from the bottom of the hole to put them at the correct heights.

Fence posts

Lay out and set the end or corner posts of a fence first; then add the intermediate posts. Dig the holes by hand or with a power digger ❶. To promote drainage, place several inches of gravel at the bottom of the hole for the post to rest on. Checking with a carpenter's level, plumb the post vertically and brace it with scrap lumber nailed to stakes ❷. Then add a few more inches of gravel around the post's base.

If your native soil compacts well, you can fix posts in place with tamped earth. Add the soil gradually, tamping it continuously with a heavy iron bar or 2x4. Check regularly with a level to see that the post doesn't get knocked out of plumb. This technique suits rustic or informal fences, where misalignments caused by shifting posts aren't noticeable or damaging.

For more formal fences, or where soils are loose or fence panels are buffeted by gusting winds, it's prudent to fix posts in concrete ❸. Mix enough concrete to set the two end posts; as a rule of thumb, figure one 80-lb. bag of premixed concrete per post. As you shovel it in, prod the con-

Setting a fence post

Post — Slope top surface for drainage.

3 ft. (typical)

Concrete and rubble (shown), or tamped earth

Coarse gravel

1 ft. (typical)

❶ Position the end or corner posts; then dig holes for them.

❷ Plumb the post, checking on adjacent faces with a level. Hold it in position with stakes and braces.

❸ Fill the hole with concrete and rubble.

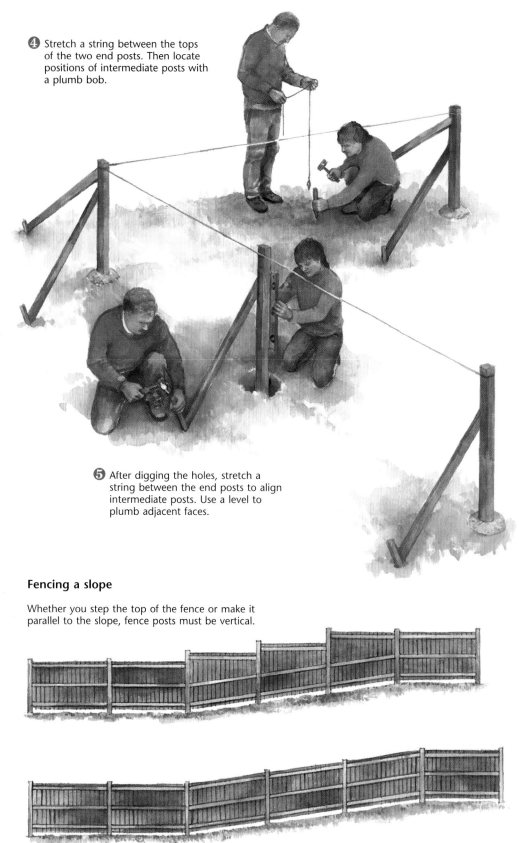

❹ Stretch a string between the tops of the two end posts. Then locate positions of intermediate posts with a plumb bob.

❺ After digging the holes, stretch a string between the end posts to align intermediate posts. Use a level to plumb adjacent faces.

Fencing a slope

Whether you step the top of the fence or make it parallel to the slope, fence posts must be vertical.

crete with a stick to settle it, particularly if you've added rubble to extend the mix. Build the concrete slightly above grade and slope it away from the post to aid drainage.

Once the end posts are set, stretch a string between them. (The concrete should cure for 24 hours before you nail or screw rails and panels in place, but you can safely stretch string while the concrete is still wet.) Measure along the string to position the intermediate posts; drop a plumb bob from the string at each intermediate post position to gauge the center of the hole below **❹**. Once all the holes have been dug, again stretch a string between the end posts, near the top. Set the intermediate posts as described previously; align one face with the string and plumb adjacent faces with the carpenter's level **❺**. Check positions of intermediate posts a final time with a tape measure.

If the fence is placed along a slope, the top of the slats or panels can step down the slope or mirror it (as shown in the bottom drawing at left). Either way, make sure that the posts are plumb, rather than leaning with the slope.

Arbor posts

Arbor posts are installed just like fence posts, but you must take extra care when positioning them. The corners of the structure must be right angles, and the sides must be parallel. Locating the corners with batter boards and string is fussy but accurate. Make the batter boards by nailing 1x2 stakes to scraps of 1x3 or 1x4, and position them about 1 ft. from the approximate location of each post as shown in the boxed drawing on the facing page. Locate the exact post positions with string; adjust the string so the diagonal measurements are equal, which ensures that the corners of the structure will be right angles.

At the intersections of the strings, locate the postholes by eye or with a plumb bob. (See **❶** on the facing page.) Remove the strings and dig the holes; then reattach the strings to position the posts exactly **❷**.

Plumb and brace the posts carefully. Check positions with the level and by measuring between adjacent posts and across diagonals. Diagonal braces between adjacent posts will stiffen them and help align their faces ❸. Then add concrete ❹ and let it cure for a day.

To establish the height of the posts, measure up from grade on one post; then use a level and straightedge to mark the heights of the other posts from the first one. Where joists will be bolted to the faces of the posts, you can install the joists and use their top edges as a handsaw guide.

Batter boards

Set L-shaped batter boards at each corner and stretch string to position the posts exactly.

1x2 stakes and 1x3 boards

Taut string

Taut string

18 to 24 in.

For square or rectangular post layout, diagonal measurements should be equal.

Setting arbor posts

❶ Position the posts with batter boards, taut string, and a plumb bob.

Batter board

Plumb bob

❷ Remove the string to dig the holes; then reattach it and align the outer faces of the posts with the string while you plumb and brace them.

Taut string

❸ Check distances between posts at top. Add diagonal bracing between posts to fix positions.

❹ Cement posts in place.

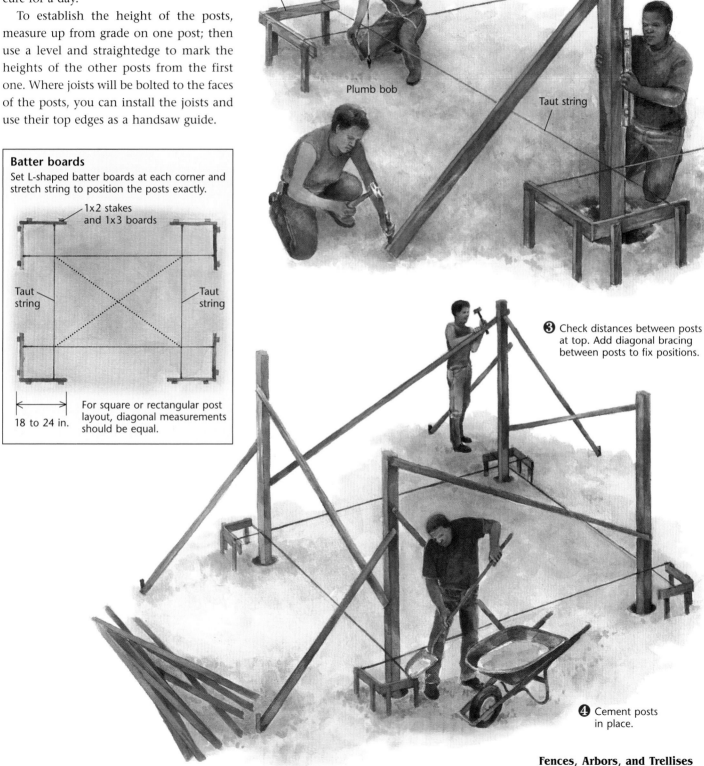

Joints

The components of the fences, arbors, and trellises used in this book are attached to the posts and to each other with the simple joints shown below. Because all the parts are made of dimension lumber, the only cuts you'll need to make are to length. For strong joints, cut ends as square as you can, so the mating pieces make good contact. If you have no confidence in your sawing abilities, many lumberyards will cut pieces to length for you for a modest fee.

Beginners often find it difficult to keep two pieces correctly positioned while trying to drive a nail into them, particularly when the nail must be driven at an angle, called "toenailing." If you have this prob-lem, predrill for nails, or use screws, which draw the pieces together. Or use metal connectors, which can be nailed or screwed in place on one piece and then attached to the mating piece.

In one of the Portfolio designs, you need to attach lattice panels to posts. The panels are made by sandwiching store-bought lattice between frames of dimen-

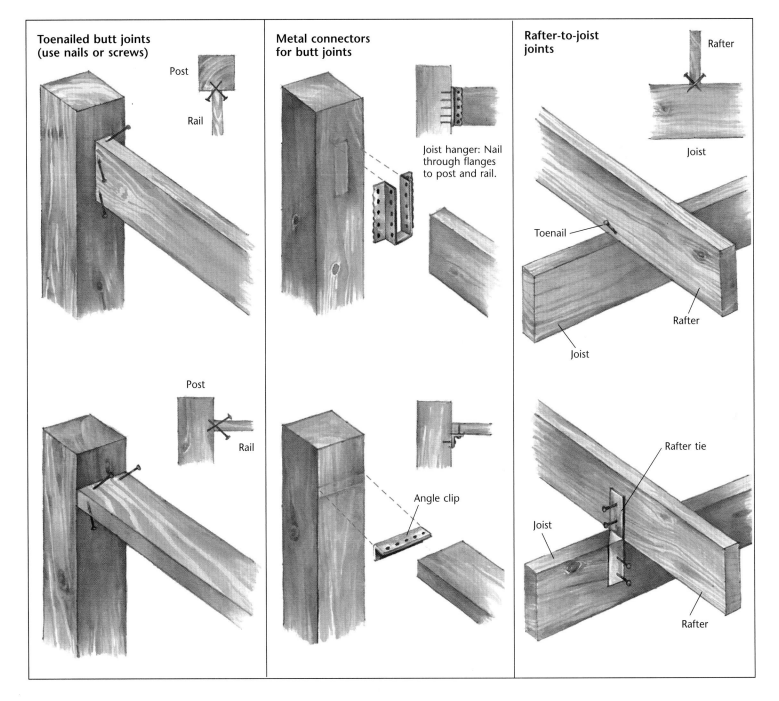

Toenailed butt joints (use nails or screws)

Post

Rail

Post

Rail

Metal connectors for butt joints

Joist hanger: Nail through flanges to post and rail.

Angle clip

Rafter-to-joist joints

Rafter

Joist

Toenail

Rafter

Joist

Rafter tie

Joist

Rafter

sion lumber (construction details are given on the following pages). While the assembled panels can be toenailed to the posts, novices may find that the job goes easier using one or more types of metal connector, as shown in the drawing at right below. Attach the angle clips or angle brackets to the post; then position the lattice panel and fix it to the connectors. For greatest strength and ease of assembly, attach the connectors with self-tapping screws driven by an electric screwdriver.

In the following pages, we'll show and comment on construction details of the fences, arbors, and trellises presented in the Portfolio of Designs. (Page numbers indicate the design.) Where the basic joints discussed here can be used, we have shown the parts but left choice of fasteners to you. Typical fastenings are indicated for other joints. We have kept the constructions shown here simple and straightforward. They are not the only possibilities, and we encourage experienced builders to adapt and alter constructions as well as designs to suit differing situations and personal preferences.

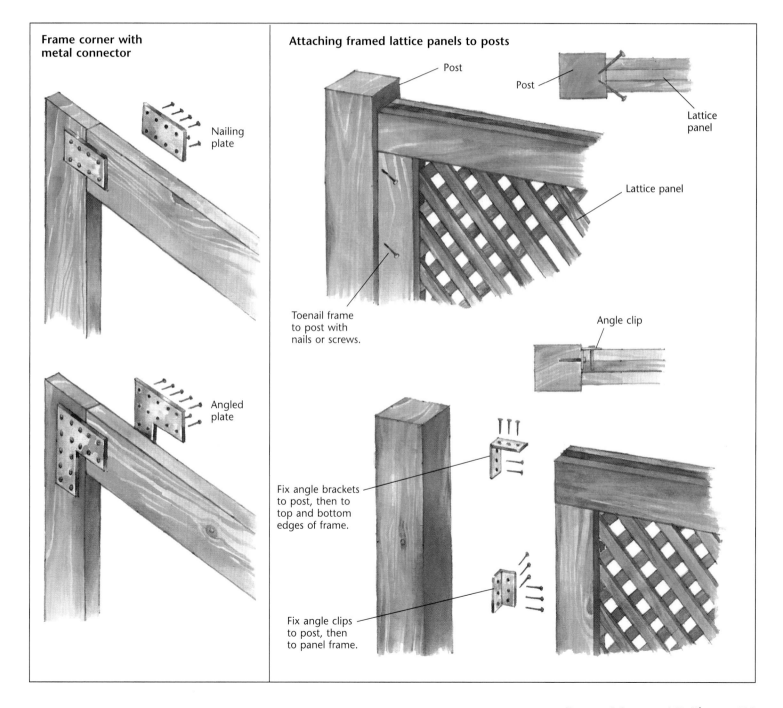

Frame corner with metal connector

Nailing plate

Angled plate

Attaching framed lattice panels to posts

Post

Post

Lattice panel

Lattice panel

Toenail frame to post with nails or screws.

Angle clip

Fix angle brackets to post, then to top and bottom edges of frame.

Fix angle clips to post, then to panel frame.

Lattice-panel screen
(pp. 24–25)

This screen serves as a decorative embellishment in the design on p. 24, but it can make an effective enclosure if you wish. The lattice is held in a frame made of 1x2s sandwiched between 1x3s and 1x4s. (The 1x4s add visual weight to the bottom of the screen.) Note how the parts overlap at the corners of the frame to form an interlocking joint.

Panels wider than 6 ft. are awkward to construct and to install. It is easiest to construct the panels on a large flat surface (a garage or basement floor). Lay out the 1x3s and 1x4 that form one face of the panel frame ❶. Then position and nail the 1x2s to them ❷. Add the lattice, then the other layer of 1x3s and 1x4 ❸. As you work, regularly check that the panel is square, its corners at right angles. (Use a framing square or measure across the diagonals to check that they are equal.) Lattice varies in thickness; if yours rattles in its groove, you can add 3/4-in. quarter round as shown in the lower box to tighten the fit.

Depending on whether you have more confidence as a post setter or as a panel builder, you can build the panels first and then use them to space the posts, or you can set the posts first (see pp. 120–122) and build the panels to fit. Either way, attach the panels to the posts by toenailing (with nails or screws) or with metal connectors along the lengths of the upright members. Add the 1x4 cap after attaching the panels to the posts. Finials in a variety of styles are available at home and garden stores.

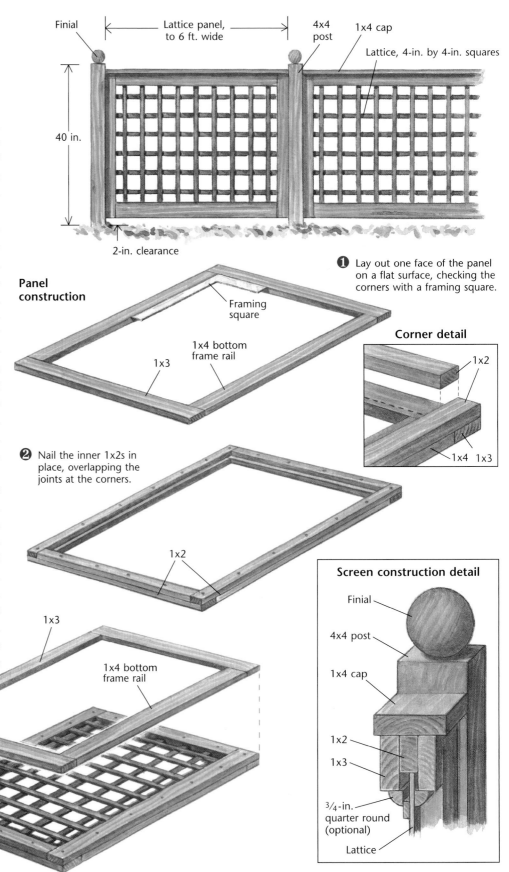

Finial

Lattice panel, to 6 ft. wide

4x4 post

1x4 cap

Lattice, 4-in. by 4-in. squares

40 in.

2-in. clearance

Panel construction

Framing square

1x4 bottom frame rail

1x3

❶ Lay out one face of the panel on a flat surface, checking the corners with a framing square.

Corner detail

1x2

1x4   1x3

❷ Nail the inner 1x2s in place, overlapping the joints at the corners.

1x2

1x3

1x4 bottom frame rail

❸ Place the lattice inside the 1x2 frame. Then nail the other face pieces in place, again overlapping the corner joints.

Screen construction detail

Finial

4x4 post

1x4 cap

1x2

1x3

3/4-in. quarter round (optional)

Lattice

Homemade lattice trellis
(pp. 40–43)

The trellis shown here supports climbing plants to make a vertical garden of a blank wall (or tall fence). Make two panels 48 in. wide for the design on p. 41. For the wide trellis on p. 43, we recommend making three 32-in.-wide modules (as shown here), which are simpler to make and handle than a single 8-ft.-wide trellis. Hung on L-hangers, these trellises are easy to remove when you need to paint the wall or fence behind. The design can readily be altered to suit other sizes and situations.

Start by cutting all the pieces to length. (Here we'll call the horizontal members "rails" and the vertical members "stiles.") Working on a large flat surface, nail or screw the two outer stiles to the top and bottom rails, checking the corners with a framing square. The 2x2 rails provide ample material to house the L-hangers.

Carefully attach the three intermediate stiles, then the 1x2 rails. Cut a piece of scrap 6 in. long to use as a spacer. Fix the L-shaped hangers to the wall or fence. Buy hangers long enough to hold the trellis several inches away from the surface, allowing air to circulate behind the foliage.

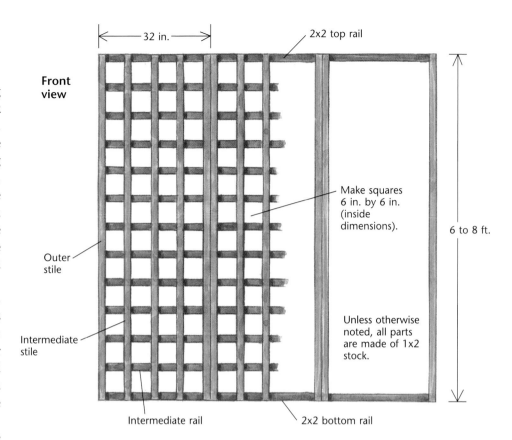

Front view

32 in.

2x2 top rail

Make squares 6 in. by 6 in. (inside dimensions).

6 to 8 ft.

Outer stile

Intermediate stile

Unless otherwise noted, all parts are made of 1x2 stock.

Intermediate rail

2x2 bottom rail

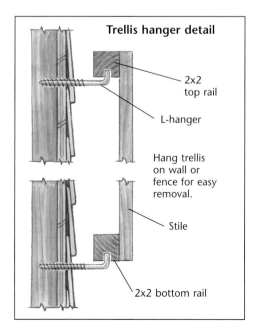

Trellis hanger detail

2x2 top rail

L-hanger

Hang trellis on wall or fence for easy removal.

Stile

2x2 bottom rail

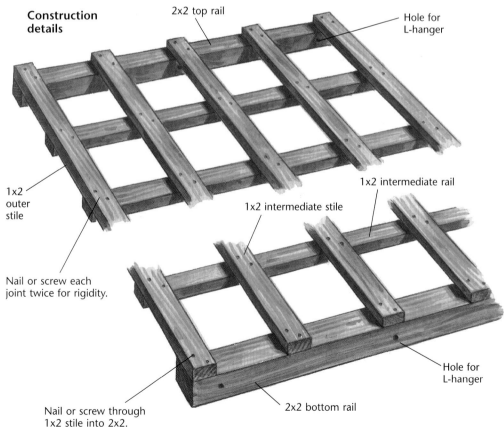

Construction details

2x2 top rail

Hole for L-hanger

1x2 outer stile

Nail or screw each joint twice for rigidity.

1x2 intermediate stile

1x2 intermediate rail

2x2 bottom rail

Nail or screw through 1x2 stile into 2x2.

Hole for L-hanger

Hideaway arbor
(pp. 44–45)

This cozy enclosure shelters a bench and supports vines to shade the occupants. Once the posts are set in place, this project can be finished in a weekend.

Build the arbor before laying the pavers under it. After setting the posts (see pp. 120–122), attach the 2x10 joists with

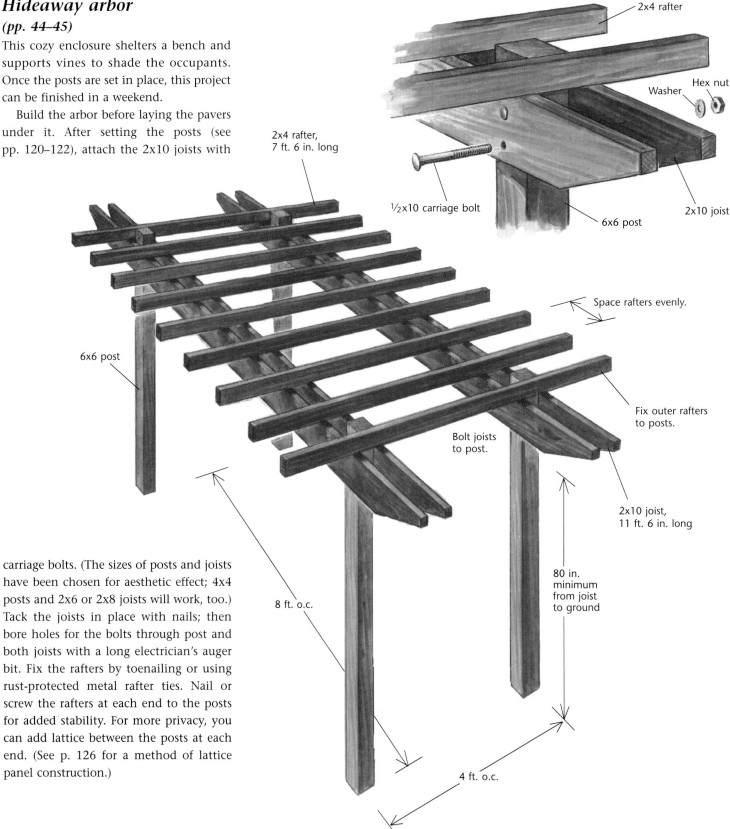

Post-to-joist detail

2x4 rafter

Hex nut

Washer

½x10 carriage bolt

6x6 post

2x10 joist

2x4 rafter, 7 ft. 6 in. long

6x6 post

Space rafters evenly.

Fix outer rafters to posts.

Bolt joists to post.

2x10 joist, 11 ft. 6 in. long

80 in. minimum from joist to ground

8 ft. o.c.

4 ft. o.c.

carriage bolts. (The sizes of posts and joists have been chosen for aesthetic effect; 4x4 posts and 2x6 or 2x8 joists will work, too.) Tack the joists in place with nails; then bore holes for the bolts through post and both joists with a long electrician's auger bit. Fix the rafters by toenailing or using rust-protected metal rafter ties. Nail or screw the rafters at each end to the posts for added stability. For more privacy, you can add lattice between the posts at each end. (See p. 126 for a method of lattice panel construction.)

Louvered fence

(pp. 48–49)

Made of vertical slats set at an angle, this 6-ft.-tall fence allows air circulation to plants and people near the patio while providing a privacy screen. Be sure to check local codes about height and setback from property lines.

The slats are supported top and bottom by 2x4 rails; a 2x6 beneath the bottom rail stiffens the entire structure, keeps the slat assembly from sagging, and adds visual weight to the design. Set the posts (see pp. 120–122); then cut the rails to fit between them. Toenailed nails or screws or metal connectors are strong enough, but you can add a 2x4 nailer between the rails (as shown in the drawing at bottom right) to make positioning and assembly easier.

Position the 1x6 slats with a spacer block 1$\frac{1}{2}$ in. wide and angled 45° at its ends. Nailing or screwing down through the top rail is easy. Nailing up through the bottom rail is more difficult; instead, you could toenail through the edges or faces of the slats into the bottom rail. You may need to cut the final slat narrower to maintain the uniform spacing.

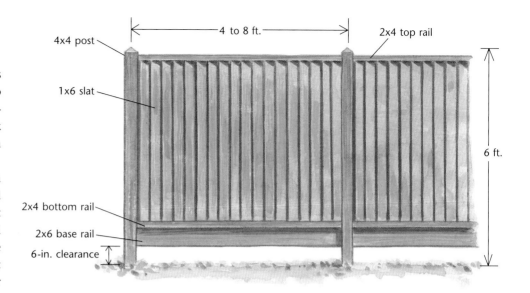

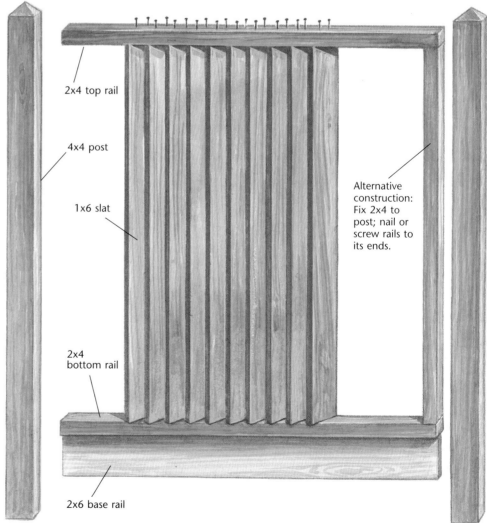

Slat assembly

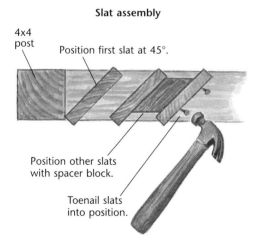

4x4 post

Position first slat at 45°.

Position other slats with spacer block.

Toenail slats into position.

Recycling-center screen
(pp. 88–89)

Draped with vines, this is an attractive but unobtrusive screen between the recycling area and the rest of the backyard.

The screen is a snap to build. After setting the posts (see pp. 120–122), add the top and bottom rails. Cut the ends of those for the angled corners at 45° and toenail or screw them to the posts. Trim the ends of the "pickets" at a 45° angle and fix them with a nail or screw into each rail. Position the pickets before fastening them to ensure even spacing. If you want a more solid-looking screen, offset the pickets so that those on one side fill the gaps left by those on the other. You can vary the size of the screen and the materials shown here. Keep in mind that the proportions are what make this simple design look good.

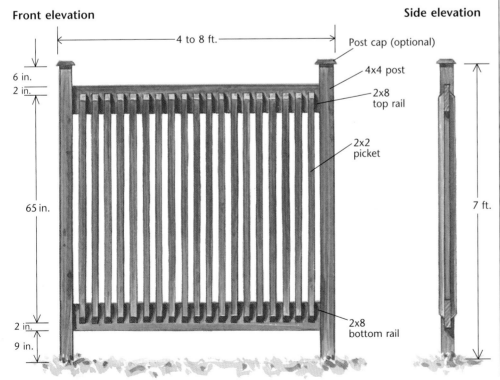

Plan view

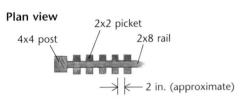

4x4 post
2x2 picket
2x8 rail
2 in. (approximate)

Front elevation

6 in.
2 in.
4 to 8 ft.
Post cap (optional)
4x4 post
2x8 top rail
2x2 picket
65 in.
2 in.
9 in.
2x8 bottom rail

4x4 post
2x8 top rail
2x2 picket
2x8 bottom rail

Side elevation

7 ft.

Scene-setting fence
(pp. 60–63)

This design provides privacy and an attractive backdrop for a perennial border. If the fence is used on a property line, be sure to check local codes for restrictions on placement and height.

This is a simple fence to construct. Assemble the panels on a flat surface, nailing or screwing the slats to the three 2x4 rails. You can lay out the arc at the top of each panel by "springing" a thin strip of wood, as shown on the facing page. Place the strip against a nail driven into a slat at the highest point of the arc in the center of the panel ❶. Enlist a couple of assistants to bend each end of the strip down to nails near each edge of the panel indicating the lowest points of the arc ❷. Pencil in the arc against the strip ❸. Then cut to the line. (A handheld electric jigsaw does the job quickly, but the curve is gentle enough to cut with a handsaw.)

View from back of fence

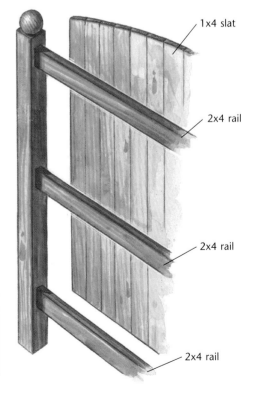

1x4 slat
2x4 rail
2x4 rail
2x4 rail

Set the posts (see pp. 120–122) according to the widths of the finished panels. The 6x6 posts shown here add an eye-pleasing heft to the fence, an effect emphasized by setting the face of the panel 1 in. back from the faces of the posts. (Posts made of 4x4s will work just as well.) Metal connectors are the easiest means of attaching the completed panels to the posts. To allow yourself access to the rails when mounting the metal connectors, leave the last slats at each end off when you assemble the panels. We've shown a spherical finial attached to the top of each post; you can buy finials of various types at home centers.

Springing an arc

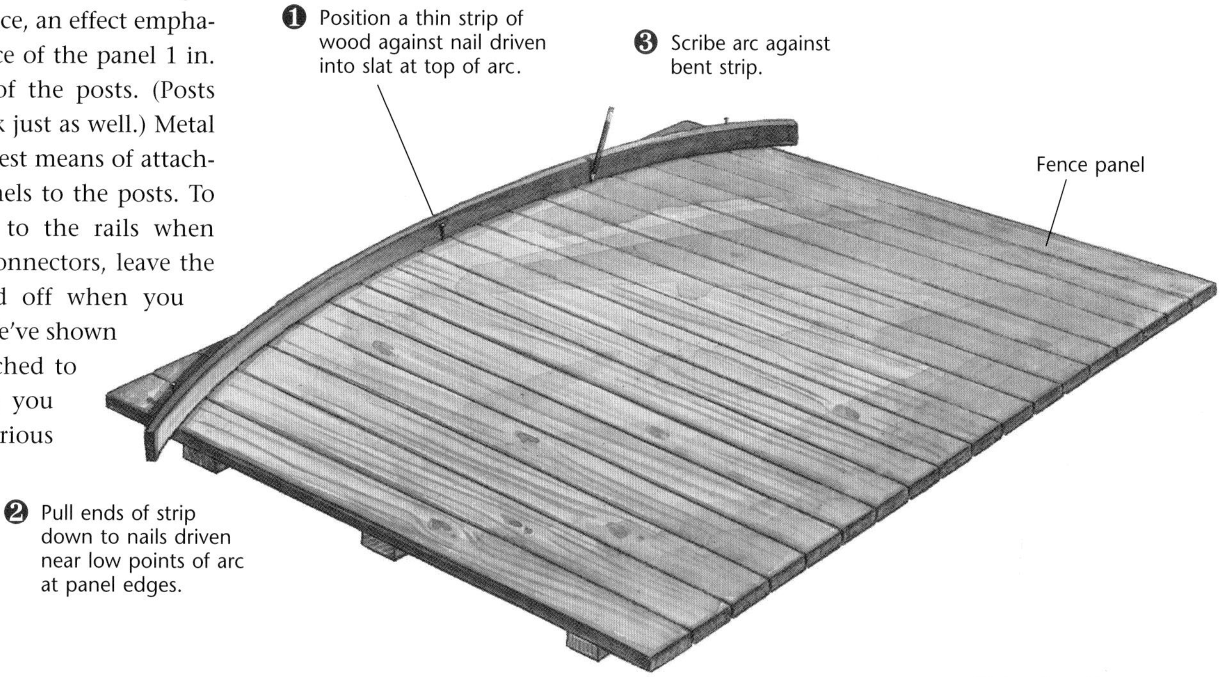

❶ Position a thin strip of wood against nail driven into slat at top of arc.

❸ Scribe arc against bent strip.

Fence panel

❷ Pull ends of strip down to nails driven near low points of arc at panel edges.

Front elevation

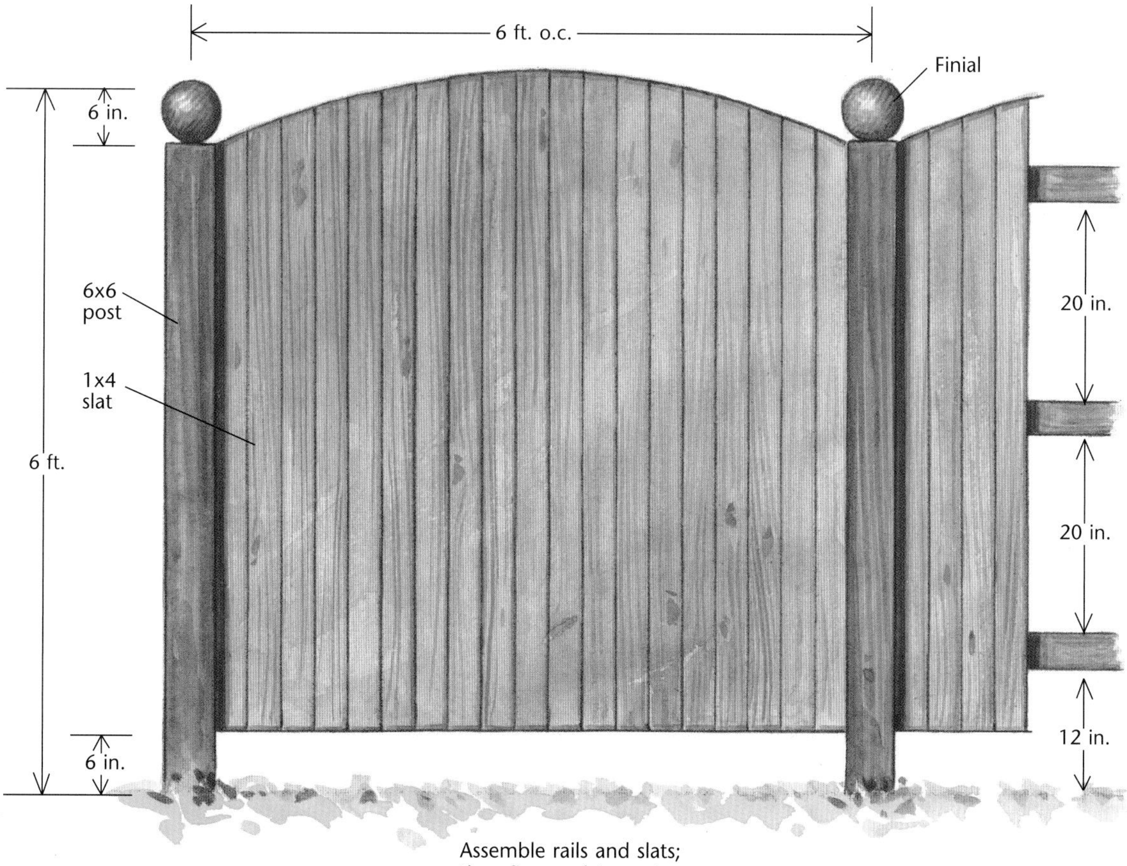

6 ft. o.c.

6 in.

Finial

6x6 post

1x4 slat

6 ft.

6 in.

20 in.

20 in.

12 in.

Assemble rails and slats; then fix panel to posts.

Side elevation

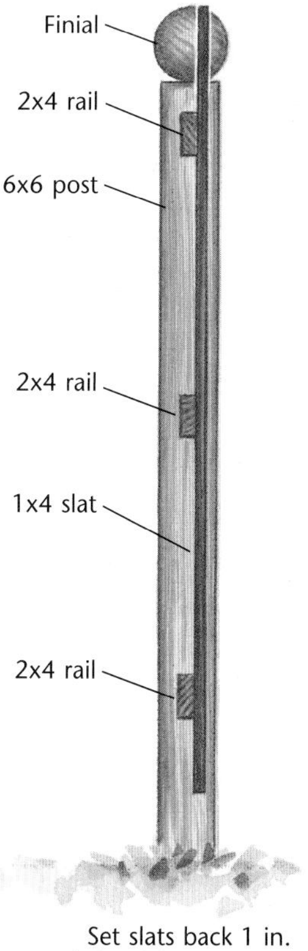

Finial

2x4 rail

6x6 post

2x4 rail

1x4 slat

2x4 rail

Set slats back 1 in. behind face of post.

Entry arbor and fence
(pp. 84–87)

This arbor makes an event of the passage from sidewalk to front door or from one part of your property to another. Two versions are shown in the Portfolio. One features a stand-alone arbor; the other adds a stylized picket fence. Construction details for both are shown here.

When the arbor stands on its own, a ladderlike trellis on each side gives the clematis something to climb. To provide a bit of visual interest, the spaces between

Detail of arbor pediment

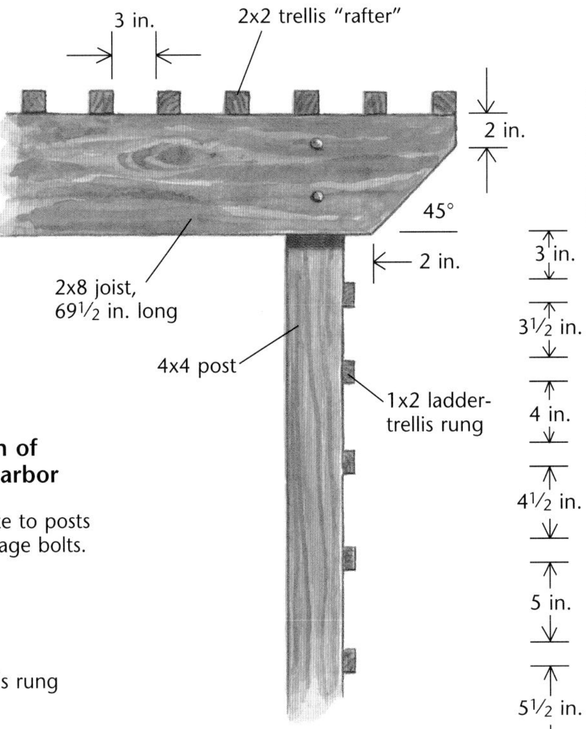

3 in.

2x2 trellis "rafter"

2 in.

45°

2 in.

2x8 joist, 69½ in. long

4x4 post

1x2 ladder-trellis rung

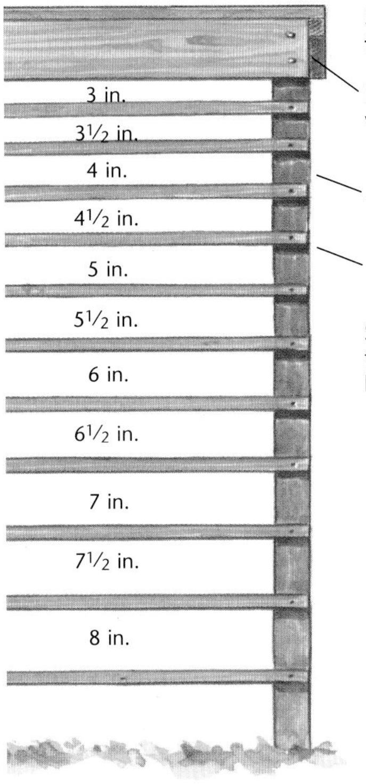

Side elevation of arbor with fence assembly

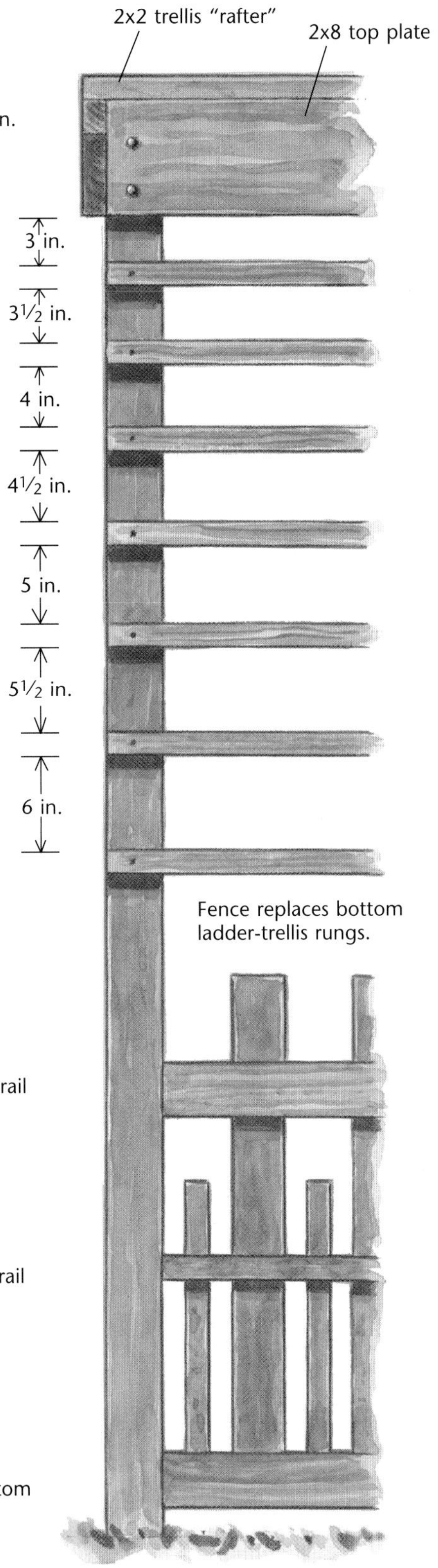

2x2 trellis "rafter"

2x8 top plate

3 in.

3½ in.

4 in.

4½ in.

5 in.

5½ in.

6 in.

Fence replaces bottom ladder-trellis rungs.

Side elevation of freestanding arbor

Fix 2x8 top plate to posts with ⅜x6 carriage bolts.

3 in.

3½ in.

4 in.

4½ in.

5 in.

5½ in.

6 in.

6½ in.

7 in.

7½ in.

8 in.

4x4 post

1x2 ladder-trellis rung

Starting at the top, increase the distance between each ladder-trellis rung by ½ in.

Elevation of fence

4x4 fence post

1x4 slat, 34 in. long

1x2 slat, 21½ in. long

2x4 top rail

9 in.

34 in.

11 in.

2x2 midrail

2x4 bottom rail

2-in. clearance

Space slats 1½ in. apart.

the 1x2 rungs decrease from bottom to top. The drawings show how the fence is incorporated into the design. You can install ladder-trellis rungs above the fence as shown. If you want a more open arbor, replace the trellis rungs with heavy wires to support the vines.

Arbor and fence are both simple to make. The fence will go up quickest if you cut rails to length and nail or screw slats to them, and then attach these assembled sections to the posts.

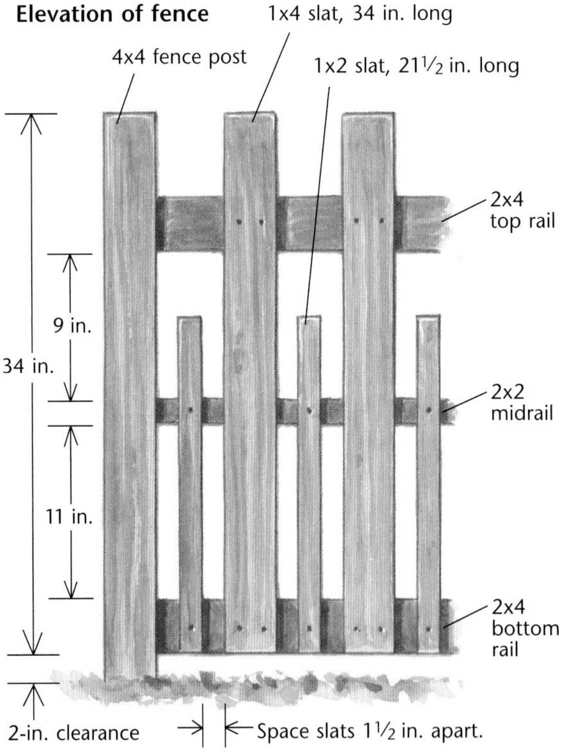

Arbor and fence

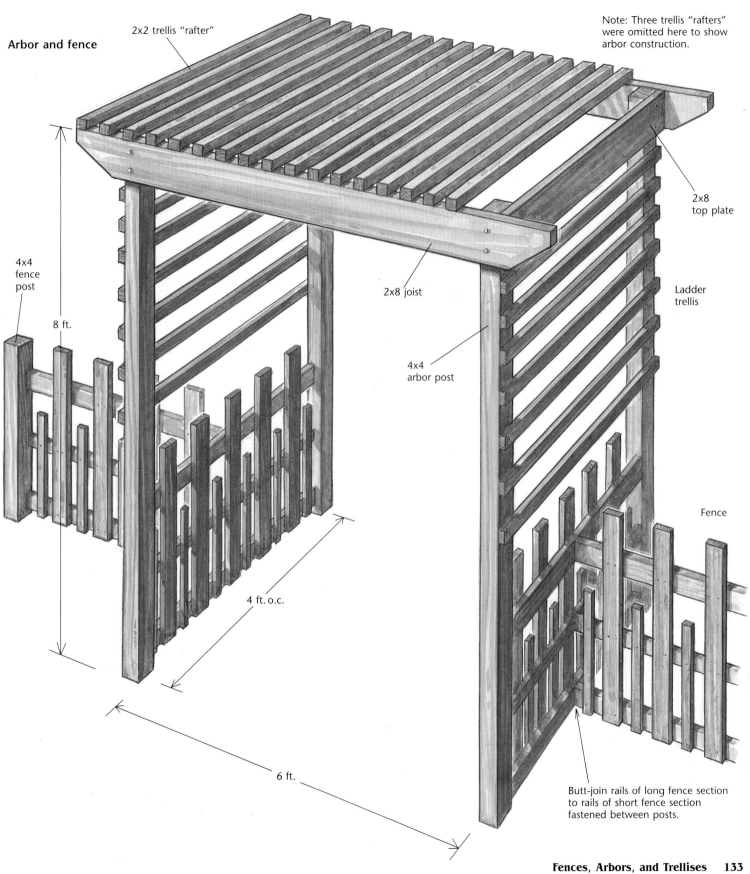

2x2 trellis "rafter"

Note: Three trellis "rafters" were omitted here to show arbor construction.

2x8 top plate

4x4 fence post

8 ft.

2x8 joist

Ladder trellis

4x4 arbor post

4 ft. o.c.

Fence

6 ft.

Butt-join rails of long fence section to rails of short fence section fastened between posts.

Preparing the Soil for Planting

The better the soil, the better the plants. Soil quality affects how fast plants grow, how big they get, how good they look, and how long they live. But on many residential lots, the soil is shallow and infertile. Unless you're lucky enough to have a better-than-average site where the soil has been cared for and amended over the years, perhaps for use as a vegetable garden or flower bed, you should plan to improve your soil before planting in it.

If you were planting just a few trees or shrubs, or planting a bed of perennials on a rocky hillside, you could prepare individual planting holes for the plants and leave the surrounding soil undisturbed. However, for nearly all the plantings in this book, digging individual holes is impractical, and it's much better for the plants if you prepare the soil throughout the entire area that will be planted. (The major exception is when you're planting under a tree, which we'll discuss on p. 136.)

For most of the situations shown in this book, you could prepare the soil with hand tools—a spade, digging fork, and rake. The job will go faster and amendments will mix in better if you use a gas-powered rototiller. Unless you grow vegetables, you probably won't use a rototiller often enough to justify buying one yourself, but you can easily borrow or rent a rototiller or hire someone with a tiller to come and prepare your site.

Loosen the soil

After you've removed any sod or other vegetation from the designated area (see pp. 100–101), the first step is digging or tilling to loosen the soil ❶. Do this on a day when the soil is moist—not so wet that it sticks to your tools or so dry that it makes dust. Start at one end of the bed and work back and forth until you reach the other end. Try to dig down at least 8 in., deeper if possible. If the ground is very compacted, you'll need to make repeated passes with a tiller to reach 8 in. deep. Toss aside any large rocks, roots, or debris that you encounter. When you're working near a house or other buildings, be sure to locate buried wires, cables, and pipes before

Preparing the soil for planting

❶ Use a spade, digging fork, or tiller to dig at least 8 in. deep and break the soil into rough clods. Discard rocks, roots, and debris. Watch out for underground utilities.

❷ Spread a 2- to 3-in. layer of organic matter on top of the soil.

❸ Sprinkle measured amounts of fertilizer and mineral amendments evenly across the entire area, and mix thoroughly into the soil.

digging. Most local governments and utility companies have a number you can call to request help locating buried utilities.

After this initial digging, the ground will likely be very rough and lumpy. Whump the clods with the back of a digging fork or make another pass with the tiller. Continue until you've reduced all the clumps to the size of apples.

Once you've loosened the existing soil and dug it as deeply as possible, you may need to add topsoil to fill in low spots, refine the grade, or raise the planting area above the surrounding grade for better drainage or to make favorite plants easier to see. Unless you need just a small amount, order topsoil by the cubic yard. Consult the staff at your local nursery to find a reputable supplier of topsoil.

Add organic matter

Common soil (and purchased topsoil, too) consists mainly of rock and mineral fragments of various sizes—which are mostly coarse and gritty in sandy soil, and dust-fine in clay soil. One of the best things you can do to improve any kind of soil for landscape and garden plants is to add some organic matter.

Organic materials used in gardening and landscaping are derived from plants and animals and include ground bark, peat moss, compost, and composted manures. Organic matter can be bought in bags or in bulk at nurseries and many municipal recycling centers. If possible, purchase only composted or aged material to amend your soil. Fresh manure can "burn" plant roots. Fresh bark and sawdust can "steal" nitrogen from the soil as they decay. If you buy uncomposted materials, ask at your nursery how best to use them as amendments (some require supplemental nitrogen).

How much organic matter should you use? Compost or aged material can be spread 2 to 3 in. thick across the entire area you're working on ❷. At this thickness, a cubic yard (about one heaping pickup-truck load) of bulk material will

Common soil amendments and fertilizers

The following materials serve different purposes. Follow soil-test recommendations or the advice of an experienced gardener in choosing which amendments and fertilizers would be best for your soil. If so recommended, you can apply two or three of these at the same time, using the stated rate for each one.

Material	Description	Amount for 100 sq. ft.
Compost	Amendment. Decomposed or aged plant parts and animal manures.	1 cu. yd.
Wood by-products	Amendment. Finely ground bark or sawdust, composted or not. Add nitrogen to uncomposted material.	1 cu. yd.
All-purpose fertilizer	Synthetic fertilizer containing various amounts of nitrogen, phosphorus, and potassium.	According to label
Organic fertilizer	Derived from a variety of organic materials. Provides nutrients in slow-release form.	According to label
Composted manure	Weak nitrogen fertilizers. Bagged steer manure is common.	6 to 8 lb.

cover 100 to 150 sq. ft. If you're working on a large area and need several cubic yards of organic matter, have it delivered and dumped close to your project area. You can spread a lot of material in just a few hours if you don't need to cart it very far. Composted and aged manures, such as the bagged steer manure sold at nurseries, contain higher concentrations of nitrogen and should be applied at much lower rates than other composts. They are more commonly used as slow-release fertilizers than as soil-improving amendments.

Add fertilizers and mineral amendments

Organic matter improves the soil's workability and helps it retain water and nutrients, but these materials usually lack essential nutrients. To provide the nutrients that plants need, you typically need to use organic or synthetic fertilizers and powdered minerals, such as lime. It's most helpful if you mix these materials into the soil before you do any planting, putting them down into the root zone as shown in the drawing ❸, but you can also sprinkle them on top of the soil in subsequent years to maintain a planting.

Getting a sample of soil tested is the most accurate way to determine how much of the various nutrients and minerals is needed. (To locate a soil-testing lab, look in the Yellow Pages or ask your Cooperative Extension Service.) Most soil just needs a moderate, balanced dose of nutrients and minerals. Less expensive, though less precise, home test kits can give you rough approximations. Although test results or a local soil expert can suggest soil needs, large deficiencies are uncommon.

The key thing is to avoid using too much of any fertilizer or mineral. Don't guess at this; measure and weigh carefully.

Calculate your plot's area. Follow your soil-test results or instructions on a commercial product's package. If necessary, weigh out the appropriate amount, using a kitchen or bathroom scale. Apply the material evenly across the plot with a spreader or by hand.

Mix and smooth the soil

Finally, use a digging fork or tiller and go back and forth across the bed again until the added materials are mixed thoroughly into the soil and everything is broken into nut-size or smaller lumps ❹. Then use a rake to smooth the surface ❺.

At this point, the soil level may look too high compared with adjacent pavement or lawn, but don't worry. Once the soil gets wet, it will settle a few inches and end up close to its original level.

Working near trees

Plantings under the shade of an old tree can be cool lovely oases. But to establish the plants, you'll need to contend with the tree's roots. Contrary to popular belief, most tree roots are in the top few inches of the soil, and they usually extend beyond the perimeter of the tree's canopy. Always try to disturb as few roots as possible when planting beneath established trees. To do so, it's often best to dig individual planting holes. Avoid cutting large roots. To start ground covers and perennials, you can add up to 6 in. of soil under the canopy of many trees. Keep the new soil and mulch away from the trunk. Covering roots with too much soil can starve them of oxygen, damaging or killing them; soil or mulch next to the trunk can rot the bark.

Plantings beneath existing cedar, fir, and hemlock trees are normally problematic because the additional water needed to maintain the planting may damage or kill these trees. If you're uncertain about whether or how to plant beneath any established tree, or if your landscape plans call for significant grade changes beneath it, consult with a certified arborist.

❹ Use a tiller or digging fork to mix everything together, again working as deep as possible.

❺ Finish by smoothing the surface with a rake.

Making neat edges

All but the most informal landscapes look best if you define and maintain neat edges between the lawn and any adjacent plantings. There are several ways to do this, varying in appearance, effectiveness, cost, and convenience. Attractive, easy-to-install edges include cut, brick or stone, and plastic strip. If you plan to install an edging, put it in after you prepare the soil but before you plant the bed.

Cut edge

Lay a hose or rope on the ground to mark the line where you want to cut. Then cut along the line with a sharp spade or edging tool. Lift away any grass that was growing into the bed (or any existing plants that were running out into the lawn). Use a rake or hoe to smooth out a shallow trench on the bed side of the cut. Keep the trench empty; don't let it fill up with mulch.

Pros and cons: Free. Good for straight or curved edges, level or sloped sites. You have to recut the edge every four to eight weeks during the growing season, but you can cut 50 to 100 ft. in an hour or so. Don't cut the trench too deep; if a mower wheel slips down into it, you scalp the lawn. Weedy grasses and other weeds may sprout in the exposed soil; if this happens, hoe or pull them out.

Brick mowing strip

Dig a trench about 8 in. wide and 4 in. deep around the edge of the bed. Fill it halfway with sand; then lay bricks on top, setting them level with the soil on the lawn side. You'll need three bricks

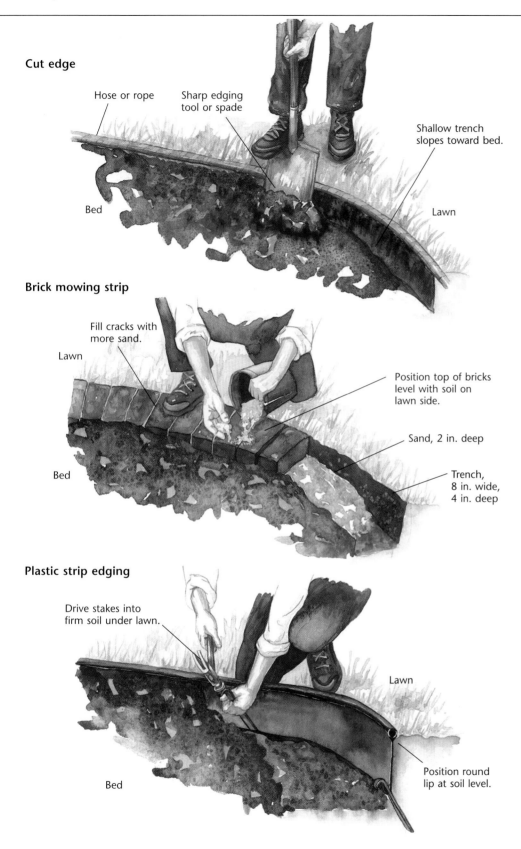

Cut edge

Hose or rope

Sharp edging tool or spade

Shallow trench slopes toward bed.

Bed

Lawn

Brick mowing strip

Fill cracks with more sand.

Lawn

Position top of bricks level with soil on lawn side.

Sand, 2 in. deep

Bed

Trench, 8 in. wide, 4 in. deep

Plastic strip edging

Drive stakes into firm soil under lawn.

Lawn

Bed

Position round lip at soil level.

per foot of edging. Sweep extra sand into any cracks between the bricks. In cold-winter areas, you'll probably need to reset a few frost-heaved bricks each spring. You can substitute cut stone blocks or concrete pavers for bricks.

Pros and cons: Good for straight or curved edges on level or gently sloped sites. Looks good in combination with brick walkways or brick house. Fairly easy to install and maintain. Some kinds of grass and plants will grow under, between, or over the bricks.

Plastic strip edging

Garden centers and home-improvement stores sell heavy-duty plastic edging in strips 5 or 6 in. wide and 20 or 50 ft. long. To install it, use a sharp tool to cut straight down through the sod around the edge of the bed. Hold the edging so the round lip sits right at soil level, and drive the stakes through the bottom of the edging and into the undisturbed soil under the lawn. Stakes, which are supplied with the edging, should be at least 8 in. long and set about 3 ft. apart.

Pros and cons: Good for straight or curved edges, but only on relatively level sites. Neat and carefree when well installed, but installation is a two- or three-person job. If the lip isn't set right on the ground, you're likely to hit it with the mower blade. Liable to shift or heave unless it's very securely staked. Hard to drive stakes in rocky soil. Some kinds of grass and ground covers can grow across the top of the edging.

Buying Plants

Once you have chosen and planned a landscape project, make a list of the plants you want and start thinking about where to get them. You'll need to locate the kinds of plants you're looking for, choose good-quality plants, and get enough of the plants to fill your design area.

Where and how to shop

You may already have a favorite place to shop for plants. If not, look in the Yellow Pages under the headings "Nurseries," "Nurserymen," and "Garden Centers," and choose a few places to visit. Take your shopping list, find a salesperson, and ask for help. The plants in this book are commonly available in the Northwest, but you may not find everything you want at one place. The salesperson may refer you to another nursery, offer to special-order plants, or recommend similar plants that you could use as substitutes.

If you're buying too many plants to carry in your car or truck, ask about delivery—it's usually available, though it may cost extra. Some nurseries offer to replace plants that fail within a limited guarantee period, so ask about that, too.

The staff at a good nursery or garden center will normally be able to answer most of the questions you have about which plants to buy and how to care for them. If you can, go shopping on a weekday when business is slow so staff will have time to answer your questions.

Don't be lured by the low prices of plants for sale at supermarkets or stores that sell plants for only a few months unless you're sure you know exactly what you're looking for and what you're looking at. The staff at these stores rarely have the time or knowledge to offer you much help, and the plants are often disorganized, unlabeled, and stressed by poor care.

If you can't find a plant locally or have a retailer order it for you, you can always order it yourself from a mail-order nursery. Most mail-order nurseries produce good plants and pack them well, but if you haven't dealt with a business before, be smart and place a minimum order first. Judge the quality of the plants that arrive; then decide whether or not to order larger quantities from that firm.

Choosing particular plants

If you need, for example, five azaleas and the nursery or garden center has a whole block of them, how do you choose which five to buy? Because the sales staff may be too busy to help you decide, you may need to choose by yourself.

Most plants today are grown in containers, so it's possible to lift them one at a time and examine them from all sides. Following the guidelines shown in the drawings below, evaluate each plant's shape, size, health and vigor, and root system.

Trees and shrubs are sometimes sold "balled-and-burlapped," that is, with a ball

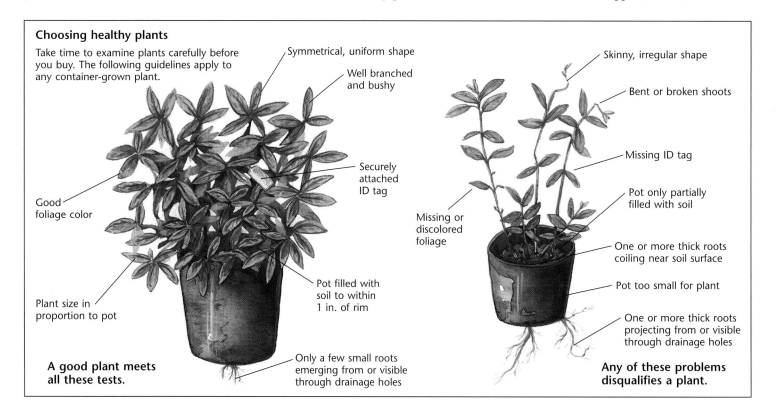

Choosing healthy plants

Take time to examine plants carefully before you buy. The following guidelines apply to any container-grown plant.

Symmetrical, uniform shape

Well branched and bushy

Securely attached ID tag

Good foliage color

Plant size in proportion to pot

Pot filled with soil to within 1 in. of rim

A good plant meets all these tests.

Only a few small roots emerging from or visible through drainage holes

Skinny, irregular shape

Bent or broken shoots

Missing ID tag

Pot only partially filled with soil

Missing or discolored foliage

One or more thick roots coiling near soil surface

Pot too small for plant

One or more thick roots projecting from or visible through drainage holes

Any of these problems disqualifies a plant.

of soil and roots wrapped tightly in burlap. For these plants, look for strong limbs with no broken shoots, an attractive profile, and healthy foliage. Then press your hands against the burlap-covered root ball to make sure that it feels firm, solid, and damp, not loose or dry. (If the ball is buried within a bed of wood chips or sawdust, carefully pull the material aside; then push it back after inspecting the plant.)

To make the final choice when you're considering a group of plants, line them up side by side and select the ones that are most closely matched in height, bushiness, and foliage color. If your design includes a hedge or mass planting where uniformity is very important, it's a good idea to buy a few extra plants as potential replacements in case of damage or loss—it may not be so easy to find matches later. Plant the extras in a spare corner so you'll have them if you need them.

Sometimes a plant will be available in two or more sizes. Which is better? That depends on how patient you are. The main reason for buying bigger plants is to make a landscape look impressive right away. If you buy smaller plants and set them out at the same spacing, the planting will look sparse at first, but it will soon catch up. A year after planting, you can't tell if a perennial came from a 4-in. or a gallon-size pot: they will look the same. For shrubs, the difference between one size pot and the next usually represents one year's growth.

Timing

It's a good idea to plan ahead and start shopping for plants before you're ready to put them in the ground. That way, if you can't find everything on your list, you'll have time to keep shopping around, place special orders, or choose substitutes. Most nurseries will let you "flag" an order for later pickup or delivery, and they'll take care of the plants in the meantime. Or you can bring the plants home; just remember to check the soil in the containers every day and water if needed.

The Planting Process

Throughout the Northwest, fall and early spring, with their cooler weather, are the best times for planting. At those times of year, new plants have the upcoming wet season to become established before the onset of dry summer weather.

Although it's handy to plant a whole bed at once, you can divide the job, setting out some plants in fall and adding the rest in spring, or vice versa. If possible, do the actual planting on a cloudy day or evening when rain is forecast. Compared with preparing the soil, putting plants in the ground goes quite quickly. If you're well prepared, you can plant a whole bed in just an hour or two. On the following pages we'll give an overview of the process and discuss how to handle individual plants. If you're installing an irrigation system, remember that some of the components may need to be put in place after the soil is prepared but before planting.

Try to stay off the soil

Throughout the planting process, do all you can by reaching in from outside the bed. Stepping on a newly prepared bed compacts the soil and makes it harder to dig planting holes. If you do need to step on the soil, use short boards or scraps of plywood as temporary steppingstones. As soon as you can decide where to put them, lay permanent steppingstones for access to plants that need regular maintenance.

Check placement and spacing

The first step in planting is to mark the position of each plant. It's easy to arrange most of the plants themselves on the bed; use empty pots or stakes to represent plants that are too heavy to move easily. Follow the site plan for the design, checking the spacing with a yardstick as you place the plants.

Then step back and take a look. What do you think? Should any of the plants be adjusted a little—moved to the left or right, a little closer together or farther apart? Don't worry if the planting looks a little sparse. It *should* look that way at first. Plants almost always get bigger than you can imagine when you're first setting them out. And it's almost always better to wait for them to fill in rather than having to prune and thin a crowded planting in a few years. (You might fill between young plants with low-growing annuals, as suggested in the box on p. 140.)

Planting pointer
When working on top of prepared soil, kneel on a piece of plywood to distribute your weight.

Moving through the job

When you're satisfied with the arrangement, mark the position of each plant with a stake or stone, and set the plants aside, out of the way, so you won't knock them over or step on them as you proceed. Start planting in order of size. Do the biggest plants first; then move on to the medium-size and smaller plants. If all the plants are about the same size, start at the back of the bed and work toward the front, or start in the center and work to the edges.

Using annuals as fillers

The plants in our designs have been spaced so they will not be crowded at maturity. Buying more plants and spacing them closer may fill things out faster, but in several years (for perennials; longer for shrubs) you'll need to remove plants or prune them frequently.

If you want something to fill the gaps between young plants for that first year or two, use some annuals. The best annual fillers are compact plants that grow only 6 to 10 in. tall. These plants will hide the soil or mulch and make a colorful carpet. Avoid taller annuals, because they can shade or smother your permanent plantings. And don't forget, filler plants will need water.

The annuals listed here are all compact, easy to grow, readily available, and inexpensive. Seeds of those marked with a symbol (❀) can be sown directly in the garden. For the others, buy six-packs or flats of plants. Thin seedlings or space plants 8 to 12 in. apart.

Ageratum: Fluffy blue, lavender, or white flowers. Choose dwarf types. Full sun (if watered) or partial shade.

Annual chrysanthemum: Bears white, pink, or yellow daisies all summer. Full sun.

Dusty miller: Silvery foliage, often lacy-textured. Full sun or partial shade.

❀ **Dwarf calendula:** Flowers in warm yellow and orange tones. Full sun.

Garden verbena: Bright red, pink, purple, or white flowers. Full sun.

Geranium: Red, pink, purple, or white flowers. Good for full sun.

Impatiens: Flowers in many colors. Slugs usually avoid them. Shade.

Lobelia: Dark blue, magenta, or white flowers. Best in full sun.

Pansy and viola: Multicolored flowers. Grow best in cool weather. Full sun.

❀ **Sweet alyssum:** Months of fragrant white or lilac flowers. Prefers cool weather. Full sun (if watered) or partial shade.

Wax begonia: Rose, pink, or white flowers. Good for shady sites but takes sun if watered regularly.

Position trees and shrubs to show their best side

Most trees and shrubs are slightly asymmetric. There's usually enough irregularity in their branching or shape that one side looks a little fuller or more attractive than the other sides do. After you've set a tree or shrub into its hole, step back and take a look. Then turn it partway, or try tilting or tipping it a little to one side or the other. Once you've decided which side and position looks best, start filling in the hole with soil. Stop and check again before you firm the soil into place.

The fine points of spacing

When you're planting a group of the same kind of plants, such as perennials, bulbs, ferns, or ground covers, it normally looks best if you space them in slightly curved or zigzag rows, with the plants in one row offset from those of the next row. Don't arrange plants like soldiers in single file unless you want to emphasize a line, such as the edge of a bed. In that case, make the row perfectly straight by sighting down it and adjusting any plants that are out of line. (Stretch a string for long rows.)

After planting, step back and evaluate the effect. If you want to adjust the placement or position of any plant, now is the time to do so.

Rake, water, and mulch

Use a garden rake to level out any high and low spots that remain in the bed after planting. Water enough to settle the soil into place around the roots. You can use a hose or watering can and water each plant individually, or you can set up a sprinkler to do the whole planting at once. Mulch the entire planting area with 1 to 3 in. of bark, wood chips, or compost.

Mulch is indispensable for controlling weeds and regulating the moisture and temperature of the soil. If you're running out of time, you don't have to spread the mulch right away, but try to do so within a week or so after planting.

Planting Basics

Planting container-grown plants

① Dig a hole about twice as wide as the container but not as deep.

② Remove the plant from the container.

③ Unwind any large, coiled roots and cut them off short. Cut vertical slits through masses of fine roots.

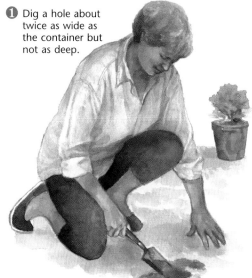

④ Position the plant in the hole and fill around it with soil.

Most of the plants that you buy for a landscaping project today are grown and sold in individual plastic containers. A few large shrubs and trees may be balled-and-burlapped, and some deciduous plants are sold bare-root. Ground covers are sometimes sold in flats. In any case, the basic concern is the same: Be careful what you do to a plant's roots. Spread them out; don't fold or coil them or cram them into a tight hole. Keep them covered; don't let the sun or air dry them out. And don't bury them too deep; the top of the root ball should be level with or slightly above the surface of the surrounding soil.

Planting container-grown plants

The steps are the same for any plant, no matter what size container it's growing in. Dig a hole about twice as wide as the container but not quite as deep—the top of the soil in the container should be slightly higher than the surrounding soil **①**. Dig several holes at a time, at the positions that you've already marked out.

Remove the container **②**. With one hand, grip the plant at the base of its stems or leaves, like pulling a ponytail, while you tug on the pot with the other hand. (Avoid squeezing the stems.) If the pot doesn't slide off easily, don't pull harder on the stems. Try whacking the pot with your trowel; if it still doesn't slide off, use a strong knife to cut or pry it off.

Examine the plant's roots **③**. If there are any thick, coiled roots, unwind them and cut them off close to the root ball, leaving short stubs. If the root ball is a mass of fine, hairlike roots, use the knife to cut three or four slits from top to bottom, about 1 in. deep. Pry the slits apart and tease the cut roots to loosen them. This cutting or slitting may seem drastic, but it's actually good for the plant because it forces new roots to grow out into the surrounding soil. Work quickly. Once you've taken a plant out of its container, get it in the ground as soon as possible. If you want to prepare several plants at a time, cover them with a wet sheet or tarp to keep the roots from drying out.

Set the root ball into the hole **④**. Make sure that the plant is positioned right, with its best side facing out, and that the top of the root ball is level with or slightly higher than the surface of the bed. Then add enough soil to fill in the hole, and pat it down firmly.

Planting a balled-and-burlapped shrub or tree

Some nurseries often grow shrubs and trees in fields, then dig them with a ball of root-filled soil and wrap a layer of burlap snugly around the ball to keep it intact. The main drawback with this system is that even a

Balled-and-burlapped

The top of the ball should be level with the surrounding soil. Cut twine that wraps around the trunk. Fold down the burlap, but don't remove it.

Ground covers in flats

Remove a clump of little plants, tease their roots apart, and plant them quickly.

Bare-root plants

Dig a hole wide enough that you can spread out the roots. A stick helps you position the plant at the correct depth as you fill the hole with soil.

Bulbs

Plant bulbs with the pointed end up, at a depth and spacing determined by the size of the bulb.

when the plants are dormant; cut back the tops; and clean all the soil off the roots, to save space and weight when storing and shipping them. If you receive a bare-root plant, unwrap it, trim away any roots that are broken or damaged, and soak the roots in a pail of water for several hours.

To plant, dig a hole large enough that you can spread the roots across the bottom without folding them. Start covering the roots with soil, then lay a stick across the top of the hole and hold the plant against it to check the planting depth, as shown in the drawing. Raise or lower the plant if needed in order to bury just the roots, not the buds. Add more soil, firming it down around the roots, and continue until the hole is full.

Planting ground covers from flats

Sometimes ground covers are sold in flats of 25 or more rooted cuttings. Start at one corner, reach underneath the soil, and lift out a portion of the flat's contents. Working quickly, because the roots are exposed, tease the cuttings apart, trying not to break off any roots, and plant them individually. Then lift out the next portion and continue planting.

Planting bulbs

Plant daffodils, tulips, crocuses, and other spring-blooming bulbs in October and November, when fresh bulbs are available at local garden centers or delivered by catalog merchants. If the soil in the bed was well prepared, you can use a trowel to dig holes for planting individual bulbs; where you have room, you can dig a wider hole or trench for planting a group of bulbs all at once. The perennials, ground covers, shrubs, and trees you planted earlier in the fall or in the spring will still be small enough that planting bulbs among them won't unduly disturb their root systems. As a rule of thumb, plant small (grape- or cherry-size) bulbs about 2 in. deep and 3 to 5 in. apart, and large (walnut- or egg-size) bulbs 4 to 6 in. deep and 6 to 10 in. apart.

small ball of soil is heavy. If the ball is more than a foot wide, moving the plant is usually a two-person job. If you're buying a tree with a ball bigger than that, consider having the nursery deliver and plant it. Here's how to proceed with plants that are small enough that you can handle them.

Dig a hole several inches wider than the root ball but not quite as deep as the root ball is high. (Step in the bottom of the hole to firm the soil so the plant won't settle deeper.) Set the plant into the hole, and lay a stick across the top of the root ball to make sure it's at or a little higher than

grade level. Rotate the plant until its best side faces out. Be sure to cut or untie any twine that wraps around the trunk. Fold the burlap down around the sides of the ball, as shown in the drawing. Don't try to remove the burlap—roots can grow out through it, and it will eventually decompose. Fill soil all around the sides of the ball and pat it down firmly. Spread only an inch of soil over the top of the ball.

Planting bare-root plants

Mail-order nurseries sometimes dig perennials, roses, and some deciduous plants

Planting on a hillside

Successful planting on a hillside depends on keeping the bare soil and young plants from blowing or washing away while they establish themselves. Here are some tips. Rather than digging and amending all the soil, prepare individual planting holes. Work from the top of the slope to the bottom. Push one or more wooden shingles into the slope just below a plant to help hold it in place. Mulch with heavier materials, such as wood chips, that won't wash or blow away. If the soil is loose, spread water-permeable landscape fabric over it to help hold it in place; slit the fabric and insert plants through the openings. Water with drip irrigation, which is less likely to erode soil than sprinklers are.

Basic Landscape Care

The landscape plantings in this book will grow increasingly carefree from year to year as the plants mature, but of course you'll always need to do some regular maintenance. This ongoing care may require as much as a few hours a week during the season or as little as a few hours a year. You'll have to control weeds, use mulch, water as needed, and do spring and fall cleanups. Trees, shrubs, and vines may need staking or training at first and occasional pruning or shearing afterward. Perennials, ground covers, and grasses may need to be cut back, staked, deadheaded, or divided. Performing these tasks, which are explained on the following pages, is sometimes hard work, but for many gardeners it is enjoyable labor, a chance to get outside in the fresh air. Also, spending time each week with your plants helps you identify and address problems before they become serious.

Mulches and fertilizers

Covering the soil in all planted areas with a layer of organic mulch does several jobs at once: it improves the appearance of your garden while you're waiting for the plants to grow, reduces the number of weeds that emerge, retards water loss from the soil during dry spells, moderates soil temperatures, and adds nutrients to the soil as it decomposes. Inorganic mulches such as landscape fabric and gravel also provide some of these benefits, but their conspicuous appearance and the difficulty of removing them if you ever want to change the landscape are serious drawbacks.

Many materials are used as mulches; the box on p. 144 presents the most common, with comments on their advantages and disadvantages. Consider appearance, availability, cost, and convenience when you're comparing different products. Most garden centers have a few kinds of bagged mulch materials, but for mulching large areas, it's easier and cheaper to have a nursery or other supplier deliver a truckload of bulk mulch. A landscape looks best if you see the same mulch throughout the entire planting area, rather than a patchwork of different mulches. You can achieve a uniform look by spreading a base layer of newspaper, hay, or other inexpensive material and topping that with a neater-looking material such as wood chips, shredded bark, or compost.

It takes at least a 1-in. layer of mulch to suppress weeds, but there's no need to spread it more than 3 in. deep. As you're spreading it, don't put any mulch against the stems of any plants, because that can lead to disease or insect problems. So put mulch around plants but not right up to them. Check the mulch during your spring and fall cleanups. Be sure it's pulled back away from the plant stems. Rake the surface of the mulch lightly to loosen it, and top it up with a fresh layer if the old material has decomposed.

Fertilizer

Decomposing mulch frequently supplies enough nutrients to grow healthy plants, but using fertilizer helps if you want to boost the plants—to make them grow faster, get larger, or produce more flowers. Young plants or those growing in poor soils also benefit from occasional applications of fertilizer. There are dozens of fertilizer products on the market—liquid and granular, fast-acting and slow-release, organic and synthetic. All give good results if applied as directed. And observe the following precautions: Don't overfertilize, don't fertilize when the soil is dry, and don't fertilize tender plants after late summer, because they need to slow down and finish the season's growth before cold weather comes.

Controlling weeds

Weeds are not much of a problem in established landscapes. Once the "good" plants have grown big enough to merge together, they tend to crowd or shade out all but the most persistent undesirable plants. But weeds can be troublesome in a new landscape unless you take steps to prevent and control them.

There are two main types of weeds: those that mostly sprout up as seedlings and those that keep coming back from perennial roots or runners. Try to identify and eliminate any perennial weeds before you start a landscaping project (see p. 100). Then you'll only have to deal with new weed seedlings later, which is easier.

Annual and perennial weeds that commonly grow from seeds include annual bluegrass, bindweed, dandelions, oxalis, plantain, and spurge. Trees and shrubs

---

Mulch materials

Bark products. Bark nuggets, chipped bark, shredded bark, ground bark, and composted bark, usually from conifers, are available in bags or in bulk. All are attractive, long-lasting, medium-price mulches.

Chipped tree trimmings. The chips available from utility companies and tree services are a mixture of wood, bark, twigs, and leaves. Excellent for paths, these chips cost less than pure bark products (you may be able to get a load for free), but they don't look as good and you have to replace them more often, because they decompose fast.

Sawdust and shavings. These are cheap at sawmills and woodshops. They make good path coverings, but they aren't ideal mulches. The microorganisms that break down the wood fibers compete with landscape plants for nitrogen in the soil. Sawdust also tends to pack down into a dense, water-resistant surface.

Hulls and shells. Ground coconut hulls, cocoa hulls, and nut shells can be picked up at food-processing plants and are sometimes sold at garden centers. They're all attractive, long-lasting mulches. Price varies from free to quite expensive, depending on where you get them.

Tree leaves. A few big trees may supply all the mulch you need, year after year. You can just rake the leaves onto a bed in fall, but it's better to chop them up with the lawn mower, pile them in compost bins for the winter, and spread them where needed in late spring.

Grass clippings. A 1- to 2-in. layer of dried grass clippings makes an acceptable mulch that decomposes within a single growing season. Don't pile clippings too thick, though. If you do, the top surface dries and packs into a water-resistant crust, and the bottom layer turns into nasty slime.

Hay and straw. Farmers sell hay that's unsuitable for fodder as "mulch" hay. Hay is cheap but is likely to include weed seeds. Straw—the stems of grain crops such as wheat—contains fewer seeds, but it can be more expensive. Both hay and straw are more suitable for mulching vegetable gardens than landscape plantings because they decompose quickly and must be renewed each year. They also tend to attract rodents.

Gravel. A mulch of pea gravel or crushed rock, spread 1 to 2 in. thick, helps keep the soil cool and moist, and many plants grow very well with a gravel mulch. However, compared with organic materials such as bark or leaves, it's much more tiring to apply a gravel mulch in the first place; it's harder to remove leaves and litter that accumulate on the gravel or weeds that sprout up through it; it's annoying to dig through the gravel if you want to replace or add plants later; and it's tedious to remove the gravel itself, should you ever change your mind about having it there. Gravel mulches also reflect heat and can make a yard hotter than normal.

Landscape fabrics. Various types of synthetic fabrics, usually sold in rolls 3 to 4 ft. wide and 20, 50, or 100 ft. long, can be spread over the ground as a weed barrier. Unlike plastic, these fabrics allow water and air to penetrate into the soil. A topping of gravel, bark chips, or other mulch can anchor the fabric and hide it from view. If you're planting small plants, you can spread the fabric and insert the plants through X-shaped slits cut in the fabric where needed. You can plant larger plants first, then cut and snug the fabric around them. Drip irrigation is best laid on top of the fabric, to make it easier to see clogs and leaks. It's also useful to lay fabric under paths, although it can be difficult to secure the fabric neatly and invisibly along the edges of adjacent planting beds. Removing fabric—if you change your mind—is a messy job. However, there are newer biodegradable fabrics that break down after a few years.

Clear or black plastic. Don't even think about using any kind of plastic sheeting as a landscape mulch. The soil underneath a sheet of plastic gets bone-dry, while water accumulates on top. Any loose mulch you spread on plastic won't stay in an even layer. No matter how you try to secure them, the edges of plastic sheeting always pull loose, appear at the surface, degrade in the sun, and shred into tatters. Use landscape fabrics instead.

such as big-leaf maple, alder, cottonwood, and Scotch broom produce weedy seedlings, too. For any of these weeds that grow from seeds, the strategy is twofold: try to keep the weed seeds from sprouting, and eliminate any seedlings as soon as you see them, while they are still small.

Almost any patch of soil includes weed seeds that are ready to sprout whenever that soil is disturbed. Preparing the soil for planting will probably cause an initial flush of weeds, but you'll never see that many weeds again if you leave the soil undisturbed in subsequent years. You don't have to hoe, rake, or cultivate around perennial plantings. If you leave the soil alone, fewer weeds will appear. Using mulch helps even more; by shading the soil, it prevents weed seeds from sprouting. And if weed seeds blow in and land on top of the mulch, they'll be less likely to germinate there than they would on bare soil.

In the Northwest, weed seedlings can emerge almost anytime except the drier months of August and September. Pull or cut them off while they're young and small, just a few inches tall. Don't let them mature and go to seed. Also, weeds that overwinter will be much stronger and harder to pull the following spring.

Using herbicides

Two kinds of herbicides can be very useful and effective in maintaining home landscapes, but only if used correctly. You need to choose the right product for the job and follow the directions on the label regarding dosage and timing of application exactly.

Preemergent herbicides. Sold in granular or liquid form, these herbicides are designed to prevent weed seeds, particularly weed grasses and other annual weeds, from sprouting. Make the first application in late fall before the first rain. You'll probably need to make another application in spring before hot weather sets in. Follow package directions to determine how long to wait between applications.

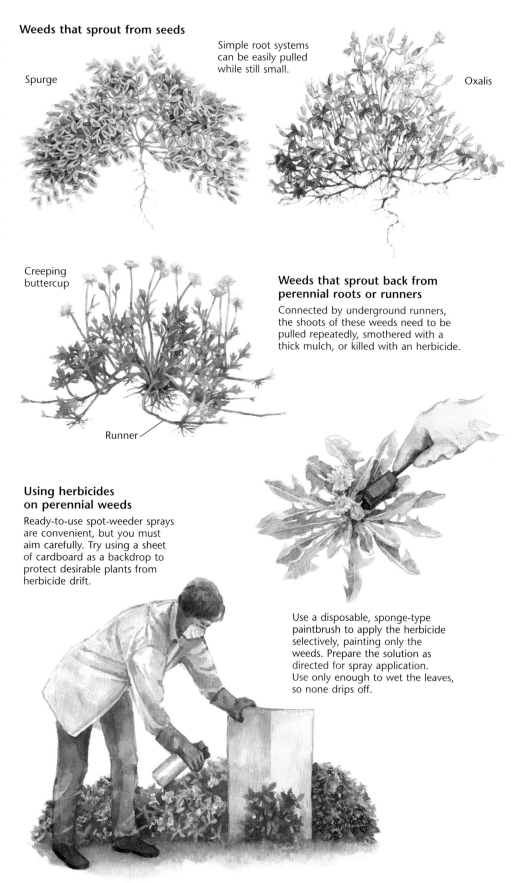

Weeds that sprout from seeds

Spurge

Simple root systems can be easily pulled while still small.

Oxalis

Creeping buttercup

Runner

Weeds that sprout back from perennial roots or runners

Connected by underground runners, the shoots of these weeds need to be pulled repeatedly, smothered with a thick mulch, or killed with an herbicide.

Using herbicides on perennial weeds

Ready-to-use spot-weeder sprays are convenient, but you must aim carefully. Try using a sheet of cardboard as a backdrop to protect desirable plants from herbicide drift.

Use a disposable, sponge-type paintbrush to apply the herbicide selectively, painting only the weeds. Prepare the solution as directed for spray application. Use only enough to wet the leaves, so none drips off.

Read the label carefully, and make sure the herbicide you buy is registered for use around the kinds of ground covers, perennials, shrubs, or other plants you have. Granular forms are often used in smaller areas, liquid in larger areas. Apply them exactly as described on the product label. Wear a dust mask and heavy rubber gloves that are rated for use with farm chemicals, not common household rubber gloves, and follow the safety precautions on the label.

Postemergent herbicides. These chemicals are used to kill growing plants. Some kill only the aboveground parts of a plant; others are absorbed into the plant and kill it, roots and all. Postemergent herbicides are typically applied as sprays, which you can buy ready-to-use or prepare by mixing a concentrate with water. Look for those that break down quickly into less-toxic substances. Follow label instructions carefully for safety and registered applications.

Postemergent herbicides work best if applied when the weeds are growing vigorously. You usually have to apply enough to thoroughly wet the plant's leaves, and do it during a spell of dry weather. Applying an herbicide is an effective way to get rid of a perennial weed that you can't dig or pull up, but it's really better to do this before you plant a bed, as it's hard to spray herbicides in an established planting without getting some on your good plants. (Some postemergent herbicides are more selective, affecting only certain types of plants.) Aim carefully, shielding nearby plants as shown in the drawing on p. 145, and don't spray on windy days. Brushing or sponging the herbicide on the leaves is slower than spraying, but you're sure to avoid damaging adjacent plants.

Using postemergent herbicides in an established planting is a painstaking job, but it may be the only way to get rid of a persistent perennial weed, such as creeping buttercup. For young weed seedlings, it's usually easier and faster to pull them by hand than to spray them.

Watering

Watering, as we've discussed previously (see pp. 102–103), is a summertime necessity for most residential landscapes in the Northwest. To use water efficiently and effectively, it is helpful to know how to gauge when your plants need water, how much water they need, and how to ensure that you supply the desired amounts.

Deciding if water is needed

Many experienced gardeners can judge whether a plant needs water simply by looking at its leaves. But drooping or dull leaves can be caused by pests, disease, and overwatering as well as by water stress. A surer way to decide whether you need to water is to examine the soil. If the top 3 to 4 in. is dry, most annuals, perennials, and shallow-rooted shrubs such as rhododendrons will need to be watered. Most trees and larger shrubs need water if the top 6 to 8 in. is dry. To check soil moisture, you can get down on your knees and dig. But digging in an established planting can be awkward as well as harmful to crowded roots.

There are several less invasive methods of checking moisture. In the loose soil of a prepared bed, you can use a paint stirrer or similar piece of unfinished, light-colored wood as though it were a dipstick. Push it down through the mulch and 6 to 8 in. into the soil. Leave it there for an hour or so, and pull it out to see if moisture has soaked in and discolored the wood. If so, the soil is moist enough for plants. If not, it's time to water.

Where ground is more compacted or where you want to gauge moisture at greater depths, you can push a $1/4$- to $1/2$-in.-diameter iron bar into the soil. The bar will move easily through wet soil. When it encounters dry soil, the bar will become harder to push or it will feel different as you push. Note that a layer of hardpan beneath the soil can also slow down or stop the bar's penetration.

Paying attention to rainfall also helps you gauge when plants may need water. In the Northwest, most landscape plants thrive if they get several inches of rain a month. Install a simple rain gauge on your

Checking soil moisture

Stick a paint stirrer or similar piece of light-colored, unfinished wood down through the mulch and into the soil. Pull it up after an hour. If the bottom of the stick looks and feels damp, the soil is moist enough for plants.

Monitoring a sprinkler

Set several tuna-fish cans throughout the area, and let the sprinkler run until about 1 in. of water has collected in each can.

property and listen to weather reports. Mark significant rainfall amounts on a calendar for easy reference. During the drier summer months, you'll need to supply most if not all of your plants' water needs.

New plantings, even those of drought-tolerant plants, require frequent watering during the first year or two until the plants are established. In summer, new plantings may require water twice a week or more. Also, plants under eaves or in other protected areas can suffer from dryness in any season, not just in the heat of summer.

Early in the morning is the best time of day to water. The wind is calm, evaporation is low, and plant foliage will have plenty of time to dry off before nightfall, which helps reduce fungal growth.

How much to water

Determining how much water to apply and how often to apply it is one of gardening's greatest challenges. Water too much and plants drown. Water too little and they dry out and die. The key to watering enough but not too much is to be a good observer. Examine your soil often, keep an eye on your plants, and make adjustments with the weather.

Established landscape plants vary in their water needs. When you do water, it is always best to water deeply, wetting a large portion of the plant's root zone. Shallow watering encourages shallow rooting, and shallow-rooted plants dry out fast and need watering more frequently. Furthermore, a water-stressed plant is also more susceptible to disease and insect damage.

If you decide your plants need a certain amount of water, you need to know how long to run your system to provide it. Different watering systems, from hose-end sprinklers to automated drip systems, deliver water at different rates. Manufacturers often provide rates for their products. You can determine a sprinkler's rate by setting tuna-fish cans in the area it covers and timing how long it takes to deposit an inch of water in one or more cans.

Caring for Woody Plants

A well-chosen garden tree, such as those recommended in this book, grows naturally into a pleasing shape, won't get too large for its site, is resistant to pests and diseases, and doesn't drop messy pods or other litter. Once established, these trees need very little care from year to year.

Regular watering is the most important concern in getting a tree off to a good start. Don't let it suffer from drought for the first few years. To reduce competition, don't plant ground covers or other plants within 2 ft. of the tree's trunk. Just spread a thin layer of mulch there.

Arborists now dismiss some care ideas that once were common practice. According to current thinking, you don't need to fertilize a tree when you plant it (in fact, unless they show obvious signs of deficiency or grow poorly, most landscape trees never need fertilizing). Keep pruning to a minimum at planting time; remove only dead or damaged twigs, not healthy shoots. Finally, research has shown that tree trunks grow stronger when they're not supported by stakes. However, newly planted trees often need some support. A sturdy stake, 3 to 4 ft. above ground, placed on the upwind side of the trunk works well. Tie the trunk loosely to the stake, and remove the tie after no more than a year. Ask your nursery for specifics about proper staking for your tree.

Shaping young trees

As a tree grows, you can affect its shape by pruning once a year, usually in winter. But don't prune just for the sake of pruning;

Pruning basics

Proper pruning keeps plants healthy and looking their best. There are two basic types of pruning cuts: heading and thinning. Heading cuts are made along the length of a branch or stem, between its tip and its base. These cuts induce vigorous growth in the dormant buds below the cut. Such growth is useful for filling in hedges and rejuvenating shrubs and perennials. But heading can drastically change the appearance of a plant, even destroying its natural shape. Heading larger limbs can also produce weakly attached new growth in trees and shrubs.

Thinning cuts remove stems and branches at their origin (the plant's crown or where the branch attaches to the trunk or a larger limb). Unlike heading, thinning does not produce vigorous growth. Instead, thinning opens the plant's interior to light and air, which

Bushier growth

For many plants, simple heading cuts can produce fuller, bushier growth. Cut off the ends of stems to induce growth from lower buds.

New growth

improves its health. And, by reducing congested growth, thinning often enhances the natural appearance of the plant. In most cases, thinning is the preferred pruning technique, especially for trees and shrubs.

Pruning roses

Roses are vigorous, fast-growing shrubs that need regular pruning to keep them shapely and attractive. Most of this pruning is done in late winter to early spring, just as the buds start to swell but before the new leaves start to unfold. Always use sharp pruning shears and cut back to a healthy bud, leaving no stub. Right after pruning is a good time to add fresh mulch around the plant.

Prune hybrid tea roses, such as 'Just Joey', to keep them neat, compact, and continuously producing long-stemmed flowers. Remove skinny or weak stems plus a few of the oldest stems (their bark is tan or gray instead of green) by cutting them off at their base. Prune off any shoots that got frozen or broken during the winter, remove old or weak shoots and crossing or crowded stems, and trim back any asymmetric or unbalanced shoots. Don't be afraid of cutting back too hard; it's better to leave just a few strong shoots than a lot of weak ones. If you cut old stems off 3 to 4 in. above ground level, new ones will grow to replace them. Cut damaged or asymmetric stems back partway and they will branch out. Cut just above an outward-facing bud to keep the center of the rose open.

Hybrid tea roses bloom on new growth, so if you prune in early spring, before new growth, you won't be cutting off flower buds. During the growing season, make a habit of removing the flowers as soon as they fade. This keeps the plant neat and makes it bloom longer and more abundantly. At least once a week, locate each faded flower, follow down its stem to the first or second five-leaflet leaf, and prune just above one of those leaves. (Follow the same steps to cut roses for a bouquet.)

Shrub roses, such as 'Flower Carpet' and *Rosa rugosa* 'Dwarf Pavement', as well as floribundas and other landscape roses also bloom on new growth. In winter, cut these bushy plants back by one-third to one-half. As for other roses, remove diseased or damaged canes when you see them. Try to cut stems at their base to avoid leaving stub ends, which are more susceptible to disease. In summer, remove spent flowers to keep plants tidy and promote additional bloom.

Pruning a hybrid tea rose

In late winter or early spring, remove old, weak, or damaged shoots; stems that are crossing or crowded; and stems that stick out too far and look asymmetric. Don't be afraid to cut a lot away.

Removing flowers

Rose flowers can look messy as they fade. Cut them off by pruning the stem back to the first healthy five-leaflet leaf.

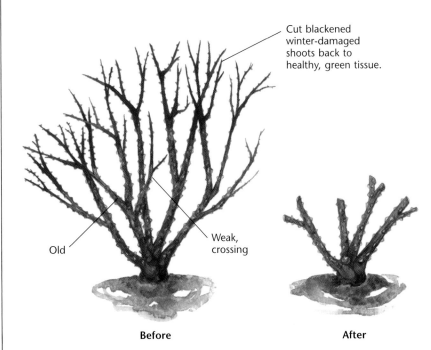

Cut blackened winter-damaged shoots back to healthy, green tissue.

Old

Weak, crossing

Before

After

Five-leaflet leaf

that does more harm than good. If you don't have a good reason for making a cut, don't do it. Follow these guidelines:

• *Use sharp pruning shears,* loppers, or saws, which make clean cuts without tearing the wood or bark.

• *Cut branches back* to a healthy shoot, leaf, or bud, or cut back to the branch collar at the base of the branch, as shown at right. Don't leave any stubs; they're ugly and prone to decay.

• *Remove any dead* or damaged branches at their base, as well as any twigs or limbs that are very spindly or weak.

• *Where two limbs* cross over or rub against each other, save one limb—usually the one that will grow into a place you want to fill—and prune off the other one.

• *Prune or widen* narrow crotches. Places where a branch and trunk or two branches form a narrow V are weak spots, liable to split apart as the tree grows. Where the trunk of a young tree exhibits such a crotch or where either of two shoots could continue the growth of a branch, prune off the weaker of the two. Where you wish to keep the branch, insert a piece of wood as a spacer to widen the angle, as shown in the drawings below. Leave the spacer in place for a year or so.

One trunk or several?

If you want a young tree to have a single trunk, identify the leader, or central shoot,

Where to cut

When removing the end of a branch, cut back to a healthy leaf, bud, or side shoot. Don't leave a stub. Use sharp pruning shears to make a neat cut that slices the stem rather than tears it.

and let it grow straight up, unpruned. The trunk will grow thicker faster if you leave the lower limbs in place for the first few years, but if they're in the way, you can remove them. At whatever height you choose—usually about 8 ft. off the ground if you want to walk or see under the tree—select the shoots that will become the main limbs of the tree. Be sure they are evenly spaced around the trunk, pointing outward at wide angles. Remove any lower or weaker shoots. As the tree matures, the only further pruning required will be an annual checkup to remove dead, damaged, or crossing shoots.

Several of the trees in this book, including vine maple, Japanese maple, Japanese

When removing an entire branch, cut just outside the slightly thickened area, called the branch collar, where the branch grows into the trunk.

snowbell, and saucer magnolia, are often grown with multiple trunks, for a graceful, clumplike appearance. When buying a multiple-trunk tree, choose one with trunks that diverge at the base. The more space between them, the better, so they can grow without squeezing each other. Prune multiple-trunk trees as previously described for single-trunk trees. Remove some of the branches that are growing toward the center of the clump, so the center doesn't get too dense and tangled.

Pruning shrubs

Shrubs are generally carefree plants, but they almost always look better if you do some pruning at least every other year. At

Avoiding narrow crotches

A tree's limbs should spread wide, like outstretched arms. If limbs angle too close to the trunk or to each other, there isn't room for them to grow properly and they may split apart after a few years, ruining the tree.

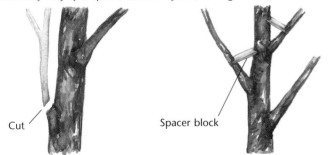

Single-trunk trees: Correct narrow crotches on a young tree by removing the less desired limb or by widening the angle with a wooden spacer block. Choose well-spaced shoots to become the main limbs of a shade tree.

Multiple-trunk trees: Whether the stems of a multiple-trunk tree emerge from the ground or from a single trunk near the ground, widen angles if necessary to keep the trunks from touching.

Selective pruning

Remove weak, spindly, bent, or broken shoots (red). Where two branches rub on each other, remove the weakest or the one that's pointing inward (orange). Head back long shoots to a healthy, outward-facing bud (blue).

Severe pruning

In late winter or early spring, before new growth starts, cut all the stems back close to the ground.

Shearing

Trim with hedge clippers to a neat profile.

a minimum, remove dead twigs each spring, and if any branches are broken by storms or accidents, remove them as soon as possible, cutting back to a healthy bud or branch or to the plant's crown. Also, unless the shrub produces attractive seedpods or berries, it's a good idea to trim off the flowers after they fade.

Beyond this routine pruning, some shrubs require more attention. (The entries in the Plant Profiles, pp. 156–183, give more information on when and how to prune particular shrubs.) Basically, shrub pruning falls into three categories: selective pruning, severe pruning, and shearing.

Selective pruning means using pruning shears to head back or thin individual shoots in order to refine the shape of the bush and maintain its vigor, as well as limit its size. (See the drawing at left.) This job takes time but produces a very graceful and natural-looking bush. Cut away weak or spindly twigs and any limbs that cross or rub against each other, and head all the longest shoots back to a healthy, outward-facing bud or to a pair of buds. You can do selective pruning on any shrub, deciduous or evergreen, at any time of year.

Severe pruning means using pruning shears or loppers to cut away most of a shrub's top growth, leaving just short stubs or a gnarly trunk. This kind of cutting back is usually done once a year in late winter or early spring. Although it seems drastic, severe pruning is appropriate in several situations.

It makes certain fast-growing shrubs, such as bigleaf hydrangea and butterfly bush, flower more profusely. It keeps others, such as spirea and 'Powis Castle' artemisia, compact and bushy.

One or two severe prunings done when a shrub is young can make it branch out at the base, producing a bushier specimen or a fuller hedge plant. Nurseries often do this pruning as part of producing a good plant, and if you buy a shrub that's already bushy,

you don't need to cut it back yourself. Older shrubs that have gotten tall and straggly sometimes respond to a severe pruning by sprouting out with renewed vigor, sending up lots of new shoots that bear plenty of foliage and flowers. This strategy doesn't work for all shrubs, though — sometimes severe pruning kills a plant. Don't try it unless you know it will work (check with a knowledgeable person at a nursery) or are willing to take a chance.

Shearing means using hedge shears or an electric hedge trimmer to trim the surface of a shrub, hedge, or tree to a neat, uniform profile, producing a solid mass of greenery. Both deciduous and evergreen shrubs and trees can be sheared; those with small, closely spaced leaves and a naturally compact growth habit usually look best. A good time for shearing most shrubs is late spring, after the new shoots have elongated but before the wood has hardened, but you can shear at other times of year. You may need to shear some plants more than once a year.

If you're planning to shear a plant, start when it is young and establish the shape — cone, pyramid, flat-topped hedge, or whatever. Looking at the profile, always make the shrub wider at the bottom than on top; otherwise the lower limbs will be shaded and won't be as leafy. Shear off as little as needed to maintain the shape as the shrub grows. Once it gets as big as you want it, shear as much as you have to in order to keep it that size.

Making a hedge

To make a hedge that's dense enough that you can't see through it, choose shrubs that have many shoots at the base. If you can only find skinny shrubs, prune them severely the first spring after planting to stimulate bushier growth.

Hedge plants are set in the ground as described on pp. 141–143 but are spaced closer together than they would be if planted as individual specimens. We took that into account in creating the designs and plant lists for this book; just follow the spacings recommended in the designs. If you're impatient for the hedge to fill in, you can space the plants closer together, but don't put them farther apart.

A hedge can be sheared, pruned selectively, or left alone, depending on how you want it to look. Slow-growing, small-leaved plants such as certain hollies make rounded but natural-looking hedges with no pruning at all, or you can shear them into any profile you choose and make them perfectly neat and uniform. (Be sure to keep them narrower at the top.) Choose one style and stick with it. Once a hedge is established, you can neither start nor stop shearing it without an awkward transition that may last a few years before the hedge looks good again.

Getting a vine off to a good start

Nurseries often sell akebia, clematis, honeysuckle, and other vines as young plants with a single stem fastened to a stake. To plant the vine, remove the stake and cut off the stem right above the lowest pair of healthy leaves, usually about 4 to 6 in. above the soil ❶. This forces the vine to send out new shoots low to the ground. As soon as those new shoots have begun to develop (typically a month or so after planting), cut them back to their first pairs of leaves ❷. After this second pruning, the plant will become bushy at the base. Now, as new shoots form, use sticks or strings to direct them toward the base of the support they are to climb ❸.

Once they're started, twining vines such as the ones named at left can scramble up a lattice trellis, although it helps if you tuck in any stray ends. The plants can't climb a smooth surface, however. To help them cover a fence with wide vertical slats or a porch post, you need to provide something the vine can wrap around. Screw a few eyebolts to the top and bottom of such a support and stretch wire, nylon cord, or polypropylene rope between them. (The wires or cords should be a few inches out from the fence, not flush against it.)

Some clinging vines, such as climbing hydrangea, can climb any surface by means of their adhesive rootlets and need no further assistance or care to get them well established.

After the first year, most vines need annual spring pruning to remove any dead, damaged, or straggly stems. If vines grow too long, you can cut them back anytime and they will branch out from below the cut. Don't prune a vine severely right before it blooms.

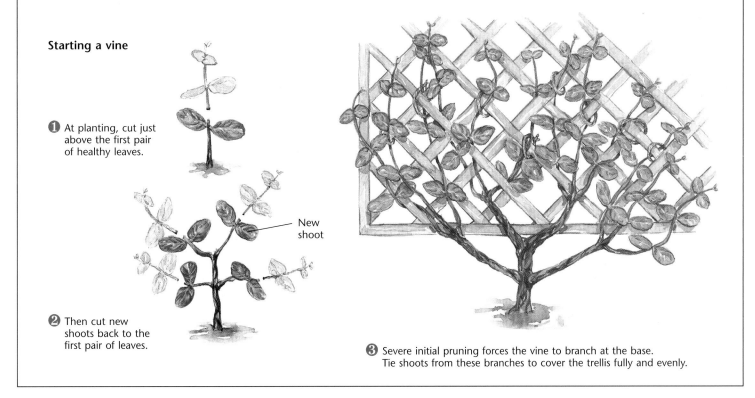

Starting a vine

❶ At planting, cut just above the first pair of healthy leaves.

New shoot

❷ Then cut new shoots back to the first pair of leaves.

❸ Severe initial pruning forces the vine to branch at the base. Tie shoots from these branches to cover the trellis fully and evenly.

Caring for Perennials

Perennials are simply plants that send up new growth year after year. A large group, perennials include flowering plants such as daylilies and purple coneflower as well as grasses, ferns, and hardy bulbs. Although some perennials need special conditions and care, most of the ones in this book are adaptable and easygoing. Get them off to a good start by planting them in well-prepared soil, adding a layer of mulch, watering as often as needed throughout the first year, and keeping weeds away. After that, keeping perennials attractive and healthy typically requires just a few minutes per plant each year. Some will need dividing every few years to keep them vigorous.

Routine annual care

Some of the perennials that are used as ground covers, such as ajuga, lilyturf, mondo grass, and thyme, need virtually no care. On a suitable site, they'll thrive for decades even if you pay them almost no attention at all.

Most garden perennials, though, look and grow better if you clean away the old leaves and stems at least once a year. When to do this depends on the type of plant. Perennials such as daylily, hosta, and Siberian iris have leaves and stalks that turn tan or brown after they're frosted in fall. Cut these down to the ground in late fall or early spring; either time is okay.

Perennials such as geranium, blue fescue grass, coralbells, and columbine are more or less evergreen, depending on the severity of the winter. For those plants, wait until they've bloomed or until the fall; then cut back any leaves or stems that are discolored or shabby-looking. Don't leave cuttings lying on the soil, because they may contain disease spores. To avoid contaminating your compost, send diseased stems or leaves to the dump.

Right after you've cleared away the dead material is a good time to renew the mulch on the bed. Use a fork, rake, or cultivator to loosen the existing mulch, and add some fresh mulch if needed. Also, if you want to sprinkle some granular fertilizer on the bed, do that now, when it's easy to avoid getting any on the plants' leaves. Fertilizing perennials is optional, but it does make them grow bigger and bloom more than they would otherwise.

Pruning and shearing perennials

Some perennials that bloom in summer or fall respond well to being pruned earlier in the growing season. Chrysanthemum, New England aster, Russian sage, and 'Autumn Joy' sedum all form tall clumps of stems topped with lots of little flowers. Unfortunately, tall stems are liable to flop over, and

Pruning a perennial

Prune to create neater, bushier clumps of some summer- and fall-blooming perennials such as New England aster, chrysanthemums, and 'Autumn Joy' sedum. When the stalks are about 1 ft. tall, cut them all back by one-third. Remove the weakest stalks at ground level.

even if they don't, too-tall clumps can look leggy or top-heavy. To prevent floppiness, prune these plants when the stems are about 1 ft. tall. Remove the weakest stems from each clump by cutting them off at the ground; then cut all the remaining, strong stems back by about one-third. Pruning in this way keeps these plants shorter, stronger, and bushier, so you don't have to bother with installing stakes to keep them upright.

Some plants, such as 'Powis Castle' artemisia, are grown more for their foliage than for their flowers. You can use hedge shears to keep them neat, compact, and bushy, shearing off the tops of the stems once or twice in spring and summer.

Remove faded flowers

Removing flowers as they fade (called "deadheading") makes the garden look neater, prevents unwanted self-sown seedlings, and often stimulates a plant to continue blooming longer than it would if you left it alone, or to bloom a second time later in the season. (This is true for shrubs and annuals as well as for perennials.)

Pick large flowers such as daisies, daylilies, irises, and lilies one at a time, snapping them off by hand. Use pruning shears on perennials such as hosta, epimedium, lavender, coralbells, and yarrow that produce tall stalks crowded with lots of small flowers, cutting the stalks back to the height of the foliage. Use hedge shears on bushy plants that are covered with lots of small flowers on short stalks, such as ajuga, salvia, 'Moonbeam' coreopsis, basket-of-gold, and evergreen candytuft, cutting the stems back by about one-half their length.

Instead of removing them, you may want to let the flowers remain on purple coneflower, Siberian iris, 'Autumn Joy' sedum, and the various grasses. These plants all bear conspicuous seedpods or seed heads on stiff stalks that remain standing and look interesting throughout the fall and winter.

Dividing perennials

Most perennials send up more stems each year, forming denser clumps or wider patches. Dividing is the process of cutting or breaking apart these clumps or patches. This is an easy way to make more plants to expand your garden, to control a plant that might otherwise spread out of bounds, or to renew an old specimen that doesn't look good or bloom well anymore.

Most perennials can be divided as often as every year or two if you're in a hurry to make more plants, or they can go for several years if you don't have any reason to disturb them. Early spring is the best time to divide most perennials, but you can also do it in fall.

There are two main approaches to dividing perennials, as shown in the drawings at right. You can leave the plant in the ground and use a sharp spade to cut it apart, like slicing a pie, and then lift out one chunk at a time. Or you can dig around and underneath the plant and lift it out all at once, shake off the extra soil, and lay the plant on the ground or a tarp where you can work with it.

Some plants, such as ajuga, yarrow, and some ferns, are easy to divide. They almost fall apart when you dig them up. Others, such as 'Autumn Joy' sedum, daylily, and most grasses, have very tough or tangled roots and you'll have to wrestle with them, chop them with a sharp butcher knife, pry them apart with a strong screwdriver or garden fork, or even cut through the roots with a hatchet or pruning saw. However you approach the job, before you insert any tool, take a close look at the plant right at ground level, and be careful to divide *between*, not *through*, the biggest and healthiest buds or shoots. Using a hose to wash loose mulch and soil away makes it easier to see what you're doing.

Don't make the divisions too small; they should be the size of a plant that you'd want to buy, not just little scraps. If you have more divisions than you need or want, choose just the best-looking ones to replant and discard or give away the others. Replant new divisions as soon as possible in freshly prepared soil. Water them right away, and water again whenever the soil dries out over the next few weeks or months, until the plants are growing again.

Divide hardy bulbs such as daffodils and crocuses every few years. Dig clumps after bloom but before the foliage turns yellow. Shake the soil off the roots, pull the bulbs apart, and replant them promptly, setting them as deep as they were buried before.

Dividing perennials

You can divide a clump or patch of perennials by cutting down into the patch with a sharp spade, like slicing a pie or a pan of brownies, and then lifting out the separate chunks.

Or you can dig up the whole clump, shake the extra soil off the roots, and pull or pry it apart into separate plantlets.

Problem Solving

Some plants are much more susceptible than others to damage by severe weather, pests, or diseases. In this book, we've recommended plants that are generally trouble-free, especially after they have had a few years to get established in your garden. But even these plants are subject to various mishaps and problems. The challenge is learning how to distinguish which problems are really serious and which are just cosmetic, and deciding how to solve—or, better yet, prevent—those problems that are serious.

Identify, then treat

Don't jump to conclusions and start spraying chemicals on a supposedly sick plant before you know what (if anything) is actually wrong with it. That's wasteful and irresponsible, and you're likely to do the plant (and your local ecosystem) more harm than good. Pinpointing the exact cause of a problem is difficult for even experienced gardeners, so save yourself frustration and seek out expert help.

If it seems that there's something wrong with one of your plants—for example, if the leaves are discolored, have holes in them, or have spots or marks on them—cut off a sample branch, wrap it in damp paper towels, and put it in a plastic bag (so it won't wilt). Take the sample to the nursery or garden center where you bought the plant and ask for help. If the nursery can't help, contact the nearest office of your state's Cooperative Extension Service or a public garden in your area and ask if they have a staff member who can diagnose plant problems.

Meanwhile, look around your property and around the neighborhood, too, to see if any other plants (of the same or different kinds) show similar symptoms. If a problem is widespread, you shouldn't have much trouble finding someone who can identify it and tell you what, if anything, to do. If only one plant is affected, it's often harder to diagnose the problem, and you may just need to wait and see what happens to it. Keep an eye on the plant, continue with watering and other regular maintenance, and see if the problem gets worse or goes away. If nothing more has happened after a few weeks, stop worrying. If the problem continues, intensify your search for expert advice.

Plant problems stem from a number of causes: insect and animal pests, diseases, and poor care, particularly in winter. Remember that plant problems are often caused by a combination of these; all the more reason to consult with experts about their diagnosis and treatment.

Pests, large and small

Deer and rabbits are liable to be a problem if your property is surrounded by or adjacent to fields or woods. You may not see them, but you can't miss the damage they do—they bite the tops off or eat whole plants of daylilies and many other perennials. Deer also eat the leaves and stems of maples, azaleas, and many other trees and shrubs. Commercial or homemade repellents that you spray on the foliage may be helpful if the animals aren't too hungry and you use them often. (See the box at right for thoughts on deer-proof plants.) But in the long run, the only solution is to fence out deer and to trap and remove smaller animals.

Squirrels are cute but naughty. They normally don't eat much foliage, but they do eat some kinds of flowers and several kinds of bulbs. They also dig up new transplants, and they plant nuts in your flower beds and lawns. Meadow voles and field mice can kill trees and shrubs by stripping the bark off the trunk, usually near the ground. Gophers eat the roots of shrubs, trees, and perennials. Moles don't eat plants, but their digging makes a mess of a lawn or flower bed. Persistent trapping is the most effective way to control all of these little critters. (You can protect the roots of some plants from gophers by planting the plants in wire cages, sold at many nurseries.)

Aphids, crane fly, cutworms, caterpillars, grubs, spider mites, scale insects, slugs, snails, weevils, and countless other pests can cause minor or devastating damage in a home landscape. Most plants can afford to lose part of their foliage or sap without suffering much of a setback, so don't panic if you see a few holes chewed in a leaf. However, whenever you suspect that insects or related pests are attacking one of your plants, try to catch one of them in a glass jar and get it identified, so you can decide what to do.

There are several new kinds of insecticides that are quite effective but much safer to use than the older products. For example, insecticidal soap, a special kind of detergent, quickly kills aphids and other soft-bodied insects, but it's nontoxic to mammals and birds and it breaks down quickly, leaving no harmful residue. Horticultural oil, a highly refined mineral oil, is a good control for scale insects, which frequently infest deciduous trees and shrubs and broad-leaved evergreens such as camellias. Most garden centers stock these and other relatively safe insecticides.

Deer-proof plants?

Planting from lists of deer-proof plants often results in disappointment. What's deer-proof in one area may not be in another. And if deer are really hungry, they'll eat almost anything. If you live in an area where deer are common, check with local nurseries for planting solutions or stroll through your neighborhood to see what's nibbled and what's not.

Deer-control fencing

Deer have been known to jump very tall fences. Experience shows that a wide mid-height fence is one of the best ways to keep deer out. This fence is suitable for a larger property. It is about 6 ft. wide and 5 ft. high and consists of angled poles fixed to posts spaced about 10 ft. apart. Attach wires at 12-in. intervals to the poles. For advice on deer fences that work best in your area, consult your Cooperative Extension Service.

Before using any insecticide, study the fine print on the label to make sure that the product is registered to control your particular pest. Carefully follow the directions for how to apply the product, or it may not work.

Diseases

Several types of fungal, bacterial, and viral diseases can attack garden plants, causing a wide range of symptoms such as disfigured or discolored leaves or petals, powdery or moldy-looking films or spots, mushy or rotten stems or roots, and overall wilting. As with insect problems, if you suspect that a plant is infected with a disease, gather a sample of the plant and show it to someone who can identify the problem before you do any spraying.

In general, plant diseases are hard to treat, so it's important to take steps to prevent problems. These steps include choosing plants adapted to your area, choosing disease-resistant plants, spacing plants far enough apart so that air can circulate between them, and removing dead stems and litter from the garden.

Perennials that would otherwise be healthy are prone to fungal infections during spells of cool humid weather, especially if the plants are crowded together or if they have flopped over and are lying on top of each other or on the ground. If your garden has turned into a jungle, look closely for moldy foliage, and if you find any, prune it off and discard (don't compost) it. It's better to cut the plants back severely than to let the disease spread.

Plan to avoid repeated problems by dividing the perennials, replanting them farther apart, and pruning them early in the season so they don't grow so tall and floppy again. Crowded shrubs are also subject to fungal problems in the summer and fall and should be pruned so that air can flow around them.

Winter damage

Even though most of the Northwest enjoys cool, mild winters, occasional cold spells that damage normally hardy plants are not uncommon. After a cold spell, wait until at least midsummer to assess the severity of the damage. At that time, new growth will tell you just how far back a plant has been killed, and you can prune out limbs that are brown and dead.

Plant Profiles

Plants are the heart of the designs in this book. In this section, you'll find descriptions of all the plants used in the designs, along with information on planting and maintaining them. These trees, shrubs, perennials, grasses, bulbs, and vines are all dependable performers in the Northwest. They offer a wide spectrum of lovely flowers and fruits, handsome foliage, and striking forms. Most contribute something of note in at least two seasons. You can use this section as an aid when installing the designs in this book and as a reference for selecting desirable plants for other home-landscaping projects.

Using the plant profiles

All of these plants are proven performers in many of the soils, climates, microclimates, and other conditions commonly found in the Northwest. But they will perform best if planted and cared for as explained in the Guide to Installation, beginning on p. 96. In the following descriptions and recommendations, "full sun" means a site that gets at least eight hours a day of direct sun throughout the growing season. "Partial sun" and "partial shade" both refer to sites that get direct sun for part of the day but are shaded the rest of the time by a building, fence, or tree. Plants preferring partial sun or shade often do best with morning sun and afternoon shade. "Full shade" means sites that don't receive direct sunlight.

The plants are organized here alphabetically by their scientific name. If you are browsing, page references direct you to the designs in which the plants appear. Numbers in **bold italic** type indicate the page where you can find a photo of the plant.

Acanthus mollis
BEAR'S BREECHES

Abelia × *grandiflora* 'Edward Goucher' ABELIA

Acer circinatum VINE MAPLE

Abelia × *grandiflora* 'Edward Goucher'

'EDWARD GOUCHER' ABELIA. A dependable semi-evergreen shrub that bears countless small rosy purple flowers in the summer and attracts butterflies. The sepals, small leaflike structures below the flower, turn copper in late summer through fall and are very showy even after the flowers have dropped. Lustrous pointed leaves are bronzy green in spring, dark green in summer, purple-bronze in winter. This cultivar grows 3 to 5 ft. tall. It needs full or partial sun and is drought tolerant. To keep the plants compact, in summer cut new shoots in half. Then each year in late winter to early spring cut a third of the old stems close to the ground. Pages: 44, 49, 73.

Acanthus mollis

BEAR'S BREECHES. A perennial with bold, deeply lobed, dark green leaves that grow up to 2 ft. long. Tall spikes of white to pinkish purple flowers bloom in late spring, reaching 2 to 3 ft. above the foliage. Grows best in moist shade but can take some sun. Cut back flowers after bloom. Divide crowded plants in spring. A vigorous plant, it can be invasive. Pages: 38, 51, 53, 79.

Acer circinatum

VINE MAPLE. This Northwest native can be a large, spreading, bushy, multistemmed deciduous shrub or a small single-stemmed tree growing 25 ft. tall. Leaves are green in summer and turn yellow, red, and purple in fall. Grows in full sun to shade. Plants in sunnier spots have more intense fall color. Tolerant of a wide range of soils, vine maples thrive in moist areas but also adapt to very dry soils. Can be shaped as a large multitrunked shrub or tree. Pages: 18, 22, 90.

Acer davidii

STRIPEBARK MAPLE. A deciduous tree with a rather narrow habit, reaching 20 to 30 ft. tall. Showy chainlike clusters of greenish yellow flowers in spring are followed by chains of small winged seeds that drop in summer. Fall color is yellow, red, and purple. The bark, especially showy in winter, is green with obvious white striping. Prefers partial shade. Carefree. Pages: 78, *79.*

Acer ginnala

AMUR MAPLE. A deciduous shrub or small tree growing to about 20 ft. tall, often sold with multiple trunks. Bears clusters of very fragrant yellow flowers in early spring. Bright clusters of red-winged seeds follow. In fall, the glossy green lobed leaves turn yellow, red, and purple. Full or partial sun. Leaves color best in full sun. Tolerant of a wide range of soil conditions. Pages: 20, *22*.

Acer palmatum

JAPANESE MAPLE. A neat, small to medium-size deciduous tree with delicate-looking serrated leaves. There are many kinds with leaves that are green, bronze, or red in summer. All are colorful in fall. Plants are sold as seed-grown (pp. 47, 76) or as named cultivars. Seed-grown plants often grow faster. Named cultivars are more expensive but have more dependable traits. 'Bloodgood' (pp. 92, **95**) grows to 20 ft. tall and stays dark red spring through fall. Coralbark maple (*A. p.* 'Sango Kaku', pp. 70, **70**) grows 15 ft. or taller and has foliage that is reddish in spring, light green in summer, and yellow in fall. Twigs turn bright coral-red in winter and early spring. Red laceleaf Japanese maple (*A. p.* 'Dissectum Atropurpureum', pp. 68, **70**) is a short spreading tree with deeply cut red leaves. Mature height varies from 3 to 8 ft. Japanese maples grow slower than some trees, so buy the biggest tree you can afford. Plants are sold balled-and-burlapped or in containers. All grow best in full sun to partial shade and in rich, moist soil covered with mulch. Prune to preserve the tree's natural shape.

Achillea 'Moonshine'

'MOONSHINE' YARROW. A perennial with flat clusters of small lemon yellow flowers on stiff stalks about 2 ft. tall. Finely divided gray-green leaves have a pungent aroma. Spreads to form a patch 2 to 3 ft. wide. Needs full sun and well-drained soil. Cut off old flower stalks when the blossoms fade. Divide every few years in spring or fall. Page: 84.

Acorus gramineus 'Variegatus'

VARIEGATED SWEET FLAG. A perennial grasslike plant that grows 1 ft. tall and spreads by rhizomes. Looks good near water. Leaves are striped creamy white and green. Flowers bloom in midsummer but are inconspicuous. Prefers constantly moist soil in full or partial shade but will adapt to drier, fertile soils. Page: 63.

Ajuga reptans

AJUGA. A low, mat-forming perennial used as a ground cover. Erect 6-in. spikes densely packed with blue flowers are very showy for a few weeks in

Acer palmatum
JAPANESE MAPLE

Achillea 'Moonshine'
YARROW

Acorus gramineus 'Variegatus'
VARIEGATED SWEET FLAG

spring. Glossy evergreen foliage is typically green, but 'Burgundy Glow' (pp. 49, 51, 73) has multicolored purple, green, and white leaves. Several other cultivars have dark purple-bronze leaves. Prefers partial shade but tolerates full sun in sites with moist, well-drained soil; it doesn't like "wet feet." After flowers fade, cut them off with a string trimmer, lawn mower, or hedge shears. Spreads quickly and will invade a lawn unless you keep cutting along the edge or install a mowing strip. Pages: 95, **95**.

Ajuga reptans 'Burgundy Glow'
AJUGA

Akebia quinata

AKEBIA. A fast-growing vine that spreads to 25 ft. or more and climbs by twining stems. The dark green leaves are attractive all summer and can be evergreen in a mild winter. A careful look in the spring will reveal lots of small, interesting, and fragrant purple flowers. Tolerates sun or shade and grows in any well-drained soil. Prune plants when young so they branch at the base. Established plants need no care. May die back in cold winters but will usually resprout from the roots. Pages: 83, *83*.

Amelanchier × grandiflora 'Autumn Brilliance'

'AUTUMN BRILLIANCE' SERVICEBERRY. A small deciduous tree up to 25 ft. tall, often trained to a single trunk. Interesting most of the year. Masses of white flowers in early spring are followed by blue or purplish summer berries loved by birds, and bright red-orange fall foliage. Smooth gray bark adds winter interest. Full or partial sun. Pages: 29, 66.

Amelanchier × grandiflora 'Autumn Brilliance' SERVICEBERRY

Aquilegia

COLUMBINE. A large group of wonderfully delicate flowering perennials with lovely spurred flowers in many single and multicolored shades. Plants bloom in spring and early summer and form neat mounds of blue-green, scalloped leaves. Flower stalks range from 12 to 48 in. tall. Many hybrids and species to choose from. The Dragonfly hybrids (p. 84) have strong stems and large flowers with long spurs. Columbines grow best in light shade but can also take full sun. Carefree, they are short-lived but self-seed easily. Pages: 16, *19*.

Arbutus unedo 'Compacta'

COMPACT STRAWBERRY TREE. A striking evergreen shrub with multiple trunks, shiny green leaves, and peeling bark. Clusters of pendulous white bell-shaped flowers bloom in fall around the time the previous year's fruit is turning a beautiful orange-red. The fruit is edible and birds feast on the fermented windfall. Prefers well-drained soil in sun or shade. Prune only to expose the beautiful bark. Pages: 16, 19.

Arctostaphylos uva-ursi 'Massachusetts' KINNIKINNICK

Arctostaphylos uva-ursi 'Massachusetts'

'MASSACHUSETTS' KINNIKINNICK. One of a group of native evergreen ground covers with shiny brown bark and lustrous deep green foliage. Small white to pink spring flowers produce berries that are red in the fall. This cultivar is an excellent ground cover less than a foot tall and spreading to 8 ft. wide. Disease resistant and drought tolerant; excellent for dry slopes. Plant in full sun or any degree of shade. Pages: 25, 53, 69.

Armeria maritima 'Alba'

'ALBA' THRIFT. A perennial that forms a neat tuft of narrow evergreen leaves and bears spherical white flower heads on stiff stalks about 1 ft. tall. Blooms generously in spring, with scattered blossoms throughout the summer and fall. Needs full sun and well-drained soil. Looks best with occasional water. Remove flowers as they fade to encourage a longer blooming season. Trim back old foliage almost to the ground in early spring. Pages: 84, *86*.

Artemisia

ARTEMISIA. Shrubby perennials, woody at the base, with fragrant, gray-green, finely divided leaves. Beautiful accent plants. They rarely flower. A. 'Powis Castle' (pp. 29, *31*) forms a dome-shaped mound of deeply cut silver foliage 2 to 3 ft. tall and 4 to 5 ft. wide. *A. ludoviciana* var. *albula* 'Silver King' (pp. 49, *51*) has smaller, lance-shaped, woolly silver-gray leaves that turn red in the fall. Plant in full sun. Will tolerate dry soil but grows faster with watering. Cut back hard in early spring to encourage new growth and to keep plant compact.

Aster

ASTER. Carefree clump-forming perennials that bear daisylike flowers from summer through fall, most having a vibrantly colored ring of rays surrounding

Aster × frikartii FRIKART'S ASTER

Aster × frikartii 'Monch' FRIKART'S ASTER

a yellow or orange center. Frikart's aster (*A. × frikartii*, p. 76) grows 2 to 3 ft. tall and bears light purple flowers. *A. × f.* 'Monch' (pp. 73, 80, 93, 95) has deep blue flowers. New England aster (*A. novae-angliae*, pp. 93, **95**) bears large sprays of pink, purple, or violet flowers. Asters thrive in full sun and well-drained soil and are drought tolerant. Prune to the ground in early spring. Cut new stems back by a third in late spring to keep plants from getting floppy. Divide every few years in early spring.

Astilbe

ASTILBE. Among the best perennials for shady or partly shady sites. In early to midsummer, fluffy plumes of tiny flowers stand high above glossy compound leaves. Foliage is attractive all season. There are many hybrids that grow from 6 to 42 in. tall and bear white, pale pink, rose, purple, or deep red flowers (pp. 79, **79**). *A. × arendsii* 'Cattleya' (p. 39), reaching 3 ft. tall, has large open crimson-pink flowers. *A. × japonica* 'Peach Blossom' (pp. 63, **63**) grows about 2 ft. tall and has peach-pink flowers. All astilbes prefer rich, moist, well-drained soil. Grow in full or partial shade, or in full sun if you can water them regularly. Cut off flower stalks when the blooms turn brown, or leave them in place, if you like the looks of the dried flowers. Cut foliage to the ground in late fall or early spring. Divide every three to five years in early spring or late summer, using a sharp spade, ax, or old pruning saw to cut the tough woody rootstock into a few large chunks.

Aucuba japonica 'Variegata'

GOLD-DUST AUCUBA. An evergreen shrub with thick, erect stems. Grows 6 to 10 ft. tall and at least 5 ft. wide. Large, toothed, leathery leaves are dark green, speckled with yellow dots. Small maroon flowers bloom in early spring. Female plants bear cherry red berries if there's a male plant nearby. One of the best shrubs for dark shady sites. Prune in late winter to control size. Responds well to hard pruning. Pages: 79, **79**.

Bergenia cordifolia 'Bressingham White'

'BRESSINGHAM WHITE' BERGENIA. A perennial with unusually large, thick, glossy leaves that are green in summer and turn garnet in winter. Clusters of white flowers show above the foliage for a few weeks in late spring. Forms a clump about 1 ft. tall and 2 ft. wide. Prefers partial shade and moist soil but tolerates sun and garden soil. Divide every few years in spring or fall. Pages: **42**, 43.

Buddleia davidii

BUTTERFLY BUSH. A fast-growing deciduous shrub that blooms from midsummer through fall. Arching shoots make a vase-shaped clump. Spikes of small white, pink, lilac, blue, or purple flowers form at the end of each stem. The flowers have a sweet fragrance and really do attract butterflies. 'Pink Delight' (p. 61) has medium pink flowers. 'Lochinch' (pp. 26, **27**) has 8-in.-long spikes of violet-blue flowers, each with an orange eye. Plants need full sun to partial shade and well-drained soil. Cut old stems by two-thirds in early spring to promote vigorous growth and maximum flowering. Grows 5 to 8 ft. tall and wide by summer's end. Self-seeded plants have become a problem in the Northwest. To help control the plant, cut off spent flower heads.

Bulbs

The bulbs recommended in this book are all perennials that come up year after year and bloom in late winter, spring, or early summer. After they flower, their leaves continue growing until sometime in summer, when they gradually turn yellow and die down to the ground. Buy bulbs from a garden cen-

Buddleia davidii
BUTTERFLY BUSH

Recommended bulbs

Crocus, Crocus
Cup-shaped flowers on 4-in. stalks in April. Available in white, yellow, lilac, and purple. Plant in masses of 15 to 20 bulbs for a showy display. Plant bulbs 4 in. deep, 4 in. apart. Pages: 33, **35**.

Hyacinthus, Hyacinth
Very fragrant bell-shaped flowers on a spike rising from a cluster of narrow bright green leaves. Colors range from white to pink, red, or lavender. Plant 4 to 6 in. deep and 6 in. apart in the fall. Pages: 65, **67**.

Narcissus, Daffodils, jonquils, and narcissus
Bright yellow, white, or bicolor flowers, often fragrant, on stalks 6 to 18 in. tall. Different kinds bloom in sequence from early February through early May. Leaves die down in July. Plant bulbs 4 to 6 in. deep, 4 to 6 in. apart, depending on their size. Very reliable, carefree, and long-lived. Use dwarf daffodils such as 'February Gold' and 'Tête à Tête' close to the house, because after they bloom, their short leaves are less conspicuous. Use larger daffodils such as 'King Alfred' and 'Mt. Hood' for plantings viewed from a distance. Most narcissus naturalize well. Pages: 33, 34, 65, 67.

Tulipa, Tulip
Large flowers in bright or pastel shades of all colors but blue, held on stalks 6 to 20 in. tall. Different kinds bloom between February and April. Plant bulbs 4 to 6 in. deep, 4 to 6 in. apart. For the best display, every fall divide and replant existing bulbs, add new ones, and fertilize. Pages: 21, **22**, 65.

Camellia sasanqua
SASANQUA CAMELLIA

Camellia sasanqua 'Cleopatra'
'CLEOPATRA' CAMELLIA

ter or catalog in late summer or fall. Plant them promptly in a sunny or partly sunny bed with well-prepared, well-drained soil. As a rule, plant bulbs at a depth two to three times the bulb's height. In subsequent years, you need only pick off the flowers after they fade and remove (or ignore, if you choose) the old leaves after they turn yellow in summer. Most bulbs can be divided every few years if you want to grow them elsewhere. Dig them as the foliage is turning yellow, shake or pull them apart, and replant them right away. For more information on specific bulbs, see the box on p. 161.

Calluna vulgaris

SCOTCH HEATHER. An evergreen shrub that is often confused with heath. Ranging from a few inches to 3 ft. tall, its many ascending branches bear tiny scalelike leaves. Depending on cultivar, summer and winter foliage can be colorful. Small bell-shaped flowers bloom on new wood in summer. Because the dried flowers remain on the stems, heathers can appear to be in bloom through the winter. 'Robert Chapman' (pp. 53, *54*) grows to 10 in. tall, has bright red new growth that turns golden as it matures, and bears purple flowers in summer. 'Silver Knight' (p. 57) grows to 18 in. and bears mauve-pink flowers and silvery gray foliage. Heathers prefer full sun to partial shade and moist, well-drained soil with lots of organic matter. To ensure that you get plants with the winter foliage color you want, shop for plants in winter. Shear in late winter to encourage new growth. Pages: 89, *91*.

Camellia

CAMELLIA. Evergreen shrubs with glossy foliage and large, lovely white, pink, or rose flowers. There are hundreds of cultivars, differing mostly in flower color, size, and form (single or double) as well as in overall plant habit, mature size, and hardiness. Camellias are also excellent container plants; ask at your nursery for reliable varieties. Japanese camellia (*C. japonica*, pp. 79, *79*) is the most popular camellia, usually ranging in height from 6 to 12 ft. and blooming in late winter to spring. Sasanqua camellias (*C. sasanqua*, pp. 38, 42, 75) are generally smaller plants that range in height from 2 to 3 ft. upward to 10 ft. They bloom in late fall and winter. Lower growers are useful as understory plants. Favorite varieties include 'Setsugekka' (pp. *22*, 23), which has white flowers borne on an upright plant. 'Apple Blossom' (pp. 31, *31*) is a spreading plant with single white flowers that are blushed with pink. 'Cleopatra' (p. 62) forms a more upright, compact plant and bears rose-pink flowers. Camellias need moist, well-drained, acid soil with a layer of mulch, and a site that is shaded from midday sun. If needed, prune and fertilize immediately after flowering.

Campanula

BELLFLOWER. A large group of useful flowering perennials (a few are annuals) that vary in plant habit and flower form. Plant in flower beds, rock gardens, or containers. Spreading types are useful as small-scale ground covers. The ones used in our designs bloom for many weeks in the summer. Carpathian bellflower (*C. carpatica*, pp. 36, 66) is a short, compact perennial, about 1 ft. tall and wide, with light blue blooms. 'Blue Clips' (pp. 95, *95*) has sky blue flowers and medium green foliage. 'Birch Hybrid' (pp. 45, *47*, 84, 87) is a very low, spreading plant with abundant blue, open bell-shaped flowers. Campanulas grow best in partial shade but can take full sun. Water regularly. Cut back after bloom. Divide as necessary in fall or early spring.

Carex buchananii

FOX RED CURLY SEDGE. A grasslike plant that grows in clumps 2 to 3 ft. tall. Leaves curl at the tip and keep their striking reddish bronze color all year, providing texture and color contrast in the garden through the seasons. Summer flowers are insignificant. Grow in full sun or partial shade. Unlike some sedges, it does well in hot sun and well-drained soil. Self-sows to form a patch. Pages: 53, *54*.

Caryopteris × clandonensis

BLUEBEARD. A small deciduous shrub that blooms for weeks in late summer. Bright or dark blue flowers contrast with the soft gray-green foliage and gray-green stems. 'Blue Mist' bears flowers that are powdery blue. 'Dark Knight' has dark blue flowers among silvery gray foliage. Plants need full sun and well-drained soil and thrive in a warm, dry spot. Cut bluebeard close to the ground each spring for compact growth and maximum bloom. Will grow 2 to 3 ft. wide by fall. Pages: 93, 95, **95**.

Ceanothus 'Victoria'

'VICTORIA' WILD LILAC, CEANOTHUS. An evergreen shrub useful in dry landscapes, especially on slopes. Leaves are small, dark green, shiny, and crinkly. Blooms in spring with a profusion of small, deep blue flowers at branch ends. Plant in full sun and well-drained soil. No need to water once established. Grows 5 ft. or more tall and wide. Pages: 26, 29, 36.

Chamaecyparis obtusa 'Nana Gracilis'

'NANA GRACILIS' DWARF HINOKI CYPRESS. A slow-growing conifer with graceful, glossy, emerald green foliage. Its habit is naturally open and sculpted with short sprays of scalelike foliage. No pruning necessary. Prefers full to partial sun and moist, well-drained soil. Buy the largest plant you can afford. It may someday reach 8 ft. or taller and spread 3 to 4 ft. wide. Pages: 21, 38, 76.

Choisya ternata

MEXICAN ORANGE. An evergreen shrub reaching 6 ft. tall with glossy leaves that are very aromatic in the hot sun. Blooms in the spring and sporadically throughout the summer with terminal white clusters of flowers that smell somewhat like an orange-tree blossom. Plant in full sun to partial shade. It is not picky about soil conditions but will not tolerate standing water on its roots. Prune after flowering to encourage a full bushy look. May die back in cold winters but will usually resprout from the roots. Pages: 62, 80.

Chrysanthemum × morifolium

FLORIST'S CHRYSANTHEMUM. An old-time favorite perennial offering hundreds of cultivars, some growing 3 to 4 ft. tall and blooming in many colors from late summer into fall. Attractive dark green lobed leaves die back each winter. All bloom best in full sun and well-drained soil. Cut old stems to the

Ceanothus 'Victoria'
'VICTORIA' WILD LILAC

Choisya ternata
MEXICAN ORANGE

Chamaecyparis obtusa
'Nana Gracilis'
DWARF HINOKI CYPRESS

ground in early spring. To keep the plant short and less floppy when it blooms, cut new growth by half one or two times before July. Pages: 93, **95**.

Cistus × pulverulentus 'Sunset'

'SUNSET' ROCKROSE. A compact evergreen shrub reaching 2 ft. tall and 3 ft. wide, with interesting wavy gray-green leaves. Bears many magenta-pink flowers for a long period in summer. Plant in full sun and well-drained soil. Very little pruning is needed. Page: 61.

Clematis

CLEMATIS. Deciduous or evergreen vines that climb or sprawl, forming a tangle of leafy stems adorned with masses of flowers, which can be tiny or large. See the box on p. 164 for information on specific kinds. Plant in partial or full sun; be sure to mulch to keep the roots cool. Because Northwest soils are acidic, add a cup or so of ground limestone to the planting area and mix it thoroughly into the soil. Dig a planting hole deep enough to allow you to cover the root ball and base of the stem with about 2 in. of soil. Cut the stem back to the lowest set of healthy leaves to encourage the plant to branch near the base. Clematis climbs by twining petioles. Guide the new stems toward a trellis, wire, or other support, and secure them with twist-ties or other fas-

teners. Prune to control size. Some clematis bloom on old growth, some on new. An easy rule of thumb is to prune right after flowering. It takes most clematis a few years to cover a fence or trellis 6 to 8 ft. tall. Many can eventually climb 10 to 15 ft.

Recommended clematis

Clematis armandii, Evergreen clematis
In early spring, displays fragrant white flowers against glossy evergreen leaves. Climbs 15 to 20 ft. Prune after bloom. Pages: 89, *91*.

Clematis hybrids
Include many mostly deciduous cultivars. Large-flowered types produce blooms from 3 to 8 in. across. 'Comtesse de Bouchard' (p. 80) bears rosy pink flowers in summer. 'Elsa Spath' (pp. 61, *63*) has mauve-blue flowers from late spring into fall. 'The President' (pp. 84, *86*, 87) bears deep violet-blue flowers in early summer. Small-flowered types (p. 76) bloom from summer to late autumn, producing flowers in sizes from less than 1 in. to 4 in. across. Early-flowering types may bloom on last year's growth, then again later in the season on new growth. Late-flowering types bloom on new growth. Page: 40.

C. tangutica, Golden clematis
Small yellow flowers bloom throughout the summer on this deciduous vine, followed by fluffy, silvery seed heads that last throughout fall and into winter. Prune in early spring, removing older shoots and cutting others back by one-third. Pages: 44, *47*.

Clematis × jackmanii 'Comtesse de Bouchard'

Clematis vitacella 'Polish Spirit'

Coreopsis verticillata 'Moonbeam'
'MOONBEAM' COREOPSIS. Long-blooming perennial that bears hundreds of small, lemon yellow, daisy-like blossoms from summer to fall. The dark green leaves are short and threadlike. Spreads by rhizomes to form a patch 2 to 3 ft. wide and tall. Needs full sun. Remove spent flower heads to extend bloom. Cut back to a few inches above ground in fall or early spring. Pages: 40, *42*, 73.

Cornus alba 'Elegantissima'
VARIEGATED SIBERIAN DOGWOOD. A deciduous shrub with four-season interest. It has bright red stems in winter, white flowers in spring, variegated green-and-white leaves from spring through fall, and white berries in late summer. Forms a vase-shaped clump 6 to 8 ft. tall with many erect or arching stems. Plant in full sun or partial shade. Does well in most soils and thrives in soils that stay wet. Cut all the stems down close to the ground every few years (or every year, if you prefer) in early spring. After a few weeks, the plant will send up vigorous new shoots. In fall, these young shoots sport brightly colored bark. Pages: 53, 89.

Cornus canadensis
BUNCHBERRY. A semievergreen to deciduous perennial that spreads by rhizomes to form a mass of 4- to 6-in.-tall stems topped with whorls of shiny dark green leaves. Blooms from late spring into summer with small flowers that look just like dogwood blossoms. Foliage turns red in fall. A Northwest native, it grows best in shade in soil amended with generous amounts of organic matter. Can be difficult to establish but very hardy and drought tolerant thereafter. Pages: 19, 91.

Cortaderia selloana 'Pumila'
DWARF PAMPAS GRASS. An evergreen clump grass growing 5 ft. tall with long linear leaves that have very sharp margins. In the summer, plumes of pink flowers that turn wheat yellow stand high above the foliage. Thrives in hot sun and all but constantly wet soil. In early spring you can cut the foliage low to the ground or use a rake to comb out the dead leaves. Page: 26.

Cornus alba 'Elegantissima'
VARIEGATED SIBERIAN DOGWOOD

Cornus canadensis
BUNCHBERRY

Cortaderia selloana 'Pumila'
DWARF PAMPAS GRASS

Corylopsis pauciflora
WINTER HAZEL

Corylopsis pauciflora

WINTER HAZEL. A deciduous shrub known for its early-spring show of pendulous, primrose yellow flower clusters blooming on bare wood. New leaves start bronze and turn green. Grows to 8 ft. tall and has a delicate and open habit. Blooms best in full sun to partial shade. Prune right after flowering. Pages: 50, 53, 58.

Corylus avellana 'Contorta'

HARRY LAUDER'S WALKING STICK. A deciduous shrub or small tree with stems twisted and contorted in interesting swirls. Named after a vaudeville star who carried a crooked cane on stage. The green leaves, also a bit contorted, turn yellow in fall. Blooms on bare wood in late winter. Male flowers are yellow and pendulous; female flowers are tiny, red, and star shaped, and after pollination produce a small nut that squirrels love. Grows to 12 ft. Plant in full sun to partial shade. Prune after flowering to remove suckers and to keep the tree open. Pages: 44, *47*, 50.

Cotinus coggygria 'Royal Purple'

'ROYAL PURPLE' SMOKE TREE. A deciduous shrub with rounded leaves that open red, turn dark purple for the summer, and then turn gold, orange, or red in fall. Fluffy flower plumes are showy for many weeks in summer and fall. They open pink, then turn tan and look like smoke rising from the foliage. Grows about 10 ft. tall and wide if unpruned, or you can prune it hard every year to have a smaller shrub with larger leaves—a very dramatic specimen. Needs full sun for good color; turns green if shaded. Pages: 49, 57, 68.

Cotoneaster dammeri

BEARBERRY COTONEASTER. An evergreen ground cover with small white flowers in spring, followed by green berries that turn red in fall and hold on through winter. Quickly forms a solid mass. Grows about 4 in. tall and 6 ft. wide. Plant in full sun to partial shade. Needs very little watering once established. No pruning necessary. Page: 27.

Cotoneaster horizontalis

ROCKSPRAY COTONEASTER. A deciduous shrub with branches arrayed in layered sprays. Blooms in the

Cotinus coggygria 'Royal Purple'
'ROYAL PURPLE' SMOKE TREE

Cotoneaster dammeri
BEARBERRY COTONEASTER

Cotoneaster horizontalis
ROCKSPRAY COTONEASTER

Crocosmia 'Lucifer'
CROCOSMIA

Echinacea purpurea
PURPLE CONEFLOWER

Cryptomeria japonica 'Elegans'
PLUME CEDAR

Daphne odora
'Aureomarginata'
VARIEGATED WINTER DAPHNE

spring with white-tinged pink flowers. Fruit follows, turning red in the fall and staying on well after the leaves drop. Plant in full sun or partial shade. Little pruning needed. Grows 2 to 3 ft. tall and 5 ft. wide but will stay shorter with full sun and poor soil. Page: 26.

Crocosmia 'Lucifer'

'LUCIFER' CROCOSMIA. A perennial with long sword-like leaves. Nodding clusters of bright red-orange flowers bloom on branched stems from summer into fall. You may see hummingbirds drinking nectar from the flowers. Takes full sun to partial shade and needs little water once established. Cut foliage to the ground in early spring. Grows to 3 ft. Pages: 21, 27, 29.

Cryptomeria japonica 'Elegans'

PLUME CEDAR. A slow-growing conifer that forms a neat cone-shaped tree with soft needlelike foliage that is blue-green in summer and bronzy red in winter. The cinnamon-colored bark peels off in strips. Grows to 60 ft. tall after many years. If height will eventually be a problem, 'Elegans Compacta' grows only 12 ft. tall. Both cultivars need full sun and require no care. Pages: 20, 53.

Daphne odora 'Aureomarginata'

VARIEGATED WINTER DAPHNE. A compact evergreen shrub with glossy leaves that have an irregular thin gold stripe around the edges. In late winter and early spring purple buds open into small rose-tinged white flower clusters that have a powerful sweet fragrance. Grows 4 ft. tall and wide. Plant in a location with morning sun, afternoon shade, and well-drained soil. Prune after flowering to remove damaged or errant branches. Pages: 23, 42, 51, 69, 82.

Dicentra

BLEEDING HEART. Perennials that form rounded clumps of soft-textured, lacy, blue-green foliage. In late spring heart-shaped flowers dangle from delicate stalks. Leaves will die down in summer heat. Common bleeding heart, *D. spectabilis* (pp. 67, *67*), is a large showy plant growing 2 to 3 ft. tall and wide with rose-pink flowers. *D. s.* 'Alba' (pp. 19, *19*) has white flowers. *D.* 'Luxuriant' (pp. 55, 59, *59*) is smaller and bears rose-red flowers on 18-in. stalks rising above a 1-ft.-tall mass of foliage. Bleeding hearts need partial shade and fertile, moist, well-drained soil. Divide every few years in spring or fall.

Doronicum orientale 'Magnificum'

'MAGNIFICUM' LEOPARD'S BANE. A perennial that forms a mound of heart-shaped green leaves with bright yellow daisylike flowers rising on long stems in the spring. Plant in partial shade in well-drained soil amended with organic matter. Goes dormant in the heat of summer. Pages: 67, *67*.

Echinacea purpurea

PURPLE CONEFLOWER. A summer-blooming perennial that attracts bees and butterflies. Large daisylike blossoms with large center "cones" are held high on stiff branching stalks above a basal mound of dark green foliage. Grows about 3 ft. tall and 2 ft. wide. Normally this plant has pink-purple flowers, but there are a few cultivars with white flowers. 'Bright Star' (p. 80) has burgundy flower heads and grows about 30 in. tall. 'Magnus' (pp. 27, 47, 61) bears large purple flowers with orange cones. Plants need full sun. Cut back flower stalks if you choose, or let the seed heads ripen to feed the birds and provide winter interest. May self-sow but isn't weedy. Older plants can be divided in early spring.

Enkianthus campanulatus

RED-VEIN ENKIANTHUS. A slow-growing deciduous shrub whose tiered branches resemble a candelabra, with clusters of small blue-green leaves near the tips. Clusters of reddish pink flowers with creamy streaks hang bell-like beneath the leaves in late spring. Foliage turns a brilliant orange-red in the fall. Plant in partial shade or, if irrigation is available, full sun. Likes well-drained soil amended with compost and then mulched. Needs no pruning and is relatively insect and disease free. Grows up to 8 ft. in 10 years. Pages: 54, 75, 82.

Epimedium

BARRENWORT, BISHOP'S HAT. A long-lived perennial with very attractive heart-shaped foliage. Excellent ground cover under trees or shrubs. Leaves change from coppery to green to maroon over the course of the summer. They're more colorful with more sun and in years with colder winters. Small flowers bloom in spring on thin stems above the foliage in red, pink, yellow, or white. Bishop's hat, *E. grandiflorum* (pp. 79, 91), bears sprays of small, pale pink or white flowers in early spring. Slowly forms a patch about 1 ft. tall and up to several feet wide. A number of species and cultivars are known by the common name "barrenwort" (pp. **42**, 43). *E. × perralchicum* 'Fröhnleiten' (pp. 58, **59**) has long spiny leaflets and 1-in. yellow flowers. *E. pinnatum* 'Colchicum' (pp. 31, 75) is a shorter plant with less-spiny leaflets and yellow flowers. *E. × rubrum* 'Snow Queen' (p. 83) has foliage with deep red margins in early spring and small white flowers. *E. × versicolor* 'Sulphureum' (pp. **54**, 55) blooms dark yellow above many-leafleted compound leaves. All epimediums need partial or full shade. Though they adapt well to the dry soil under trees, provide regular water to get them started. Shear off all foliage to the ground in early spring to encourage a good show of flowers and new foliage. Plants spread by rhizomes and can be divided every few years.

Erica carnea

HEATH. An evergreen shrub that grows about 1 ft. tall and spreads to form a mass of small needlelike leaves. Blooms profusely in winter and early spring, bearing small, urn-shaped and long-lasting flowers. 'Springwood White' (p. 80) has white flowers. 'Springwood Pink' (pp. 69, **86**, 87) has pink. Heath does well in full sun or partial shade and well-drained soil with lots of organic matter. Space 18 in. apart for ground cover. Shear off flowers and tips of

Enkianthus campanulatus
RED-VEIN ENKIANTHUS

Epimedium grandiflorum
BISHOP'S HAT

Epimedium pinnatum
'Colchicum'
BARRENWORT

Erica carnea
HEATH

stems after bloom to encourage new growth that will set bud for the following winter. Pests don't bother this plant.

Escallonia rubra 'Newport Dwarf'

'NEWPORT DWARF' ESCALLONIA. A compact evergreen shrub densely clothed in shiny dark green leaves edged in red. In summer, small upright clusters of red flowers bloom at the ends of the branches. Prefers hot sun and well-drained soil. In cold winters it may freeze to the ground but will usually resprout from the base. Needs very little pruning. Grows about 2 to 3 ft. tall. Pages: 34, 40, 71.

Euonymus fortunei

CREEPING EUONYMUS. A versatile small shrub or ground cover with glossy evergreen leaves. There are many fine cultivars. 'Emerald 'n Gold' (pp. 89, **91**) is very popular, with yellow-edged bright green leaves that take on a pink tinge in the cold of winter. 'Silver Queen' (pp. 25, 31, 34) bears white-edged bright green leaves that also turn pinkish in winter. Adapts to sun or shade and needs well-drained soil. Shear or prune at any time to control size or shape.

Recommended ferns

Athyrium nipponicum 'Pictum'
Japanese painted fern
A colorful fern that forms rosettes of finely cut fronds marked in shades of green, silver, and maroon. They look almost iridescent. Deciduous, but can be evergreen when planted in spots where conditions are mild in winter. Grows about 1 ft. tall, 2 ft. wide. Pages: 19, 51, 55, 59, 75, 83.

Dryopteris × complexa 'Robust' male fern
A thick, lush evergreen fern growing over 3 ft. tall. Divided fronds with slightly arched tips give it a lacy look. Once established it is very drought tolerant. Page: 31.

Dryopteris filix-mas 'Barnesii'
Barnes' narrow male fern
A narrowly upright semievergreen fern with slightly ruffled pinnules (small leaflets). Can reach over 3 ft. tall over time. Does best in well-drained soil. Pages: 21, 39, 58, 65, 67.

Polystichum munitum
Sword fern
A Northwest native fern with shiny, 2- to 4-ft.-long evergreen fronds. One of the most dependable ferns for shady areas, it will also tolerate quite a bit of sun. Needs little water once established. Pages: 19, 83.

Polystichum polyblepharum
Tassel fern
An evergreen fern with stiff, glossy, finely divided fronds. Needs moist soil. Forms a clump about 2 ft. tall, 3 to 4 ft. wide. Pages: 43, 51, 91.

Polystichum setiferum
Soft shield fern
An evergreen fern with soft, gray-green to green fronds that can form a dense crown. It grows 2 ft. tall by 2 ft. wide and prefers morning sun. Pages: 23, 54, 79.

Athyrium nipponicum 'Pictum'
JAPANESE PAINTED FERN

Polystichum munitum
SWORD FERN

Polystichum polyblepharum
TASSEL FERN

Polystichum setiferum
SOFT SHIELD FERN

Where deer are a problem, plant pachysandra or periwinkle instead.

Euonymus japonicus 'Microphyllus Variegatus'
VARIEGATED BOXLEAF JAPANESE EUONYMUS. Tough, dependable evergreen shrub with a compact habit and small shiny white-and-green leaves. Has a refined look as a clipped hedge or planted closely as a ground cover. Grows 1 to 2 ft. tall and wide. Plant in full sun and well-drained soil. Shear or prune at any time to control size or shape. Mildew can be a problem in late summer. Trim off damaged shoots and hose the plant down with water. Pages: 73, *75*.

Euphorbia polychroma
CUSHION SPURGE. A perennial that is attractive in several seasons. Upright stems bear whorls of dark green leaves, forming a dome-shaped clump 1 to 2 ft. tall and wide. From spring into summer, it bears long-lasting bright yellow flowers at the tips of the stems. Leaves turn red in fall. Needs full sun or partial shade. Cut the stems back partway after bloom to keep the clump compact and tidy. Pages: 36, 57, *59*.

Ferns
Ferns are carefree, long-lived perennials. Despite their delicate appearance, they're among the most durable and trouble-free plants you can grow. Many ferns prefer shade, but some do well in partial shade or even full sun. They grow best in well-drained soil that's been amended with extra organic matter. You can divide them every few years in early spring if you want more plants, or leave them alone for decades. If you want to keep the foliage very fresh and green, you can cut all the fronds off at the crown each spring before the new fiddleheads start to unfurl. See the box at left for more information on specific ferns.

Festuca ovina var. glauca 'Elijah Blue'
'ELIJAH BLUE' BLUE FESCUE GRASS. A neat, compact perennial that forms a dense tuft about 1 ft. tall and wide of very slender, blue-green leaves. Narrow flower spikes appear in early summer and soon turn tan. 'Elijah Blue' is one of several cultivars with especially blue-colored foliage. Mass-planted in small areas, it makes a handsome, fine-textured, clumpy display. Takes full sun or partial shade; can take some drought. For fresh foliage, cut the plant close to the ground in early spring. Pages: 84, *86*.

Fragaria 'Pink Panda'

'PINK PANDA' ORNAMENTAL STRAWBERRY. A compact evergreen ground cover with pink flowers and small edible strawberry fruit in the spring. Dark green three-toothed leaves turn red in winter. Grows fast, enjoys full sun, and tolerates any soil. Mow or cut back in early spring to encourage lush green growth and to reduce crowding from the many runners it sends out. Grows 6 in. tall. Pages: 32, *35*.

Fuchsia

HARDY FUCHSIA. Evergreen and deciduous shrubs in a variety of flower colors, often with different-colored sepals and petals. The petals may be single or double (many ruffled layers). Hummingbirds are attracted to the single-petaled flowers because they can reach the nectar better. Fruits are purple and edible. The fuchsias selected for this book are hardy in the Northwest and may remain evergreen in mild winters. In cold winters they may lose their leaves or die back to the ground, but the crown will resprout and a new plant will grow the following spring. *F. magellanica* (pp. 44, 70, *70*) is an upright open shrub reaching 3 ft. tall that bears many small flowers with red sepals and purple petals all summer long. *F.* 'Riccarrtonii' (p. 87) is an upright, very hardy shrub also reaching 3 ft. and has dark green, slightly bronzy leaves and flowers with rosy pink sepals and dark purple petals. *F.* 'Maiden's Blush' (p. 62) has small pale pink flowers covering an upright shrub that grows 3 ft. tall. Fuchsias love partial shade but will do fine in full sun with some summer watering. They perform best with well-drained soil, compost over their roots, and periodic feeding with a balanced organic fertilizer. To encourage new growth, prune to the ground or reduce by one-half in early spring.

Galium odoratum

SWEET WOODRUFF. A deciduous perennial ground cover that spreads quickly, needs no care, and lasts for decades. Fine-textured foliage is bright green throughout the growing season and turns beige or tan in late fall. Thousands of tiny white flowers sparkle above the fresh new foliage in spring. Adapts to most soils, prefers partial or full shade. Shear or mow close to the ground in early spring and rake away the old foliage. Easily divided in spring or fall to make more plants. If you buy just a few plants to start with, you'll have all the plants you want in a year or two. Grows about 6 in. tall, spreads indefinitely. Pages: *54*, 55.

Garrya elliptica

SILK-TASSEL BUSH. A striking evergreen shrub or small tree that reaches about 10 ft. tall. Leaves are gray-green and wavy along the margins. Masses of long, slender, pendulous gray-green male catkins grace the tree in late winter. Plant in full sun and well-drained soil. Prune only to enhance the shape or open the center to air and light. Pages: 18, 76.

Gaultheria procumbens

WINTERGREEN. A rhizomatous evergreen ground cover with upright stems and glossy green leaves that crowd together at the tips. Small white urn-shaped flowers appear in summer, followed by red fruit in fall and winter. Foliage turns red and purple in winter. Both the leaves and the fruit smell like wintergreen when crushed. Best when protected from the afternoon sun and mulched with organic matter. Grows 6 in. tall. Pages: 16, *19*.

Gaultheria shallon

SALAL. A Northwest native evergreen shrub often used as a ground cover. Its leathery leaves are used in floral arrangements. Bell-like clusters of pinkish white flowers appear in the late spring, followed in the fall by blue-black edible fruit. Grows 6 ft. or more in the shade or 1 ft. in the sun. Spreads by underground stems and does best in soil amended with organic matter. Drought tolerant once established. No pruning necessary. Pages: 65, *67*.

Genista pilosa 'Vancouver Gold'

'VANCOUVER GOLD' SILKY LEAF WOADWAXEN. A low deciduous ground cover that forms a mat of green twiggy stems with tiny dark green leaves. In late spring and early summer, a profusion of bright yellow pealike flowers cover the entire mass. Likes full sun and tolerates drought once established. Needs very little care. Pages: 29, 44, 69, 71, 84.

Geranium

GERANIUM, CRANESBILL. Unlike the common geraniums that are grown as bedding plants and in pots, these are hardy perennials that form a compact or sprawling mound of attractive leaves with jagged edges. (See the box on p. 170 for information on specific kinds.) They bloom in spring or early summer and sporadically until fall with clusters of flowers in various shades of pink, purple, blue-purple, and white. Plant in full sun or partial shade and well-drained soil. Cut off flower stalks when the blossoms fade. If plants look tattered or get floppy

Garrya elliptica
SILK-TASSEL BUSH

Genista pilosa
'Vancouver Gold'
SILKY LEAF WOADWAXEN

in midsummer, cut them back partway and they will bush out again. Otherwise wait until late fall or early spring and cut them to the ground.

Hamamelis mollis

CHINESE WITCH HAZEL. A rather slow-growing deciduous shrub or small tree that is known for its fragrant, straplike, winter-blooming yellow flowers. The branches have a slight zigzag appearance. The long gray-green leaves turn yellow in fall. Prefers full sun and well-drained soil but will bloom well in partial shade. Prune suckers and crossing branches after flowering. May grow to 8 ft. tall. Pages: 64, 76, 88.

Helictotrichon sempervirens

BLUE OAT GRASS. A clump-forming perennial with thin, wiry, pale blue evergreen leaves. Blooms sparsely, with thin flower spikes that turn beige or tan. Plant in full sun. Do not cut foliage back. Simply comb your fingers or a garden "scratching" tool through the clump to pull out any loose, dead leaves. Old clumps may die out in the middle; if so, divide them in fall or early spring. Grows 2 to 3 ft. tall and wide. Pages: 29, *31*, 57.

Helleborus

HELLEBORE. A clump-forming evergreen perennial with dark leathery leaves and round flowers that bloom for many weeks in late winter and early spring. Christmas rose (*H. niger*, pp. 43, 91, **91**) has white flowers 3 to 4 in. wide that open some years as early as Christmas. Lenten rose (*H. orientalis*, pp. 23, 43, 53, 59, 62, 75, 83) has pink, purple, white, or greenish flowers 2 to 3 in. wide in early spring. Corsican hellebore (*H. argutifolius*, pp. 36, **39**) has sharp-toothed leaves and pale green flowers in late winter. All need partial shade and rich, well-drained soil. Hellebores are slow-growing, but they self-sow, gradually spreading to form a patch. Once established, all are carefree and long-lived. Groom once a year by cutting off any dead leaves when the flower buds appear. Established clumps are typically about 18 in. tall, 18 to 24 in. wide.

Hemerocallis

DAYLILY. One of the most reliable and popular perennials, with large lilylike flowers in summer, held above dense clumps or patches of grassy arching leaves. Most daylilies sold today are hybrids (p. 95) comprising thousands of named cultivars. Some are evergreen; others die back in winter. Some are low-growing; others have flower stalks reaching 5 ft. Flowers last only a day but are abundant. They come in many shades of white, yellow, orange, red, and purple. Plants bloom from several weeks to several months or more. Mix early-blooming, midseason, and late-blooming varieties to ensure months of color. 'Happy Returns' (yellow flowers; pp. 57, *59*) and 'Stella d'Oro' (gold-orange flowers; p. 80) bloom from early June until October and are compact plants 18 to 24 in. tall. 'Little Grapette' (deep rosy purple flowers; p. 25) blooms in early summer and

Recommended geraniums

Geranium × cantabrigiense

A compact mass of light green, seven-lobed evergreen leaves bearing many light purple flowers in the summer. Pages: 75, 76.

G. 'Johnson's Blue'

Popular and dependable, it forms a large sprawling mound, about 1 ft. tall and 2 ft. wide, with medium-size leaves and blue-purple flowers from late spring to fall. Pages: 40, 44, 65, 95.

Geranium 'Johnson's Blue'

G. macrorrhizum
Bigroot geranium

A short, compact plant that forms bushy clumps of fragrant, light green semievergreen foliage, with magenta or pink flowers in late spring. Makes a good ground cover for partial shade and dry soil. Grows up to 1 ft. tall, 18 to 24 in. wide. Pages: 31, 58, 73, 79.

Geranium macrorrhizum
BIGROOT GERANIUM

G. × riversleaianum
'Mavis Simpson' geranium

A sprawling plant with gray-green leaves and light pink flowers in summer. Pages: 57, *59*, 61.

Geranium × riversleaianum
'MAVIS SIMPSON' GERANIUM

grows 2 ft. tall and wide. All daylilies prefer full sun and well-drained soil. Water regularly during bloom. Pinch off spent flowers; cut off flower stalks after blooming is finished. Divide every few years in late summer or early spring. When planting, space shorter daylilies about 1 ft. apart, taller kinds 2 ft. apart. They will fill in in a few years.

Heuchera

CORALBELLS, HEUCHERA. Perennials that form low clumps of almost evergreen foliage and bloom from spring into summer, bearing clouds of tiny red, coral, pink, or white flowers on slender stalks about 18 in. tall. They're fine accent plants or small-scale ground covers. The fresh or dried flowers are also attractive in floral arrangements. Often sold as *H. × brizoides* or *H. sanguinea;* there are a number of other species and a variety of hybrids. *H.* 'Palace Purple' (pp. 73, 81, 93, 95) has dark bronzy purple, maple-like leaves on long stalks. Grown primarily for its foliage, it also forms sprays of tiny white flowers in summer. *H. americana* 'Velvet Night' (pp. 39, 55, 58) has deep purple leaves and brownish green flowers in spring. Heucheras do best in partial shade; leaves tend to scorch or fade in full sun. They prefer well-drained soil and some summer water. Remove flower stalks as the blossoms fade. Divide every few years, replanting the divisions an inch or two deeper than they were growing before.

Heuchera 'Palace Purple'
HEUCHERA

Hosta

HOSTA. A long-lived, carefree, shade-tolerant perennial with beautiful leaves in a wide variety of colors and sizes. Plants form dome-shaped clumps or spreading patches of foliage that look good from spring to fall and die down in winter. Lavender, purple, or white flowers bloom on slender stalks in mid- to late summer. 'Krossa Regal' (pp. 54, 93, *172*) has medium-size powdery blue-green leaves and forms vase-shaped clumps 3 ft. tall, 2 ft. wide, with pale lilac flowers on stalks 5 ft. tall. Variegated

Hamamelis mollis
CHINESE WITCH HAZEL

Helleborus
HELLEBORE

Hemerocallis 'Stella d'Oro'
DAYLILY

Hemerocallis 'Little Grapette'
DAYLILY

Hosta **171**

hostas make striking accents. 'Green Gold' (p. 63) forms a mound about 2 ft. tall and wide of large dark green leaves with yellow borders fading to cream and lavender flowers. Some hostas tolerate full sun, but most grow best in partial or full shade. All need fertile, moist, well-drained soil. Cut off flower stalks before seedpods ripen. Clumps can be divided in late summer or early spring if you want to make more plants; otherwise leave them alone. Snails and slugs can ravage some hostas. Talk to nursery staff about which varieties are most resistant to these pests. Pages: 23, 39, **39**, 53, 75, 79, 83, **83**.

Hosta

Hosta 'Green Gold'

Hosta 'Krossa Regal'

Hydrangea macrophylla

BIGLEAF HYDRANGEA. A medium-size deciduous shrub with large round leaves and very showy clusters of papery-textured blue, pink, or white flowers in summer. Grows 6 to 10 ft. tall and equally wide. There are many varieties. 'Nikko Blue' (pp. 62, **63**) is a popular cultivar with blue flowers. It grows only 4 to 6 ft. tall and wide. 'Preziosa' (pp. 24, **27**; also sold as *H. serrata*) bears smaller flowers that start out white and turn deep red, blue, or mauve. Grows 5 ft. tall. Hydrangeas are usually grown in partial shade but can be planted in full sun if regularly watered. Avoid late afternoon sun. Bigleaf hydrangea needs fertile, moist, well-drained soil. Stalks grow one year, bloom the next year. In early spring cut to the ground one-half of the stalks that have bloomed. Head back the others by cutting off their tips. You may need to add lime to the soil to produce pink flowers or aluminum sulfate to produce blue ones. Pages: 16, 75.

Hydrangea paniculata 'Grandiflora'

PEEGEE HYDRANGEA. A deciduous shrub often trained to grow as a small, single-trunk tree. It has light green leaves and big clusters of papery flowers at branch tips in mid- to late summer. Flowers open white and gradually turn pink, then tan in late fall. The dried flowers last at least partway through the winter; prune them off in spring. Can reach 15 to 20 ft. tall and wide over time or be kept smaller by annual pruning. Plant in full or partial sun. A vigorous, trouble-free plant. Both specimens in this book are trained as single-trunk trees. You can train them yourself, but purchasing already trained plants from a nursery is much easier. Pages: 16, 94.

Hydrangea petiolaris

CLIMBING HYDRANGEA. A long-lived deciduous vine that has a thick trunk with peeling bark, large glossy leaves, and lacy clusters of white flowers in June. Clings to a tree or wall and climbs by itself. Tolerates sun or shade; prefers moist, well-drained soil. Grows slowly for the first few years, then climbs several feet a year, eventually to 40 ft. or more. Prune only to keep it in bounds. Pages: 49, **51**.

Hydrangea quercifolia

OAKLEAF HYDRANGEA. A deciduous shrub with large lobed leaves emerging pale green in spring, turning dark in summer, and displaying winelike shades of red and purple in fall. The stems have wonderful peeling, cinnamon-colored bark that's attractive in winter. Clusters of papery white flowers top the stems in early summer, then turn beige or pink-tan, lasting through summer and fall. Enjoy the flowers on the plant and in floral arrangements. 'Snow Queen' has larger-than-average flowers, and 'Snowflake' has double flowers. This species adapts to sun or shade. Water regularly during long dry spells. Needs no other care. Grows fairly quickly, reaching at least 6 ft. tall and wide. Pages: 66, 76.

Hypericum

ST.-JOHNSWORT. Shrubs and perennials with neat leaves and five-petaled flowers ranging from pale yellows to golds. There are hundreds of species, many of them evergreen. *H.* 'Hidcote' (pp. 76, **79**) is a dense deciduous shrub with dark green opposite leaves and golden yellow flowers in summer. Grows 4 ft. tall and 3 ft. wide. *H.* 'Sungold' (p. 62) is also deciduous and has clusters of bright yellow flowers followed by fruit that turns bright red in fall. Grows 3 ft. tall and 4 ft. wide. Both need full sun and well-drained soil and are very hardy once established. Cut all stems by two-thirds in early spring. If you want to keep the plants shorter and more compact, prune all new shoots by half in June.

Iberis sempervirens

EVERGREEN CANDYTUFT. A bushy perennial that forms a low or sprawling mound, about 1 ft. tall and 2 to 3 ft. wide, of slender, glossy evergreen foliage. Bears clusters of bright white flowers for several weeks in March or April. 'Little Gem' (pp. 21, 47, *47*) is a compact plant growing 6 to 8 in. tall. Candytuft can be used as a ground cover. Needs full or partial sun and well-drained soil. Shear off the top half of the plants after they bloom. Needs no other care. Don't try to divide it; buy new plants if you want more. Pages: 69, *70*.

Ilex crenata

JAPANESE HOLLY. A compact shrub with dense twiggy growth and small evergreen leaves. Good for formal specimens, hedges, and foundation plantings. Some cultivars spread wider than tall; others grow upright and conical. 'Green Island' (pp. 24, 92) grows 2 ft. tall and 3 ft. wide. 'Helleri' (p. 24) is a tight compact shrub 1 ft. tall. Plants adapt to full sun or partial shade; need well-drained soil. Can be pruned or sheared to shape, or not at all.

Iris ensata

JAPANESE IRIS. A perennial that forms a clump of dark green, swordlike leaves about 2 ft. tall and produces spectacular 3- to 6-in. flowers on stalks about 3 ft. tall in summer. The broad, ruffled petals have a fragile, velvety texture and come in bright shades of blue, purple, yellow, or white. Needs full sun and rich, fertile, moist soil. Divide every few years in late summer, cutting the clump into three or four large chunks. Pages: 63, *63*.

Iris foetidissima

GLADWIN IRIS. A vigorous perennial with slender shiny leaves and clusters of purple flowers in summer. Large green seedpods split open to reveal bright orange-red seeds that last for months. This species does well in full sun or shade and is very drought tolerant once established. Grows 2 ft. tall. Pages: 31, *31*, 89.

Iris reticulata 'Harmony'

'HARMONY' RETICULATA IRIS. A miniature iris that grows only 6 in. tall. In early spring, before the

Hydrangea macrophylla
BIGLEAF HYDRANGEA

Hydrangea paniculata 'Grandiflora'
PEEGEE HYDRANGEA

swordlike leaves emerge, it bears fragrant purple-and-yellow flowers. Needs full sun and well-drained soil. Page: 16.

Iris sibirica

SIBERIAN IRIS. A carefree perennial that forms a large, vase-shaped clump of slender green leaves up to 2 ft. long and bears scores of showy flowers in late spring on stalks 2 to 3 ft. tall. 'Caesar's Brother' (pp. *70*, 71) is a popular cultivar with very dark blue-purple flowers. 'Tropic Night' (pp. 25, 39) is a 2-ft. cultivar with deep purple flowers. Other cultivars have indigo, sky blue, or yellow flowers. Let the seedpods develop if you choose; they look interesting from summer through winter, and setting seed doesn't seem to reduce the next year's display of flowers. Plants need full or partial sun. After several years, divide clumps in early fall.

Hydrangea quercifolia
OAKLEAF HYDRANGEA

Iris reticulata 'Harmony'

Iris sibirica 'Tropic Night'
SIBERIAN IRIS

Juniperus squamata 'Blue Star'
JUNIPER

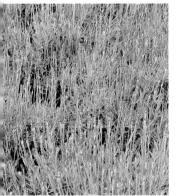

Lavandula LAVENDER

Leucothoe axillaris

Leucothoe fontanesiana
'Rainbow'

Juniperus squamata 'Blue Star'

'BLUE STAR' JUNIPER. A small, slow-growing evergreen shrub that makes an irregular mound of silver blue, prickly-textured foliage. Needs full sun, well-drained soil. Reaches 1 to 2 ft. tall, 2 to 4 ft. wide after many years. Pages: 36, 57.

Kalmia latifolia

MOUNTAIN LAUREL. An evergreen shrub with smooth leaves and very showy clusters of white, pale pink, or rosy flowers in June. Adapts to shade but blooms much more profusely in partial or full sun; needs moist, well-drained soil. Snap off flower stalks as soon as the petals drop (if you let the seedpods form, the plant will bloom only every other year). Prune at the same time to open the plant to light and air. Normally reaches 8 ft. tall and wide after many years. Some cultivars with brighter-colored flowers are more compact and only about 4 ft. tall. A few of the newer compact cultivars have smaller leaves and reach only 2 ft. tall. Pages: 82, *83*.

Lamium maculatum 'Pink Pewter'

'PINK PEWTER' LAMIUM. A creeping perennial that makes an excellent ground cover for shady areas. Gray-green heart-shaped leaves are marked with silver and topped with clusters of pink flowers in early summer. Plants form low mats less than 6 in. tall and spreading 2 ft. or wider. Foliage is evergreen. Lamiums grow best in shade but can take more sun if watered. Cut back halfway after bloom and again in early spring if plants look shabby. Divide every few years in spring or fall. Pages: 51, *51*.

Lavandula

LAVENDER. Choice evergreen shrubs ideal for dry sunny locations. They form bushy mounds of fragrant gray-green foliage topped in early summer with countless long-stalked spikes of very fragrant flowers. English lavender, *L. angustifolia,* generally grows 3 to 4 ft. tall, with 1- to 2-ft. flower spikes. 'Munstead' (pp. 49, *51*) reaches about 18 in. and has pale lavender flowers. 'Hidcote' (pp. 26, 36, 40, 44, 69, 87) grows about 1 ft. tall and wide, with gray-green foliage and dark purple flowers. *L. × intermedia* 'Provence' (pp. 40, *42*) grows 12 to 18 in. and has very deep purple flowers. All lavenders need full sun, well-drained soil, and little water. Shear flower stalks to foliage height when the petals fade. Otherwise, if you leave the stalks on, remnants of the flowers will last well into fall.

Leucothoe

LEUCOTHOE. Evergreen shrubs with arching stems and glossy leaves. In spring, clusters of small fragrant white flowers line the stems. Drooping leucothoe, *L. fontanesiana,* grows up to 4 ft. tall and wide. 'Rainbow' (p. 78) has leaves that are cream, green, and pink. *L. axillaris* (pp. 19, 66, 82) is a more compact shrub that grows 2 ft. tall by 3 ft. wide. Leucothoes need full or partial shade and moist soil.

Lonicera japonica 'Halliana'

HALL'S JAPANESE HONEYSUCKLE. A fast-growing semi-evergreen vine with dull-green leaves. Blooms for months from late spring with sweet-smelling white flowers changing to yellow. Plant in full sun to partial shade. Prune heavily each year right after flowering to reduce buildup of old wood. Pages: 29, *31*.

Magnolia × soulangiana

SAUCER MAGNOLIA. Deciduous tree with large bold leaves. Huge fragrant flowers in shades of white, pink, or purple are borne on leafless stems in early spring. There are many varieties to choose from. Often the inside and the outside of the flower differ in color. Saucer magnolias grow 15 to 25 ft. tall and spread as wide, usually with multiple trunks. They need full sun, well-drained soil, and regular water. Prune in early spring when the branching structure is still easy to see, removing only weak or crossing limbs. Pages: 84, *86*.

Mahonia repens

CREEPING MAHONIA. Spreading evergreen shrub with handsome, deeply divided, blue-green leaves; showy yellow flower clusters in spring; blackish blue berries in fall; and purple leaf tones in winter. Grows 2 to 3 ft. tall and wide, spreads by rhizomes. Mahonias can be grown in sun or shade and are very tolerant of drought. Need no pruning. Pages: 19, *19*.

Malus 'Snowdrift'

'SNOWDRIFT' CRAB APPLE. A small deciduous tree with showy white flowers in late spring that start out red in the bud. Orange-red fruits ripen in early fall and last into winter. Grows 20 to 25 ft. tall. Train young trees by spreading narrow crotches and removing lower limbs to form a crown you can walk underneath. Prune off any suckers that sprout from the base of the tree, and any water sprouts (shoots that grow straight up from a horizontal branch). Does best in full sun and well-drained soil. Unlike

Miscanthus sinensis
JAPANESE SILVER GRASS

Nandina domestica 'Moyers Red'
HEAVENLY BAMBOO

Nandina domestica 'Plum Passion'
HEAVENLY BAMBOO

Nepeta × *faassenii*
Catmint

most crab apples, 'Snowdrift' is resistant to scab, a fungal disease that disfigures leaves and fruit and causes premature leaf and fruit drop. Pages: 73, *75.*

Miscanthus sinensis

JAPANESE SILVER GRASS, MISCANTHUS. A showy grass that forms vase-shaped clumps of long arching leaves. Blooms in late summer or fall, and the fluffy seed heads last through the winter. Bloom is unreliable in the Northwest. For best flowering results, plant in hot sunny spots. 'Morning Light' (pp. 53, *54*) and 'Sarabande' (pp. 24, 27, 61) have very slender, white-striped leaves that look silvery from a distance. Both form a clump of foliage 4 to 5 ft. tall, with flower stalks about 6 ft. tall. 'Purpurascens' (pp. 47, *47*, 87) has leaves that in summer are purplish green with a pink midrib and in fall are orange-red. All miscanthus need full sun. Cut old leaves and stalks close to the ground in late winter or early spring. Divide clumps in early spring every few years.

Nandina domestica

HEAVENLY BAMBOO. An evergreen shrub that forms a clump of slender erect stems. Fine-textured compound leaves change color with the seasons, from bronze to green to red. The species (pp. 78, *79*) grows 4 to 6 ft. tall, 2 to 3 ft. wide, and bears fluffy clusters of white flowers in summer and sporadically throughout the year, followed by long-lasting orange-to-red berries. Plant two or three for better fruit set. 'Harbour Dwarf' (pp. 32, *35*, 89) is a nonflowering dwarf form that makes bushy mounds 18 to 24 in. tall and wide, with fine-textured foliage that turns bright crimson in winter. 'Wood's Dwarf' (pp. 16, *19*) is also very compact and has great scarlet-orange winter color. 'Moyers Red' (pp. 21, 75, 90) grows about 6 ft. tall and 4 ft. wide and has intense red leaves in fall and winter if it gets some sun. 'Plum Passion' (pp. 61, 81) is a newer cultivar with purple-plum new growth and winter color. All do well in full sun or shade. In spring, prune to remove old, weak, or winter-damaged stems. To keep the plant full, cut some of the stems to the ground each year to encourage new growth from the base.

Nepeta × faassenii

CATMINT. A perennial that forms a bushy mound of soft pale green foliage about 18 in. tall and wide topped with clusters of small violet-blue flowers. Blooms most in early summer but continues or repeats throughout the season. Needs full sun and well-drained soil. Shear plants back halfway after the first blooming to keep them tidy and to promote new growth. Cut to the ground in late fall or winter. May self-sow. Pages: 65, 95.

Ophiopogon planiscapus 'Ebony Knight'

'EBONY KNIGHT' BLACK MONDO GRASS. A small perennial with grassy evergreen foliage in an unusual shade of purple-black. Spreads gradually by rhizomes to form a patch under 1 ft. tall. Prefers partial sun and moist, well-drained soil. A patch fills in better if you start with several small plants in-

Osmanthus burkwoodii
HOLLY OSMANTHUS

Oxydendrum arboreum
SOURWOOD

Pennisetum setaceum 'Rubrum'
PURPLE FOUNTAIN GRASS

stead of a few large ones. Mow or shear off the top of the old foliage in early spring. Fresh new growth will look neat the rest of the year. Pages: **54**, 55.

Osmanthus burkwoodii

HOLLY OSMANTHUS. A slow-growing evergreen shrub that has dark green leaves with toothed margins. In the spring it bears a profusion of small, fragrant, tubular white flowers. Grows in full sun to shade but flowers best in sun. Can be pruned as a hedge or left to grow more loosely. Drought tolerant once established. Grows 6 ft. tall. Pages: 65, 73.

Oxydendrum arboreum

SOURWOOD. A slow-growing, multitrunked deciduous shrub or single-trunked small tree with light green, slightly folded leaves. In summer, long fingerlike clusters of cream-colored flowers hang from the branches. Small creamy seedpods that follow the flowers are very attractive and persist well into fall, when the leaves turn shades of yellow, orange, red, or purple. Does well in sun or shade and well-drained soil. Fall color is best in full sun. Grows 15 to 25 ft. tall. Page: 16.

Paeonia hybrid
PEONY

Paeonia

PEONY. Long-lived perennials that form a bushy clump of many stems, with spectacular large, fragrant flowers in late May or June and dark glossy foliage that turns purple or gold before it dies down in fall. Choose from a wide variety of hybrids offering single or double flowers in white, pale pink, or rose. Peonies need full sun and deep, well-drained, fertile soil. Plant in early spring, positioning the thick rootstock so the pink buds are no more than 1 in. deep. (If planted too deep, peonies may not bloom.) Established clumps are typically 2 to 3 ft. tall, 3 to 4 ft. wide. Pages: 25, 80.

Parrotia persica

PERSIAN PARROTIA. A slow-growing, deciduous multistemmed shrub or single-trunked small tree. Bears small clusters of spiderlike red flowers in early spring on bare wood. Leaves are oval with wavy margins and dark green in summer, changing in fall to yellow, then red, and finally purple. The gray and peeling mature bark is attractive when exposed in winter. Needs full sun and well-drained soil. Prune in spring right after flowering to remove any crossing or rubbing branches. Grows 15 ft. tall. Pages: 32, **35**.

Pennisetum

FOUNTAIN GRASS. A grass that forms a hassocklike clump of arching leaves, green in summer and gold or tan in fall. Blooms over a long season from midsummer to fall, with fluffy spikes on arching stalks. *P. alopecuroides* 'Hameln' (pp. 61, **63**), a dwarf cultivar, grows about 2 ft. tall, 3 ft. wide. *P. setaceum* (pp. 80, **83**) grows about 4 ft. tall and 3 ft. wide and bears pink or purple flower spikes. Purple fountain grass (*P. s.* 'Rubrum', p. 26) has reddish brown leaves in summer and purple flowers. *P. orientale* (pp. 36, **39**) grows about 2 ft. tall and wide and is known for its long, soft-bristled flower spikes. Fountain grass needs full sun. Cut old leaves close to the ground in late winter, or sooner if storms knock them down. Can go many years without being divided.

Perovskia

RUSSIAN SAGE. A shrubby perennial that forms an open, vase-shaped clump of straight, fairly stiff stems with sparse silver-gray foliage and tiny but abundant lavender-blue flowers. Blooms for weeks in summer and into fall. *P. atriplicifolia* 'Longin' (pp. 34, 61) has the same graceful lavender flowers but a more upright form. Grow in full sun and well-drained soil. Needs little water. Cut old stems down to 6-in. stubs in spring. Grows 3 to 5 ft. tall and wide by fall. To control size, cut stems back by one-third in early summer. Pages: 36, 71.

Phlox subulata

MOSS PHLOX. A low perennial that forms dense mats of prickly-textured evergreen foliage. Pink, magenta, lilac-blue, or white flowers completely cover the foliage for a few weeks in spring. Grows about 6 in. tall and spreads to form a patch 2 to 3 ft. wide. Needs full or partial sun. Tolerates dry sites. To promote neat, compact growth, shear the plants back halfway after they bloom. Pages: 25, *27*.

Phormium tenax

NEW ZEALAND FLAX. A perennial prized for its bold evergreen foliage. Stiff, straplike leaves form a fan-like clump about 3 to 5 ft. tall and at least as wide. Stalks bearing reddish flowers rise high above the leaves in summer. Because of the Northwest's cool summers, bloom is unreliable. Many varieties with colorful foliage are available, including 'Rubrum' (p. 73), which has deep purple-red leaves. All are excellent accent plants, but large types need lots of room. Smaller varieties, better suited to small gardens, are also available. Plant New Zealand flax in full sun. Needs little water. May not be hardy in colder parts of the Northwest or in colder microclimates. Pages: 36, *39*.

Phyllostachys aurea

GOLDEN BAMBOO. An evergreen bamboo with golden green leaves arising from jointed stems. Grows 6 to 10 ft. tall and spreads by rhizomes. Plant in full sun to partial shade. Can be invasive. To control spread, plant in heavy clay soil and prune the rhizomes each year, or surround the planting with a barrier 2 to 3 ft. deep. Make sure the barrier extends 2 to 3 in. above the soil to keep the rhizomes from growing over it. You can cut some culms to the ground each spring to thin the planting or just let all the culms grow. Pages: 38, *39*.

Picea abies 'Nidiformis'

BIRD'S-NEST NORWAY SPRUCE. A dwarf conifer with sharp, dark green needles. Grows wider than tall, typically reaching about 2 to 3 ft. tall and 3 to 5 ft. wide, and is flat or slightly concave on top—hence its common name. Grow in full sun or light shade and well-drained soil. Grows slowly, so buy the biggest plant you can afford. Doesn't need pruning and is otherwise carefree. Pages: 22, *22*.

Picea omorika

SERBIAN SPRUCE. A narrow, graceful evergreen tree that may eventually reach 50 ft. tall but only 8 ft. wide. Its needles are dark green above and whitish below. Mature bark is brown and platelike. Grows best in full sun and well-drained soil. No pruning needed. Pages: 64, *67*.

Pieris japonica

JAPANESE ANDROMEDA, LILY-OF-THE-VALLEY SHRUB. An evergreen shrub with neat, glossy green foliage; beadlike flower buds that are conspicuous all winter; and drooping clusters of white or pink blooms in late winter and early spring. Even young plants bloom abundantly. The new leaves that form after bloom are often bright gold or red and contrast beautifully with the older green leaves. Can grow to 12 ft. tall. There are many fine cultivars. Most eventually reach 4 to 8 ft. tall and wide, and some get larger. 'Mountain Fire' (pp. 75, *75*) has bright red new growth and white flowers. 'Debutante' (pp. 82, *83*) grows 3 ft. tall and bears white flowers. 'Valley Fire' (pp. 64, 83), whose new growth is also bright red, has white flowers. All need partial shade, preferably afternoon shade, and rich, moist, well-drained soil. Container-grown plants transplant easily, but because the root system is very fibrous, be sure before you plant to slit and tease apart the roots. Prune right after flowering, removing spent flowers and trimming any wayward shoots.

Pinus mugo

MUGO PINE. A slow-growing pine that forms an irregular shrubby mound, not a conical tree. Needles are dark green. Needs full sun and well-drained soil. Doesn't require pruning. Named cultivars usually stay less than 3 ft. tall. Plants grown from seedlings can exceed 10 ft. tall and wide after many years. Pages: 34, *35*.

Pinus strobus 'Nana'

DWARF EASTERN WHITE PINE. A very slow-growing evergreen shrub or small tree that makes a nice container plant or point of interest in the garden. It may eventually reach 3 to 7 ft. tall and wide. The needles are blue-green and very soft to the touch. The bark is smooth and gray and has resin blisters. Grows in full sun to partial shade and well-drained soil. Prune only to let in light and air. Page: 26.

Pratia pedunculata

BLUE STAR CREEPER. A very low (2 to 3 in.) creeping, spreading perennial ground cover with small oval green leaves. Bears tiny sky-blue starlike flowers in late spring and sporadically throughout the summer. Looks great among steppingstones and withstands light foot traffic. Plant in full sun and well-drained soil. Sometimes sold as *Laurentia fluviatilis*. Pages: 39, 51, 57.

Phormium tenax 'Rubrum'
NEW ZEALAND FLAX

Pinus strobus 'Nana'
DWARF EASTERN WHITE PINE

Pratia pedunculata
BLUE STAR CREEPER

Recommended rhododendrons

NOTE: All plants here are evergreen, except for *Rhododendron viscosum* 'Arpege'.

Rhododendron 'Bow Bells' Bell-shaped light pink flowers bloom loosely in spring on this open-habit shrub. Grows about 4 ft. tall and 5 ft. wide. Rounded leaves are green; new growth is coppery. Pages: 51, 82.

R. 'Cilpinense' Light pink flowers bloom in late winter and early spring on a compact, small-leaved shrub. Grows about 3 ft. tall and wide. Pages: 42, 76.

R. 'Dora Amateis' White flowers with green spots bloom in a loose open fashion from early to midspring on this compact semidwarf shrub. Grows about 2 ft. tall and wide. Pages: 19, *19*.

R. 'Gomer Waterer' White flowers flushed pink on the petal margins bloom in late spring. Grows up to 5 ft. tall and wide. Very tolerant of sun and drought. Pages: 44, *47*.

R. 'Hardizer's Beauty' Strikingly pink midspring flowers bloom on this compact plant with small dark green leaves. Grows about 2 ft. tall and 3 ft. wide. Pages: 84, *86*.

R. impeditum Dark purple flowers bloom in early to midspring on this compact plant with very small gray-green leaves. Tolerates sun well. Grows 1 ft. tall. Pages: 47, 69, 84.

R. 'PJM' Purple flowers in very early spring on a compact shrub about 4 ft. tall and 3 ft. wide. Has small dark green leaves. Very hardy and drought tolerant. Page: 87.

R. 'Ramapo' Violet flowers bloom in early to midspring on this low-growing shrub with gray-green leaves. Grows 2 ft. tall. Pages: 24, *27*.

R. 'Snow Lady' Clusters of fragrant white flowers with black stamens bloom in early spring on this 3-ft.-tall plant. The fuzzy light green leaves are attractive. Pages: 50, 91.

R. 'Sweet Simplicity' White flowers edged in pink bloom in late spring. Has shiny dark leaves. Grows 4 ft. tall. Page: 87.

R. viscosum 'Arpege' A deciduous azalea with very fragrant, deep yellow flowers in early spring. Has hairy stems and dark green leaves. Page: 87.

Rhododendron 'Bow Bells'

Rhododendron 'Cilpinense'

Rhododendron 'PJM'

Rhododendron 'Snow Lady'

Pulmonaria saccharata

LUNGWORT. A perennial that blooms for many weeks in early spring, with masses of tiny pink, red, or violet flowers. The large, white-spotted leaves make a good ground cover throughout the summer and fall. There are many cultivars with smaller leaves and other flower colors. Needs partial shade. Prefers rich, moist, well-drained soil but will tolerate drier conditions in shade. Cut off flower stalks when the petals fade. Divide every few years in late summer. Pages: 43, 51, 58, 67.

Rhododendron

RHODODENDRON AND AZALEA. An especially diverse and popular group of shrubs with very showy flowers between early spring and early summer. The leaves can be small or large, deciduous or evergreen. The plants can be short, medium-size, or tall, with spreading, mounded, or erect habits. See the box at left for information on specific varieties.

All rhododendrons and azaleas do best with partial shade and need fertile, moist, well-drained soil. Plant in spring or fall, mixing compost into the planting bed. Be sure not to plant too deep—the top of the root ball should be level with, or a little higher than, the surrounding soil. Azaleas are usually sold in containers. To ensure that they root well in the surrounding soil, make a few deep cuts down the root ball and tease apart some of the roots before planting. Treat container-grown rhododendrons the same way. Large rhododendron plants are often sold balled-and-burlapped; the roots were cut when the plants were dug and need no further attention. They will grow out through the burlap in time. (Remove any synthetic material.)

Azaleas and rhododendrons are shallow rooted, so mulch with a layer of compost to keep the soil cool and damp. For the first few years, water during any dry spell. Snap off spent flower heads as soon as the petals fade to prevent seed formation (which can reduce the following year's flowering) and to tidy up the plants. Prune right after flowering to control the size and shape of the plant. Deer sometimes eat rhododendrons; spraying the plants with a deer repellent offers some protection.

Rosa

ROSE. Fast-growing deciduous shrubs with glossy compound leaves, thorny stems or canes, and showy—often fragrant—flowers. *R.* 'Just Joey' (p. 94) is a vigorous tea rose with an open habit 3 to 5 ft. tall. Flowers are prolific, rounded, double, and fragrant and bloom summer to fall. They open orangish pink and turn white. *R. rugosa* 'Dwarf Pavement' (p. 71) grows only 2 ft. tall and has very thorny stems. Flowers are semidouble and pink and bloom spring to fall. *R.* 'Flower Carpet' (pp. 24, 40, 57, 95) is a ground-cover rose, 2 to 3 ft. tall and 3 to 4 ft. wide, with shiny leaves and profuse flower clusters from spring through autumn. Available in pink, white, and apple blossom.

In winter and early spring, many garden centers stock bare-root roses, with the roots packed in moist wood shavings wrapped in a plastic bag. These are a good investment if you buy them right after they arrive in the stores and plant them promptly, but their quality deteriorates as the weather warms and they begin to grow in the bag. Nurseries may also sell bare-root roses in early spring. If you buy a potted rose, you can plant it anytime, but if the rose has already leafed out, be careful not to disturb the roots in the transplant process.

All roses grow best in full sun and fertile, well-drained soil topped with a few inches of mulch. Once established, the roses recommended in this book require no more care than many other shrubs. Prune them once a year in early spring, before new growth starts. (See p. 148 for more on pruning.) The roses recommended here have good resistance to various fungal diseases but may have problems during especially moist years. To control fungal diseases such as powdery mildew or black spot, try some of the new baking soda derivatives available at nurseries. Follow label directions carefully. Aphids—soft-bodied insects the size of a pinhead—may attack new growth. Wash them away with plain or soapy water. Deer eat rosebushes, despite the thorns. Where deer are a problem, consider planting lilacs, spireas, clematis, or other plants instead.

Rosmarinus officinalis

ROSEMARY. Classic Mediterranean evergreen shrub with gray-green needlelike leaves that combine a lovely fragrance with a tasty flavor. Small blue, lilac, or white flowers bloom in late winter and early spring and sporadically throughout the year. Grows upright or spreading, 2 to 5 ft. tall. 'Tuscan Blue' (pp. 29, 40, *42*) is upright, grows 5 ft. tall, has deep blue flowers, and can be grown as a low hedge. 'Majorca Pink' (pp. 32, *35*) is a smaller upright shrub, 2 to 4 ft. tall, with lavender-pink blooms. Rosemaries are tough plants. They do best in full sun and well-drained soil. Need little water once established. Prune or shear in spring or summer. Page: 49.

Rosa 'Just Joey'
ROSE

Rosa 'Flower Carpet Pink'
ROSE

Rudbeckia 'Goldsturm'
CONEFLOWER

Rudbeckia

CONEFLOWER, BLACK-EYED SUSAN. A popular perennial wildflower that bears daisylike flowers with bright-colored petals and large conical centers in late summer. 'Goldsturm' (pp. 29, 44, 47, 84, 87) bears hundreds of cheerful yellow black-eyed flowers for several weeks in summer and into fall. Forms a robust clump 2 to 3 ft. tall and wide, with large dark green leaves at the base and stiff, erect, branching flower stalks. Gloriosa daisy (*R. hirta*, pp. 65, *67*) has large orange-yellow flowers with black centers. Grows 3 to 4 ft. tall, with upright stems. Can be grown as an annual. Some varieties are much smaller. Plant in full sun and well-drained soil. Plants look best with regular watering. Remove spent flowers. Cut down the flower stalks in fall or spring. Divide every few years in early spring.

Salvia officinalis COMMON SAGE

Sarcococca humilis LOW SARCOCOCCA

Salvia × *superba* 'Blue Queen'   *Salvia* × *superba* 'May Night'   *Sarcococca ruscifolia* FRAGRANT SARCOCOCCA

Sagina subulata

IRISH MOSS. A very low-growing, dense ground cover with tiny, linear, emerald green leaves. Miniature white flowers stand just above the foliage in spring. Not a true moss, it grows best in well-drained soil and partial shade. Looks great between rocks or steppingstones and withstands light foot traffic. Pages: 39, *39*.

Salvia officinalis

COMMON SAGE, GARDEN SAGE. A shrubby perennial with fragrant, gray-green, oval leaves and spikes of lovely blue flowers in June. Leaves are often used in cooking. Ideal for containers and small spaces near the kitchen. Grows 1 to 2 ft. tall, 2 to 3 ft. wide. 'Berggarten' (pp. 49, *51*) has a more compact habit, rounded leaves, and purple flowers. Plants need full sun and well-drained soil. Cut stems back two-thirds to a bud in early spring, and cut off flower stalks after they bloom.

Salvia × superba

SALVIA. A long-blooming perennial that forms a patch of dark green foliage topped with countless flower spikes. (This salvia is also sold as *S. nemorosa* and *S.* × *sylvestris*.) 'May Night' (pp. 27, 61) has dark indigo-purple flowers. Salvias start blooming in June and continue off and on through summer and fall. They prefer full sun and well-drained soil. Shear or trim off the old flower stalks from time to time to keep the plant blooming. Plants grow 18 to 24 in. tall, spread 2 ft. wide. Page: 16.

Sarcococca

SARCOCOCCA. Low sarcococca (*S. humilis*, pp. 31, 43, 66) is a slow-growing evergreen shrub with small, leathery, pointed leaves that are glossy green all year. Blooms in February and March; the small white flowers cluster at the bases of the leaves and are very sweet-scented. Grows 12 to 18 in. tall and 2 to 3 ft. wide. Spreads by rhizomes and can be used as a ground cover. Fragrant sarcococca (*S. ruscifolia*, pp. 23, 75, 78, 83, 90) has glossy green, wavy leaves. Small white flowers in late winter and early spring are also strongly scented. Grows about 3 ft. tall and wide. Plant sarcococcas in full or partial shade. They're carefree.

Sedum

SEDUM. Perennials that form clumps of succulent foliage on thick stems topped with flat clusters of tiny flowers. 'Autumn Joy' (pp. 16, 27, 34, 44, 47, 49, 61, 71, 84, 93) grows 2 to 3 ft. tall, with erect stems and gray-green foliage. The flowers change color from pale to deep salmon-pink to rusty red over many weeks in late summer and fall as they open, mature, and go to seed. 'Vera Jameson' (pp. 40, 93) grows about 1 ft. tall, with floppy stems, rounded leaves in an unusual shade of purple-gray, and pink flowers in August. *S. spurium* 'Dragon's Blood' (pp. 36, *39*) is evergreen, forming a low mat of fleshy bronze leaves covered in summer with clusters of tiny rosy red flowers. Sedums need full sun. Cut down old stalks in winter or early spring. Divide clumps every few years in early spring.

Sempervivum tectorum

HEN-AND-CHICKS. An evergreen perennial ground cover forming a rosette of succulent leaves with spikes of pink or mauve flowers in summer. Produces numerous plantlets (the "chicks") attached by runners. There are many species and cultivars. They grow best in full hot sun and well-drained soil. Very drought tolerant. Pages: 49, *51*.

Senecio greyi

GREY'S SENECIO. A mound-forming evergreen shrub with woolly stems and leaves that are soft to the touch. (Also sold as *Brachyglottis greyi*.) New leaves are covered with white hairs and become dark green and hairless. Yellow daisylike flowers bloom from summer to fall. *S. g.* 'Sunshine' (p. 40) grows 3 ft. tall and wide and has leaves with scalloped edges. Grow senecio in full sun or partial shade. Very drought tolerant once established. Most are grown for their gray foliage, so shear off the flowers if the leaf color is what you're after. Every few years prune older stems by two-thirds in the early spring to encourage new vibrant gray-green growth. Pages: 26, 29, 36, 49, 81.

Spiraea japonica

JAPANESE SPIREA. A deciduous shrub that forms a low mound of thin, graceful, arching stems, with sharply toothed leaves and round flat clusters of tiny flowers in summer. 'Goldflame' (pp. 16, 69, *70*; sometimes listed under the species *S.* × *bumalda*) has bright gold leaves tinged with orange in spring and turning red in fall. Flowers are pink-red. 'Little Princess' (pp. 57, *59*) has dark green leaves and rosy

Sedum 'Autumn Joy'

Sedum 'Vera Jameson'

Senecio greyi
GREY'S SENECIO

Spiraea japonica 'Shirobana'
JAPANESE SPIREA

pink flowers. 'Shirobana' (p. 76) has attractive dark green leaves and mixed white, pink, and deep rose flowers throughout the summer. All of these cultivars grow about 2 to 3 ft. tall and wide and need full or partial sun. Prune every year in spring, removing some of the older stems at ground level and cutting others back partway. In summer, shear off faded flowers to promote reblooming. Powdery mildew can be a problem late in the summer.

Stewartia pseudocamellia

JAPANESE STEWARTIA. A medium-size deciduous tree with a slightly zigzag branching pattern and four-

Stewartia pseudocamellia
JAPANESE STEWARTIA

Styrax japonicum
JAPANESE SNOWBELL

Taxus baccata 'Repandens'
SPREADING ENGLISH YEW

season appeal: silken pointed buds in spring, white camellia-like flowers in midsummer, colorful fall foliage, and flaking bark that's conspicuous in winter. Prefers fertile, moist, well-drained soil and partial or full sun. Buy a container-grown tree and plant it in spring so it has a full season to become established. Water periodically the first summer. Usually sold in small sizes, which transplant best. Prune and train carefully, making sure the main trunks and limbs diverge at wide angles. Once established, needs little pruning and no routine care. Grows 30 to 40 ft. tall, about 20 ft. wide. Pages: 24, 75, 80, 83.

Styrax japonicum

JAPANESE SNOWBELL. A deciduous single-trunked tree or large multistemmed bush that puts out a profusion of fragrant white pendulous flowers in spring. Oval green leaves appear while the tree is still in bloom and turn yellow in fall. Plant in full sun to shade. Avoid hot sites with reflected heat. The tree may eventually reach 20 to 30 ft. tall. Pages: 68, 80.

Taxus baccata 'Repandens'

SPREADING ENGLISH YEW. A low-growing, wide-spreading evergreen shrub with dark green needles. Grows about 2 ft. tall and 6 to 8 ft. wide after many years. This is a female plant, producing attractive red berries with a poisonous hard seed. Adapts to full sun, partial sun, or shade but must have well-drained soil. Prune individual branches as needed to maintain the desired shape. Pages: 53, 70, 91.

Thymus

THYME. A shrubby perennial that forms a tangle of wiry twigs covered with tiny fragrant evergreen leaves. Blooms profusely in July or August, with pink, mauve, rose, or white flowers. There are many thymes to choose from at any herb nursery or the herb section of a garden center, usually sold by common names. Woolly thyme (*T. pseudolanuginosus*, p. 27) has fuzzy gray leaves and forms a low mat a few inches tall and 1 ft. or more wide. It tolerates light foot traffic and smells good when you step on it. Creeping thyme (*T. praecox* ssp. *arcticus*, pp. 36, 45, 47, 59, *59*) has shiny green leaves that turn maroon in cold weather, grows very low, and withstands light foot traffic. Mother-of-thyme (*T. serpyllum*, pp. 76, *79*) is a bushier plant that grows 6 to 8 in. tall and about 1 ft. wide and bears purple flowers in summer. Common thyme (*T. vulgaris*, pp. 49, *51*) is another bushy type, 8 to 12 in. tall, with

bright purple to white flowers in summer. The leaves are often used in cooking. All thymes need full sun and well-drained soil. Shear old growth back halfway in early spring on the bushy forms. Divide the low-spreading ground covers as needed in spring.

Tsuga canadensis 'Pendula'

WEEPING HEMLOCK. A selected form of the Canadian hemlock with limbs that arch gracefully out and down, forming a mounded specimen. Needlelike leaves are green on top and white below. Grows slowly and spreads wider than tall, reaching 2 to 3 ft. tall and 4 to 6 ft. wide. Will eventually grow twice as tall and wide but will take many years to do so. Start with the largest specimen you can afford. Takes sun or shade but needs moist, well-drained soil. Requires no pruning and is generally trouble free, but can be subject to the woolly adelgid, an aphidlike pest that is hard to control. Pages: 22, *22*.

Tsuga mertensiana

MOUNTAIN HEMLOCK. An evergreen tree native to the higher elevations in the Northwest. The leaves are small blue-green needles arranged in spirals around the stem. Grows slowly, about 6 to 8 in. a year, and forms an irregular cone. Likes moist, well-drained soil with some protection from the hot late-afternoon sun or reflected heat. Requires no pruning. Pages: 66, *67*.

Vaccinium

VACCINIUM. Evergreen and deciduous shrubs native to the Northwest. They all bear small, pinky white, urn-shaped flowers in the spring, followed by edible fruits, some red, some blue-black, that birds also enjoy. Many will grow larger in the shade or woodland understory, and smaller in the sun. All do best in well-drained soil with lots of organic matter. Evergreen huckleberry (*V. ovatum*, pp. 18, *19*) has leaves that start out bronze in spring and turn glossy green; small, sweet, and blue-black fruit; and branches that are attractive in floral arrangements. Grows 2 to 3 ft. tall in the sun and 8 to 10 ft. in the shade. Foxberry (*V. vitis-idaea*, pp. 89, 91, *91*) is an evergreen shrub or ground cover with leaves that begin red-tinged and turn glossy green. Late-spring flowers are followed by small sour red berries. Grows 1 ft. tall and spreads by rhizomes.

Viburnum

VIBURNUM. Deciduous or evergreen shrubs with many outstanding features—showy foliage, flowers, fragrance, or fruits, or all of the above. For more information on specific plants, see the box at right. All of the viburnums recommended in this book need full or partial sun and moist, well-drained soil. Prune young plants in late winter or right after they finish flowering to encourage them to branch out and become bushy. Established plants need little pruning; when they do, prune after flowering. Insect and disease free.

Water plants

Most big garden centers offer some water plants. Specialty nurseries and mail-order water-garden specialists offer several dozen kinds. Most water plants are fast-growing, even weedy, so you need only one of each kind to start. The plants named here are all tender to frost, but you can overwinter them indoors in a pot or aquarium. There are three main groups of water plants: marginal, floating, and oxygenating. Choose one or more of each for an interesting and balanced effect.

Marginal, or emergent, plants grow well in containers covered with 2 in. or more of water; their leaves and flower stalks stand above the water surface. For example, dwarf papyrus (*Cyperus haspan*) is a popular marginal with leaves that branch out like umbrella spokes; it grows 18 in. tall.

Floating plants have leaves that rest on the water and roots that dangle into it. Water lettuce (*Pistia stratiotes*) is a floater that forms saucer-size rosettes of iridescent pale green leaves.

Oxygenating, or submerged, plants grow underwater; they help keep the water clear and provide oxygen, food, and shelter for fish. Anacharis (*Elodea canadensis*) is a popular oxygenator with tiny, dark green leaves.

Water lilies (*Nymphaea* species, pp. 53, *54*) are the most popular plant for pools and ponds. The best selection is available from specialty nurseries. There are two main groups of water lilies. Hardy water lilies survive outdoors from year to year and bloom in midsummer. They are usually the easiest to grow. Tropical water lilies need warm water and bloom over a longer season from summer through fall, but are treated as annuals. Both kinds are available in dwarf-size plants, suitable for small pools, with fragrant or scentless flowers in shades of white, yellow, and pink. Tropicals also come in shades of blue and purple. All water lilies need full sun. Plant the roots in a container of heavy, rich garden soil, and set it in the pool so about 6 in. of water covers the soil. (See p. 115 for more on planting.)

Recommended viburnums

Viburnum × *bodnantense* 'Dawn'
An upright deciduous shrub with dark green leaves that are scarlet in fall and peely brown bark. Clusters of very sweet-smelling pink flowers bloom on bare wood in late winter but can begin as early as October. Blooms best in full sun. Grows 8 to 10 ft. tall and 6 ft. wide. Pages: 31, *31*, 57.

V. carlesii 'Compactum', Compact Korean spice viburnum
A deciduous shrub with clusters of pink buds that open into spicy-scented white flowers in April. Leaves may be red or green in fall. Grows about 4 ft. tall and wide. Pages: 80, *83*.

V. davidii, David viburnum
A compact evergreen shrub with leathery, veined, dark green leaves. Flat-topped clusters of white flowers are borne on branch tips in late spring and sporadically into summer. Metallic blue fruit ripens in late fall. Each plant will produce more fruit when there are several plants in the same area. Grows 3 ft. tall in sun, 5 ft. tall in shade. Pages: 21, 31, 73.

V. tinus 'Spring Bouquet'
A compact evergreen shrub with dark green leaves borne on reddish

Viburnum davidii
DAVID VIBURNUM

Viburnum tinus 'Spring Bouquet'

stems, clusters of fragrant white flowers in spring, and metallic blue berries in late summer. Flower buds are set in fall and stay a beautiful burgundy-white all winter. Grows 6 ft. tall and about 4 ft. wide. Pages: 47, 80.

Weigela 'Java Red'

'JAVA RED' WEIGELA. A deciduous shrub with a fountainlike habit, dark purple-green foliage, and deep pink tubular flowers in early summer and sporadically after. Hummingbirds enjoy the flowers. Blooms best in full sun and well-drained soil. Will grow 6 ft. tall. To control size, you can prune before flowering, cutting one-third of the stems to the ground, or prune right after flowering, removing flowering stems back to a branch that has not bloomed. Pages: 73, *75*.

Glossary

Amendments. Organic materials or minerals used to improve the soil. Peat moss, perlite, and compost are commonly used.

Annual. A plant that grows from seed, flowers, produces new seeds, and dies during a single growing season; a perennial plant treated like an annual in that it is grown for only a single season's display and then removed.

Balled-and-burlapped. Describes a tree or shrub dug out of the ground with a ball of soil intact around the roots, the ball then wrapped in burlap and tied for transport.

Bare-root. Describes a plant dug out of the ground and then shaken or washed to remove the soil from the roots.

Balled-and-burlapped

Bare-root

Compound leaf. A leaf consisting of two or more leaflets branching from the same stalk.

Container-grown. Describes a plant raised in a pot that is removed before planting.

Crown. That part of a plant where the roots and stem meet, usually at soil level.

Cultivar. A cultivated variety of a plant, often bred or selected for some special trait such as double flowers, compact growth, cold hardiness, or disease resistance.

Deadheading. Removing spent flowers during the growing season to improve a plant's appearance, prevent seed formation, and stimulate the development of new flowers.

Deciduous. Describes a tree, shrub, or vine that drops all its leaves in winter.

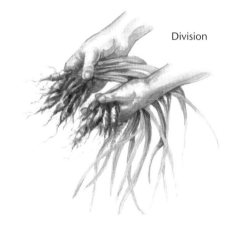

Division

Division. Propagation of a plant by separating it into two or more pieces, each piece possessing at least one bud and some roots. Plants commonly divided include perennials, bulbs, grasses, and ferns.

Drainage. Movement of water through soil. If water poured into a foot-deep hole drains completely in a few hours, the drainage is good.

Drip line. The circle of soil beneath a tree mirroring the circumference of the tree's canopy. This area benefits from direct rainfall and "drip" from leaves. Because many of the tree's feeder roots are found along the drip line and beyond, this area is the best for fertilizing and watering.

Dry-laid. Describes a masonry path or wall that is installed without mortar.

Edging. A barrier that serves as the border between lawn and a planting bed. Edgings may be shallow trenches or barriers of plastic, brick, or boards.

Exposure. The characterization of a site according to the sun, wind, and temperature acting upon it.

Formal. Describes a style of landscaping that features symmetrical layouts, with beds and walks related to adjacent buildings, and often with plants sheared to geometric or other shapes.

Foundation planting. Traditionally, a narrow border of evergreen shrubs planted around the foundation of a house. Contemporary foundation plantings often include deciduous shrubs, grasses, perennials, and other plants as well.

Frost heaving. A disturbance or uplifting of soil, pavement, or plants caused when moisture in the soil freezes and expands.

Full shade. Describes a site that receives no direct sun during the growing season.

Full sun. Describes a site that receives at least eight hours of direct sun each day during the growing season.

Garden soil. Soil specially prepared for planting to make it loose enough for roots and water to penetrate easily. Usually requires digging or tilling and the addition of some organic matter.

Grade. The angle and direction of the ground's slope in a given area.

Ground cover. A plant providing continuous cover for an area of soil. Commonly a low, spreading foliage plant such as candytuft, vinca, or ajuga.

Habit. The characteristic shape of a plant, such as upright, mounded, columnar, or vase-shaped.

Hardiness. A plant's ability to survive the winter temperatures in a given region without protection.

Hardscape. Parts of a landscape constructed from materials other than plants, such as walks, walls, and trellises made of wood, stone, or other materials.

Herbicide. A chemical used to kill plants. Preemergent herbicides are used to kill weed seeds as they sprout, and thus to prevent weed growth. Postemergent herbicides kill plants that are already growing.

Hybrid. A plant with two parents that belong to different varieties, species, or genera.

Interplant. To use plants with different bloom times or growth habits in the same bed to increase the variety and appeal of the planting.

Invasive. Describes a plant that spreads quickly, usually by runners, and mixes with or dominates adjacent plantings.

Landscape fabric. A synthetic fabric, sometimes water-permeable, spread under paths or mulch to serve as a weed barrier.

Lime, limestone. Mineral compounds applied to soil to render it less acid, thereby making nutrients more available for plants to use. Limestone also supplies calcium that plants need.

Loam. Soil rich in organic matter and with mineral particles in a range of sizes. Excellent for many garden plants.

Microclimate. A small-scale "system" of factors affecting plant growth on a particular site, including shade, temperature, rainfall, and so on.

Brick mowing strip

Mowing strip. A row of bricks or paving stones set flush with the soil around the edge of a bed, and wide enough to support one wheel of the lawn mower.

Mulch. A layer of organic or other materials spread several inches thick around the base of plants and over open soil in a bed. Mulch conserves soil moisture, smothers weeds, and moderates soil temperatures. Where winters are cold, mulches help protect plants from freezing. Common mulches include compost, shredded leaves, straw, lawn clippings, gravel, newspaper, and landscape fabric.

Native. Describes a plant that is or once was found in the wild in a particular region and was not imported from another area.

Nutrients. Elements needed by plants. Found in the soil and supplied by organic matter and fertilizers, nutrients include nitrogen, phosphorus, potassium, calcium, magnesium, sulfur, iron, and other elements, in various forms and compounds.

Organic matter. Partially or fully decomposed plant and animal matter. Includes leaves, trimmings, and manure.

Peat moss. Partially decomposed mosses and sedges. Dug from boggy areas, peat moss is often used as an organic amendment for garden soil.

Perennial. A plant with a life span of more than one year. Woody plants such as trees and shrubs are perennials, in addition to the "herbaceous perennials" more commonly cited, which have no woody tissue that persists from year to year.

Pressure-treated lumber. Softwood lumber treated with chemicals that protect it from decay.

Propagate. To produce new plants from seeds or by vegetative means such as dividing plant parts, taking root cuttings, and grafting stems onto other plants.

Retaining wall. A wall built to stabilize a slope and keep soil from sliding or eroding downhill.

Rhizome. A horizontal underground stem from which roots and shoots emerge. Some swell to store food. Branched rhizomes (those of iris, for instance) can be divided to produce new plants.

Root ball. The mass of soil and roots dug with a plant when it is removed from the ground; the soil and roots of a plant grown in a container.

Rosette. A low, flat cluster or crown of overlapping leaves.

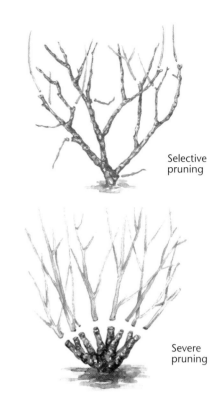

Selective pruning

Severe pruning

Selective pruning. Using pruning shears to remove or cut back individual shoots in order to refine the shape of a shrub, maintain its vigor, or limit its size.

Severe pruning. Using pruning shears or loppers to cut away most of a shrub's top growth, leaving just short stubs or a trunk.

Shearing. Using hedge shears or an electric hedge trimmer to shape the surface of a shrub, hedge, or tree and produce a smooth, solid mass of greenery.

Specimen plant. A striking plant, often providing year-round interest, placed for individual display.

Spike. An elongated flower cluster on which individual flowers are attached directly to the main stem or are on very short stalks attached to the main stem.

Tender. Describes a plant that is damaged by cold weather in a particular region.

Underplanting. Growing short plants, such as ground covers, under a taller plant, such as a shrub.

Variegated. Describes foliage with color patterns in stripes, specks, or blotches that occur naturally or result from breeding.

Photo Credits

Index

*NOTE: Page numbers in **bold italic** refer to photographs.*

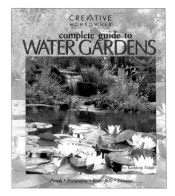

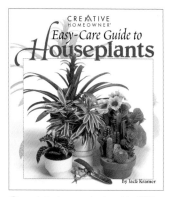
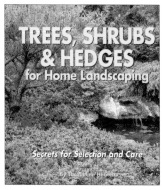

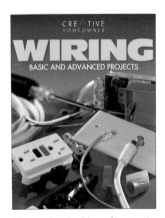
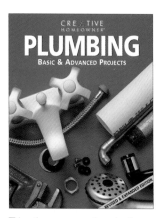
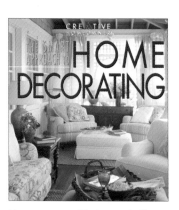
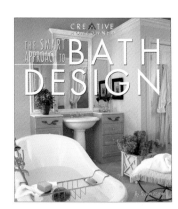